T0219758

Expert SQL Server In-Memory OLTP

Second Edition

Dmitri Korotkevitch

Apress®

Expert SQL Server In-Memory OLTP

Dmitri Korotkevitch
Land O Lakes, Florida, USA

ISBN-13 (pbk): 978-1-4842-2771-8   ISBN-13 (electronic): 978-1-4842-2772-5
DOI 10.1007/978-1-4842-2772-5

Library of Congress Control Number: 2017952536

Managing Director: Welmoed Spahr
Editorial Director: Todd Green
Acquisitions Editor: Jonathan Gennick
Development Editor: Laura Berendson
Technical Reviewer: Victor Isakov
Coordinating Editor: Jill Balzano
Copy Editor: Kim Wimpsett
Compositor: SPi Global
Indexer: SPi Global
Artist: SPi Global

Distributed to the book trade worldwide by Springer Science+Business Media New York, 233 Spring Street, 6th Floor, New York, NY 10013. Phone 1-800-SPRINGER, fax (201) 348-4505, e-mail orders-ny@springer-sbm.com, or visit www.springeronline.com. Apress Media, LLC is a California LLC and the sole member (owner) is Springer Science + Business Media Finance Inc (SSBM Finance Inc). SSBM Finance Inc is a **Delaware** corporation.

For information on translations, please e-mail rights@apress.com, or visit www.apress.com/rights-permissions.

Apress titles may be purchased in bulk for academic, corporate, or promotional use. eBook versions and licenses are also available for most titles. For more information, reference our Print and eBook Bulk Sales web page at www.apress.com/bulk-sales.

Any source code or other supplementary material referenced by the author in this book is available to readers on GitHub via the book's product page, located at www.apress.com/9781484227718. For more detailed information, please visit www.apress.com/source-code.

Printed on acid-free paper

To all my friends in the SQL Server community and outside of it.

Contents at a Glance

Contents

About the Author

Dmitri Korotkevitch is a Microsoft Data Platform MVP and Microsoft Certified Master (SQL Server 2008) with more than 20 years of IT experience, including years of experience working with Microsoft SQL Server as an application and database developer, database administrator, and database architect. He specializes in the design, development, and performance tuning of complex OLTP systems that handle thousands of transactions per second around the clock. Dmitri regularly speaks at various Microsoft and SQL PASS events, and he provides SQL Server training to clients around the world. He regularly blogs at http://aboutsqlserver.com and rarely tweets as @aboutsqlserver, and he can be reached at dk@aboutsqlserver.com.

About the Technical Reviewer

Victor Isakov is a Microsoft Certified Architect, Microsoft Certified Master, Microsoft Certified Trainer, and Microsoft MVP with more than 20 years of experience with SQL Server. He regularly speaks at conferences internationally, including IT/Dev Connections, Microsoft TechEd, and the PASS Summit. He has written a number of books on SQL Server and has worked on numerous projects for Microsoft, developing SQL Server courseware, certifications, and exams. In 2007, Victor was invited by Microsoft to attend the SQL Ranger program in Redmond. Consequently, he became one of the first IT professionals to achieve the Microsoft Certified Master and Microsoft Certified Architect certifications globally.

Acknowledgments

I would like to thank my family for their patience, understanding, and continuous support. It would have been impossible for me to write this book without them!

It would also have been impossible to write this book without help from my friend and eternal technical reviewer Victor Isakov. I just don't understand why Victor still talks to me after all my books he has reviewed!

On the same note, I would like to thank Nazanin Mashayekh, who read the manuscript and provided many great advices and suggestions. Nazanin lives in Tehran and has years of experience working with SQL Server in various roles.

I am enormously grateful to Jos de Bruijn from Microsoft who generously answered a never-ending stream of my questions. Jos is one of the few people who shaped In-Memory OLTP into its current form. I cannot understate his contribution to this book—it would never cover the technology in such depth without his help. Thank you, Jos!

Finally, I would like to thank the entire Apress team, especially Jill Balzano, Kim Wimpsett, and Jonathan Gennick. It is always a pleasure to work with all of you!

Thank you very much!

Introduction

The year 2016 was delightful for the SQL Server community—we put our hands on the new SQL Server build. This was quite a unique release; for the first time in more than ten years, the new version did not focus on specific technologies. In SQL Server 2016, you can find enhancements in all product areas, such as programmability, high availability, administration, and BI.

I, personally, was quite excited about all the enhancements in In-Memory OLTP. I really enjoyed this technology in SQL Server 2014; however, it had way too many limitations. This made it a niche technology and prevented its widespread adoption. In many cases, the cost of the required system refactoring put the first release of In-Memory OLTP in the "it's not worth it" category.

I was incredibly happy that the majority of those limitations were removed in SQL Server 2016. There are still some, but they are not anywhere near as severe as in the first release. It is now possible to migrate systems into memory and start using the technology without significant code and database schema changes.

I would consider this simplicity, however, a double-edged sword. While it can significantly reduce the time and cost of adopting the technology, it can also open the door to incorrect decisions and suboptimal implementations. As with any other technology, In-Memory OLTP has been designed for a specific set of tasks, and it can hurt the performance of the systems when implemented incorrectly. Neither is it a "set it and forget it" type of solution; you have to carefully plan for it before implementing it and maintain it after the deployment.

In-Memory OLTP is a great tool, and it can dramatically improve the performance of systems. Nevertheless, you need to understand how it works under the hood to get the most from it. The goal for this book is to provide you with such an understanding. I will explain the internals of the In-Memory OLTP Engine and its components. I believe that knowledge is the cornerstone of a successful In-Memory OLTP implementation, and this book will help you make educated decisions on how and when to use the technology.

If you read my *Pro SQL Server Internals* book (Apress, 2016), you will notice some familiar content from there. However, this book is a much deeper dive into In-Memory OLTP, and you will find plenty of new topics covered. You will also learn how to address some of In-Memory OLTP's limitations and how to benefit from it in existing systems when full in-memory migration is cost-ineffective.

Even though this book covers In-Memory OLTP in SQL Server 2016, the content should also be valid for the SQL Server 2017 implementation. Obviously, check what technology limitations were lifted there.

Finally, I would like to thank you for choosing this book and for your trust in me. I hope that you will enjoy reading it as much as I enjoyed writing it.

How This Book Is Structured

This book consists of 13 chapters and is structured in the following way:

- Chapter 1 and Chapter 2 are the introductory chapters, which will provide you with an overview of the technology and show how In-Memory OLTP objects work together.

- Chapter 3, Chapter 4, and Chapter 5 explain how In-Memory OLTP stores and works with data in memory.

- Chapter 6 shows how In-Memory OLTP allocates memory for internal objects and works with off-row columns. I consider this as one of the most important topics for successful in-memory OLTP migrations.

- Chapter 7 covers columnstore indexes that help you to support operational analytics workloads.

- Chapter 8 explains how In-Memory OLTP handles concurrency in a multi-user environment.

- Chapter 9 talks about native compilation and the programmability aspect of the technology.

- Chapter 10 demonstrates how In-Memory OLTP persists data on disk and how it works with the transaction log.

- Chapter 11 covers the In-Memory OLTP garbage collection process.

- Chapter 12 discusses best practices for In-Memory OLTP deployments and shows how to perform common database administration tasks related to In-Memory OLTP.

- Chapter 13 demonstrates how to address some of the In-Memory OLTP surface area limitations and how to benefit from In-Memory OLTP components without moving all the data into memory.

The book also includes four appendixes.

- Appendix A explains how In-Memory OLTP works with memory pointers in a multi-user environment.

- Appendix B covers how the page splitting and merging processes are implemented.

- Appendix C shows you how to analyze the state of checkpoint file pairs and navigates you through their lifetime.

- Appendix D discusses SQL Server tools and wizards that can simplify In-Memory OLTP migration.

Downloading the Code

You can download the code used in this book from the Source Code section of the Apress web site (`www.apress.com`) or from the Publications section of my blog (`http://aboutsqlserver.com`). The source code consists of a SQL Server Management Studio solution, which includes a set of projects (one per chapter). Moreover, it includes several .NET C# projects, which provide the client application code used in the examples in Chapters 2 and 13.

I have tested all the scripts in an environment with 8GB of RAM available to SQL Server. In some cases, if you have less memory available, you will need to reduce the amount of test data generated by some of the scripts. You can also consider dropping some of the unused test tables to free up more memory.

CHAPTER 1

■ ■ ■

Why In-Memory OLTP?

This introductory chapter explains the importance of in-memory databases and the problems they address. It provides an overview of the Microsoft In-Memory OLTP implementation (code name Hekaton) and its design goals. It discusses the high-level architecture of the In-Memory OLTP Engine and how it is integrated into SQL Server.

Finally, this chapter compares the SQL Server in-memory database product with several other solutions available.

Background

Way back when SQL Server and other major databases were originally designed, hardware was expensive. Servers at that time had just one or very few CPUs and a small amount of installed memory. Database servers had to work with data that resided on disk, loading it into memory on demand.

The situation has changed dramatically since then. During the last 30 years, memory prices have dropped by a factor of 10 every 5 years. Hardware has become more affordable. It is now entirely possible to buy a server with 32 cores and 1TB of RAM for less than $50,000. While it is also true that databases have become larger, it is often possible for *active* operational data to fit into the memory.

Obviously, it is beneficial to have data cached in the buffer pool. It reduces the load on the I/O subsystem and improves system performance. However, when systems work under a heavy concurrent load, this is often not enough to obtain the required throughput. SQL Server manages and protects page structures in memory, which introduces large overhead and does not scale well. Even with row-level locking, multiple sessions cannot modify data on the same data page simultaneously and must wait for each other.

Perhaps the last sentence needs to be clarified. Obviously, multiple sessions can modify data rows on the same data page, holding exclusive (X) locks on different rows simultaneously. However, they cannot update *physical* data page and row objects simultaneously because this could corrupt the in-memory page structure. SQL Server addresses this problem by protecting pages with *latches*. Latches work in a similar manner to locks, protecting internal SQL Server data structures on the physical level by serializing access to them, so only one thread can update data on the data page in memory at any given point of time.

© Dmitri Korotkevitch 2017
D. Korotkevitch, *Expert SQL Server In-Memory OLTP*, DOI 10.1007/978-1-4842-2772-5_1

In the end, this limits the improvements that can be achieved with the current database engine's architecture. Although you can scale hardware by adding more CPUs and cores, that serialization quickly becomes a bottleneck and a limiting factor in improving system scalability. Likewise, you cannot improve performance by increasing the CPU clock speed because the silicon chips would melt down. Therefore, the only feasible way to improve database system performance is by reducing the number of CPU instructions that need to be executed to perform an action.

Unfortunately, code optimization is not enough by itself. Consider the situation where you need to update a row in a table. Even when you know the clustered index key value, that operation needs to traverse the index tree, obtaining latches and locks on the data pages and a row. In some cases, it needs to update nonclustered indexes, obtaining the latches and locks there. All of that generates log records and requires writing them and the dirty data pages to disk.

All of those actions can lead to a hundred thousand or even millions of CPU instructions to execute. Code optimization can help reduce this number to some degree, but it is impossible to reduce it dramatically without changing the system architecture and the way the system stores and works with data.

These trends and architectural limitations led the Microsoft team to the conclusion that a true in-memory solution should be built using different design principles and architecture than the classic SQL Server Database Engine. The original concept was proposed at the end of 2008, serious planning and design started in 2010, actual development began in 2011, and the technology was finally released to the public in SQL Server 2014.

The main goal of the project was to build a solution that would be 100 times faster than the existing SQL Server Database Engine, which explains the code name Hekaton (Greek for "100"). This goal has yet to be achieved; however, it is not uncommon for In-Memory OLTP to provide 20 to 40 times faster performance in certain scenarios.

It is also worth mentioning that the Hekaton design has been targeted toward OLTP workloads. As we all know, specialized solutions designed for particular tasks and workloads usually outperform general-purpose systems in the targeted areas. The same is true for In-Memory OLTP. It shines with large and busy OLTP systems that support hundreds or even thousands of concurrent transactions. At the same time, the original release of In-Memory OLTP in SQL Server 2014 did not work well for a data warehouse workload, where other SQL Server technologies outperformed it.

The situation changes with the SQL Server 2016 release. The second release of In-Memory OLTP supports columnstore indexes, which allow you to run real-time operation analytics queries against *hot* OLTP data. Nevertheless, the technology is not as mature as disk-based column-based storage, and you should not consider it an in-memory data warehouse solution.

In-Memory OLTP has been designed with the following goals:

- *Optimize data storage for main memory*: Data in In-Memory OLTP is not stored on disk-based data pages, and it does not mimic a disk-based storage structure when loaded into memory. This permits the elimination of the complex buffer pool structure and the code that manages it. Moreover, regular (non-columnstore) indexes are not persisted on disk, and they are re-created upon startup when the data from memory-resident tables is loaded into memory.

- *Eliminate latches and locks*: All In-Memory OLTP internal data structures are latch- and lock-free. In-Memory OLTP uses a multiversion concurrency control to provide transaction consistency. From a user standpoint, it behaves like the regular SNAPSHOT transaction isolation level; however, it does not use a locking or tempdb version store under the hood. This schema allows multiple sessions to work with the same data without locking and blocking each other and provides near-linear scalability of the system, allowing it to fully utilize modern multi-CPU/multicore hardware.

- *Use native compilation*: T-SQL is an interpreted language that provides great flexibility at the cost of CPU overhead. Even a simple statement requires hundreds of thousands of CPU instructions to execute. The In-Memory OLTP Engine addresses this by compiling row-access logic, stored procedures, and user-defined functions into native machine code.

The In-Memory OLTP Engine is fully integrated in the SQL Server Database Engine. You do not need to perform complex system refactoring, splitting data between in-memory and conventional database servers or moving all of the data from the database into memory. You can separate in-memory and disk data on a table-by-table basis, which allows you to move active operational data into memory, keeping other tables and historical data on disk. In some cases, that migration can even be done transparently to client applications.

This sounds too good to be true, and, unfortunately, there are still plenty of roadblocks that you may encounter when working with this technology. In SQL Server 2014, In-Memory OLTP supported just a subset of the SQL Server data types and features, which often required you to perform costly code and schema refactoring to utilize it. Even though many of those limitations have been removed in SQL Server 2016, there are still incompatibilities and restrictions you need to address.

You should also design the system considering In-Memory OLTP behavior and internal implementation to get the most performance improvements from the technology.

In-Memory OLTP Engine Architecture

In-Memory OLTP is fully integrated into SQL Server, and other SQL Server features and client applications can access it transparently. Internally, however, it works and behaves very differently than the SQL Server Storage Engine. Figure 1-1 shows the architecture of the SQL Server Database Engine, including the In-Memory OLTP components.

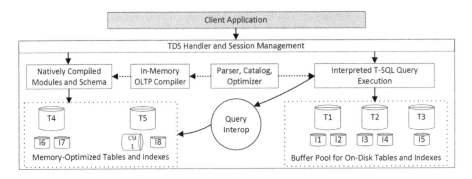

Figure 1-1. *SQL Server Database Engine architecture*

In-Memory OLTP stores the data in *memory-optimized tables*. These tables reside completely in memory and have a different structure compared to the classic *disk-based tables*. With one small exception, memory-optimized tables do not store data on the data pages; the rows are linked together through the chains of memory pointers. It is also worth noting that memory-optimized tables do not share memory with disk-based tables and live outside of the buffer pool.

■ **Note**   I will discuss memory-optimized tables in detail in Chapter 3.

There are two ways the SQL Server Database Engine can work with memory-optimized tables. The first is the *Query Interop Engine*. It allows you to reference memory-optimized tables from interpreted T-SQL code. The data location is transparent to the queries; you can access memory-optimized tables, join them with disk-based tables, and work with them in the usual way. Most T-SQL features and language constructs are supported in this mode.

You can also access and work with memory-optimized tables using *natively compiled modules*, such as stored procedures, memory-optimized table triggers and scalar user-defined functions. You can define them similarly to the regular T-SQL modules using several additional language constructs introduced by In-Memory OLTP.

Natively compiled modules have been compiled into machine code and loaded into SQL Server process memory. Those modules can introduce significant performance improvements compared to the Interop Engine; however, they support just a limited set of T-SQL constructs and can access only memory-optimized tables.

■ **Note**   I will discuss natively compiled modules in Chapter 9.

The memory-optimized tables use row-based storage with all columns combined into the data rows. It is also possible to define *clustered columnstore indexes* on those tables. These indexes are the separate data structures that store a heavily compressed copy of the data in column-based format, which is perfect for real-time operational analytics queries. In-Memory OLTP persists those indexes on disk and does not re-create them on a database restart.

■ **Note**   I will discuss clustered columnstore indexes in Chapter 7.

In-Memory OLTP and Other In-Memory Databases

In-Memory OLTP is hardly the *only* relational in-memory database (IMDB) available on the market. Let's look at other popular solutions that exist as of 2017.

Oracle

As of this writing, Oracle provides two separate IMDB offerings. The mainstream Oracle 12*c* database server includes the Oracle Database In-Memory option. When it is enabled, Oracle creates the copy of the data in column-based storage format and maintains it in the background. Database administrators may choose the tables, partitions, and columns that should be included in the copy.

This approach is targeted toward analytical queries and data warehouse workloads, which benefit from column-based storage and processing. It does not improve the performance of OLTP queries that continue to use disk-based row-based storage.

In-memory column-based data adds overhead during data modifications; it needs to be updated to reflect the data changes. Moreover, it is not persisted on disk and needs to be re-created every time the server restarts.

The same time, this implementation is fully transparent to the client applications. All data types and PL/SQL constructs are supported, and the feature can be enabled or disabled on the configuration level. Oracle chooses the data to access on a per-query basis using in-memory data for the analytical/data warehouse and disk-based data for OLTP workloads. This is different from SQL Server In-Memory OLTP where you should explicitly define memory-optimized tables and columnstore indexes.

In addition to the Database In-Memory option, Oracle offers the separate product Oracle TimesTen targeted toward OLTP workloads. This is a separate in-memory database that loads all data into memory and can operate in three modes.

> *Standalone In-Memory Database* supports a traditional client-server architecture.

> *Embedded In-Memory Database* allows applications to load Oracle TimesTen into an application's address space and eliminate the latency of network calls. This is extremely useful when the data-tier response time is critical.

> *Oracle Database Cache (TimesTen Cache)* allows the product to be deployed as an additional layer between the application and the Oracle database. The data in the cache is updatable, and synchronization between TimesTen and the Oracle database is done automatically.

Internally, however, Oracle TimesTen still relies on locking, which reduces transaction throughput under heavy concurrent loads. Also, it does not support native compilation, as In-Memory OLTP does.

It is also worth noting that both the Oracle In-Memory option and TimesTen require separate licenses. This may significantly increase implementation costs compared to In-Memory OLTP, which is available at no additional cost even in non-Enterprise editions of SQL Server.

IBM DB2

Like the Oracle Database In-Memory option, IDM DB2 10.5 with BLU Acceleration targets data warehouse and analytical workloads. It persists the copy of the row-based disk-based tables in column-based format in in-memory *shadow tables*, using them for analytical queries. The data in the shadow tables is persisted on disk and is not re-created at database startup. It is also worth noting that the size of the data in shadow tables may exceed the size of available memory.

IBM DB2 synchronizes the data between disk-based and shadow tables automatically and asynchronously, which reduces the overhead during data modifications. This approach, however, introduces latency during shadow table updates, and queries may work with slightly outdated data.

IBM DB2 BLU Acceleration puts the emphasis on query processing and provides great performance with data warehouse and analytical workloads. It does not have any OLTP-related optimizations and uses disk-based data and locking to support OLTP workloads.

SAP HANA

SAP HANA is relatively new database solution on the market; it has been available since 2010. Until recently, SAP HANA was implemented as a pure in-memory database, limiting the size of the data to the amount of memory available on the server.

This limitation has been addressed in the recent releases; however, it requires separate tools to manage the data. The applications should also be aware of the underlying storage architecture. For example, HANA supports disk-based *extended tables*; however, applications need to query them directly and also implement the logic to move data between in-memory and extended tables.

SAP HANA stores all data in a column-based format, and it does not support row-based storage. The data is fully modifiable; SAP HANA stores new rows in the *delta stores*, compressing them in the background. Concurrency is handled with Multiversion Concurrency Control (MVCC) when UPDATE operations generate new versions of the rows similarly to SQL Server In-Memory OLTP.

■ **Note** I will discuss the In-Memory OLTP concurrency model in depth in Chapter 8.

SAP claims that HANA may successfully handle both OLTP and data warehouse/ analytical workloads using the single copy of the data in column-based format. Unfortunately, it is pretty much impossible to find any benchmarks that prove this for OLTP workloads. Considering that pure column-based storage is not generally optimized for OLTP use cases, it is hard to recommend SAP HANA for the systems that require high OLTP throughput.

SAP HANA, however, may be a good choice for systems that are focused on operational analytics and BI and need to support infrequent OLTP queries.

It is impossible to cover all the in-memory database solutions available on the market. Many of them are targeted to and excel in specific workloads and use cases. Nevertheless, SQL Server provides a rich and mature set of features and technologies that may cover the wide spectrum of requirements. SQL Server is also a cost-effective solution compared to other major vendors on the market.

Summary

In-Memory OLTP was designed using different design principles and architecture than the classic SQL Server Database Engine. It is a specialized product targeted toward OLTP workloads and can improve performance by 20 to 40 times in certain scenarios. Nevertheless, it is fully integrated into the SQL Server Database Engine. The data storage is transparent to the client applications, which do not require any code changes if they use the features supported by In-Memory OLTP.

The data from memory-optimized tables is stored in memory separately from the buffer pool. All In-Memory OLTP data structures are completely latch- and lock-free, which allows you to scale the systems by adding more CPUs to the servers.

In-Memory OLTP may support operational analytics by defining the clustered columnstore indexes on memory-optimized tables. Those indexes store the copy of the data from the table in column-based storage format.

In-Memory OLTP uses native compilation to the machine code for any row-access logic. Moreover, it allows you to perform native compilation of the stored procedures, triggers and scalar user-defined functions, which dramatically increase their performance.

CHAPTER 2

■ ■ ■

In-Memory OLTP Objects

This chapter provides a high-level overview of In-Memory OLTP objects. It shows how to create databases with an In-Memory OLTP filegroup and how to define memory-optimized tables and access them through the Interop Engine and natively compiled modules.

Finally, this chapter demonstrates performance improvements that can be achieved with the In-Memory OLTP Engine when a large number of concurrent sessions insert the data into the database and latch contention becomes a bottleneck.

Preparing a Database to Use In-Memory OLTP

The In-Memory OLTP Engine has been fully integrated into SQL Server and is always installed with the product. In SQL Server 2014 and 2016 RTM, In-Memory OLTP is available only in the Enterprise and Developer editions. This restriction has been removed in SQL Server 2016 SP1, and you can use the technology in every SQL Server edition.

You should remember, however, that non-Enterprise editions of SQL Server have a limitation on the amount of memory they can utilize. For example, buffer pool memory in SQL Server 2016 Standard and Express editions is limited to 128GB and 1,410MB of RAM, respectively. Similarly, memory-optimized tables cannot store more than 32GB of data *per database* in Standard and 352MB of data in Express editions. The data in memory-optimized tables will become read-only if In-Memory OLTP does not have enough memory to generate new versions of the rows.

■ **Note** I will discuss how to estimate the memory required for In-Memory OLTP objects in Chapter 12.

In-Memory OLTP is also available in the Premium tiers of the SQL Databases in Microsoft Azure, including the databases in the Premium Elastic Pools. However, the amount of memory the technology can utilize is based on DTUs of the service tier. As of this writing, Microsoft has provided 1GB of memory for each 125DTU or eDTU of the tier. This may change in the future, and you should review the Microsoft Azure documentation when you decide to use In-Memory OLTP with SQL Databases.

© Dmitri Korotkevitch 2017
D. Korotkevitch, *Expert SQL Server In-Memory OLTP*, DOI 10.1007/978-1-4842-2772-5_2

You do not need to install any additional packages or perform any configuration changes on the SQL Server level to use In-Memory OLTP. However, any database that utilizes In-Memory OLTP objects should have a separate filegroup to store memory-optimized data.

With an *on-premise* version of SQL Server, you can create this filegroup at database creation time or alter an existing database and add the filegroup using the CONTAINS MEMORY_OPTIMIZED_DATA keyword. It is not required, however, with SQL Databases in Microsoft Azure, where the storage level is abstracted from the users.

Listing 2-1 shows an example of the CREATE DATABASE statement with the In-Memory OLTP filegroup specified. The FILENAME property of the filegroup specifies the folder in which the In-Memory OLTP files would be located.

Listing 2-1. Creating a Database with the In-Memory OLTP Filegroup

```
create database InMemoryOLTPDemo
on primary
(
    name = N'InMemoryOLTPDemo'
    ,filename = N'M:\Data\InMemoryOLTPDemo.mdf'
),
filegroup HKData CONTAINS MEMORY_OPTIMIZED_DATA
(
    name = N'InMemory_OLTP_Data'
    ,filename = N'H:\HKData\InMemory_OLTP_Data'
),
filegroup LOGDATA
(name = N'LogData1', filename = N'M:\Data\LogData1.ndf'),
(name = N'LogData2', filename = N'M:\Data\LogData2.ndf'),
(name = N'LogData3', filename = N'M:\Data\LogData3.ndf'),
(name = N'LogData4', filename = N'M:\Data\LogData4.ndf')
log on
(
    name = N'InMemoryOLTPDemo_log'
    ,filename = N'L:\Log\InMemoryOLTPDemo_log.ldf'
)
```

Internally, In-Memory OLTP utilizes a streaming mechanism based on the FILESTREAM technology. While coverage of FILESTREAM is outside the scope of this book, I will mention that it is optimized for sequential I/O access. In fact, In-Memory OLTP does not use random I/O access at all by design. It uses sequential append-only writes during a normal workload and sequential reads on the database startup and recovery stages. You should keep this behavior in mind and place In-Memory OLTP filegroups into the disk arrays optimized for sequential performance.

Similar to FILESTREAM filegroups, the In-Memory OLTP filegroup can include multiple containers placed on the different disk arrays, which allows you to spread the load across them.

It is worth noting that In-Memory OLTP creates the set of files in the filegroup when you create the first In-Memory OLTP object. Unfortunately, SQL Server does not allow you to remove an In-Memory OLTP filegroup from the database even after you drop all memory-optimized tables and objects. However, you can still remove the In-Memory OLTP filegroup from the database while it is empty and does not contain any files.

■ **Note** You can read more about FILESTREAM at https://docs.microsoft.com/en-us/sql/relational-databases/blob/filestream-sql-server.

I will discuss how In-Memory OLTP persists data on disk in Chapter 10 and cover the best practices in hardware and SQL Server configurations in Chapter 12.

DATABASE COMPATIBILITY LEVEL

As the general recommendation, Microsoft suggests that you set the database compatibility level to match the SQL Server version when you use In-Memory OLTP in the system. This will enable the latest T-SQL language constructs and performance improvements, which are disabled in the older compatibility levels.

You should remember, however, that the database compatibility level affects the choice of cardinality estimation model along with Query Optimizer hotfix servicing model formerly controlled by the trace flag T4199. This may and will change the execution plans in the system even when you enable the LEGACY_CARDINALITY_ ESTIMATION database-scoped configuration.

You should carefully plan that change when you migrate the system from the old versions of SQL Server regardless if you utilize In-Memory OLTP or not. You can use the new SQL Server 2016 component called the *Query Store* to capture the execution plans of the queries before changing the compatibility level and force the old plans to the system-critical queries in case of regressions.

Creating Memory-Optimized Tables

Syntax-wise, creating memory-optimized tables is similar to disk-based tables. You can use the regular CREATE TABLE statement specifying that the table is memory-optimized.

The code in Listing 2-2 creates three memory-optimized tables in the database. Please ignore all unfamiliar constructs; I will discuss them in detail later in the chapter.

Listing 2-2. Creating Memory-Optimized Tables

```
create table dbo.WebRequests_Memory
(
    RequestId int not null identity(1,1)
        primary key nonclustered
        hash with (bucket_count=1048576),
    RequestTime datetime2(4) not null
        constraint DEF_WebRequests_Memory_RequestTime
        default sysutcdatetime(),
    URL varchar(255) not null,
    RequestType tinyint not null, -- GET/POST/PUT
    ClientIP varchar(15) not null,
    BytesReceived int not null,

    index IDX_RequestTime nonclustered(RequestTime)
)
with (memory_optimized=on, durability=schema_and_data);

create table dbo.WebRequestHeaders_Memory
(
    RequestHeaderId int not null identity(1,1)
        primary key nonclustered
        hash with (bucket_count=8388608),
    RequestId int not null,
    HeaderName varchar(64) not null,
    HeaderValue varchar(256) not null,

    index IDX_RequestID nonclustered hash(RequestID)
    with (bucket_count=1048576)
)
with (memory_optimized=on, durability=schema_and_data);

create table dbo.WebRequestParams_Memory
(
    RequestParamId int not null identity(1,1)
        primary key nonclustered
        hash with (bucket_count=8388608),
    RequestId int not null,
    ParamName varchar(64) not null,
    ParamValue nvarchar(256) not null,

    index IDX_RequestID nonclustered hash(RequestID)
    with (bucket_count=1048576)
)
with (memory_optimized=on, durability=schema_and_data);
```

Each memory-optimized table has a DURABILITY setting. The default SCHEMA_AND_DATA value indicates that the data in the tables is fully durable and persists on disk for recovery purposes. Operations on such tables are logged in the database transaction log.

SCHEMA_ONLY is another value, which indicates that data in memory-optimized tables is not durable and would be lost in the event of a SQL Server restart, crash, or failover to another node. *Operations against nondurable memory-optimized tables are not logged in the transaction log.* Nondurable tables are extremely fast and can be used if you need to store temporary data in use cases similar to temporary tables in tempdb. As the opposite to temporary tables, SQL Server persists the schema of nondurable memory-optimized tables, and you do not need to re-create them in the event of a SQL Server restart.

The indexes of memory-optimized tables must be created inline and defined as part of a CREATE TABLE statement. You cannot add or drop an index or change an index's definition after a table is created.

SQL Server 2016 allows you to alter the table schema and indexes. This, however, creates the new table object in memory, copying data from the old table there. This is an offline operation, which is time- and resource-consuming and requires you to have enough memory to accommodate multiple copies of the data.

■ **Tip**   You can combine multiple ADD or DROP operations into a single ALTER statement to reduce the number of table rebuilds.

In SQL Server 2016, memory-optimized tables support at most eight indexes. Durable memory-optimized tables should have a unique PRIMARY KEY constraint defined. Nondurable memory-optimized tables do not require the PRIMARY KEY constraint; however, they should still have at least one index to link the rows together. It is worth noting that the eight-index limitation will be removed in SQL Server 2017.

Memory-optimized tables support two main types of indexes, HASH and NONCLUSTERED. Hash indexes are optimized for point-lookup operations, which is the search of one or multiple rows with equality predicates. This is a conceptually new index type in SQL Server, and the Storage Engine does not have anything similar to it implemented. Nonclustered indexes, on the other hand, are somewhat similar to B-Tree indexes on disk-based tables. Finally, SQL Server 2016 allows you to create clustered columnstore indexes to support operational analytics queries in the system.

Hash and nonclustered indexes are never persisted on disk. SQL Server re-creates them when it starts the database and loads memory-optimized data into memory. As with disk-based tables, unnecessary indexes in memory-optimized tables slow down data modifications and use extra memory in the system.

■ **Note**   I will discuss hash indexes in detail in Chapter 4 and nonclustered indexes in Chapter 5. I will cover columnstore indexes in Chapter 7.

Working with Memory-Optimized Tables

You can access data in memory-optimized tables either using interpreted T-SQL or from natively compiled modules. In interpreted mode, SQL Server treats memory-optimized tables pretty much the same way as disk-based tables. It optimizes queries and caches execution plans, regardless of where the table is located. The same set of operators is used during query execution. From a high level, when SQL Server needs to get a row from a table and the operator's GetRow() method is called, it is routed either to the Storage Engine or to the In-Memory OLTP Engine, depending on the underlying table type.

Most T-SQL features and constructs are supported in interpreted mode. Some limitations still exist; for example, you cannot truncate a memory-optimized table or use it as the target in a MERGE statement. Fortunately, the list of such limitations is small.

Listing 2-3 shows an example of a T-SQL stored procedure that inserts data into the memory-optimized tables created in Listing 2-2. For simplicity's sake, the procedure accepts the data that needs to be inserted into the dbo.WebRequestParams_Memory table as the regular parameters, limiting it to five values. Obviously, in production code it is better to use table-valued parameters in such a scenario.

Listing 2-3. Stored Procedure That Inserts Data into Memory-Optimized Tables Through the Interop Engine

```
create proc dbo.InsertRequestInfo_Memory
(
   @URL varchar(255)
   ,@RequestType tinyint
   ,@ClientIP varchar(15)
   ,@BytesReceived int
   -- Header fields
   ,@Authorization varchar(256)
   ,@UserAgent varchar(256)
   ,@Host varchar(256)
   ,@Connection varchar(256)
   ,@Referer varchar(256)
   -- Hardcoded parameters.. Just for the demo purposes
   ,@Param1 varchar(64) = null
   ,@Param1Value nvarchar(256) = null
   ,@Param2 varchar(64) = null
   ,@Param2Value nvarchar(256) = null
   ,@Param3 varchar(64) = null
   ,@Param3Value nvarchar(256) = null
   ,@Param4 varchar(64) = null
   ,@Param4Value nvarchar(256) = null
   ,@Param5 varchar(64) = null
   ,@Param5Value nvarchar(256) = null
)
```

```
as
begin
    set nocount on
    set xact_abort on

    declare
        @RequestId int

    begin tran
        insert into dbo.WebRequests_Memory
            (URL,RequestType,ClientIP,BytesReceived)
        values
            (@URL,@RequestType,@ClientIP,@BytesReceived);

        select @RequestId = SCOPE_IDENTITY();

        insert into dbo.WebRequestHeaders_Memory
            (RequestId,HeaderName,HeaderValue)
        values
            (@RequestId,'AUTHORIZATION',@Authorization)
            ,(@RequestId,'USERAGENT',@UserAgent)
            ,(@RequestId,'HOST',@Host)
            ,(@RequestId,'CONNECTION',@Connection)
            ,(@RequestId,'REFERER',@Referer);

        ;with Params(ParamName, ParamValue)
        as
        (
            select ParamName, ParamValue
            from (
                values
                    (@Param1, @Param1Value)
                    ,(@Param2, @Param2Value)
                    ,(@Param3, @Param3Value)
                    ,(@Param4, @Param4Value)
                    ,(@Param5, @Param5Value)
                ) v(ParamName, ParamValue)
            where
                ParamName is not null and
                ParamValue is not null
        )
        insert into dbo.WebRequestParams_Memory
            (RequestID,ParamName,ParamValue)
        select @RequestID, ParamName, ParamValue
        from Params;
    commit
end
```

15

As you can see, the stored procedure that works through the Interop Engine does not require any specific language constructs to access memory-optimized tables.

Natively compiled modules are also defined with a regular CREATE statement, and they use the T-SQL language. However, there are several additional options that must be specified at the creation stage.

The code in Listing 2-4 creates the natively compiled stored procedure that accomplishes the same logic as the dbo.InsertRequestInfo_Memory stored procedure defined in Listing 2-3.

Listing 2-4. Natively Complied Stored Procedure

```
create proc dbo.InsertRequestInfo_NativelyCompiled
(
    @URL varchar(255) not null
    ,@RequestType tinyint not null
    ,@ClientIP varchar(15) not null
    ,@BytesReceived int not null
    -- Header fields
    ,@Authorization varchar(256) not null
    ,@UserAgent varchar(256) not null
    ,@Host varchar(256) not null
    ,@Connection varchar(256) not null
    ,@Referer varchar(256) not null
    -- Parameters.. Just for the demo purposes
    ,@Param1 varchar(64) = null
    ,@Param1Value nvarchar(256) = null
    ,@Param2 varchar(64) = null
    ,@Param2Value nvarchar(256) = null
    ,@Param3 varchar(64) = null
    ,@Param3Value nvarchar(256) = null
    ,@Param4 varchar(64) = null
    ,@Param4Value nvarchar(256) = null
    ,@Param5 varchar(64) = null
    ,@Param5Value nvarchar(256) = null
)
with native_compilation, schemabinding, execute as owner
as
begin atomic with
(
    transaction isolation level = snapshot
    ,language = N'English'
)
    declare
        @RequestId int

    insert into dbo.WebRequests_Memory
        (URL,RequestType,ClientIP,BytesReceived)
    values
        (@URL,@RequestType,@ClientIP,@BytesReceived);
```

```
select @RequestId = SCOPE_IDENTITY();

insert into dbo.WebRequestHeaders_Memory
(RequestId,HeaderName,HeaderValue)
    select @RequestId,'AUTHORIZATION',@Authorization union all
    select @RequestId,'USERAGENT',@UserAgent union all
    select @RequestId,'HOST',@Host union all
    select @RequestId,'CONNECTION',@Connection union all
    select @RequestId,'REFERER',@Referer;

insert into dbo.WebRequestParams_Memory
(RequestID,ParamName,ParamValue)
    select @RequestID, ParamName, ParamValue
    from
    (
        select @Param1, @Param1Value union all
        select @Param2, @Param2Value union all
        select @Param3, @Param3Value union all
        select @Param4, @Param4Value union all
        select @Param5, @Param5Value
    ) v(ParamName, ParamValue)
    where
        ParamName is not null and
        ParamValue is not null;
end
```

You should specify that the module is natively compiled using the WITH NATIVE_ COMPILATION clause. All natively compiled modules are schema-bound, and they require you to specify the SCHEMABINDING option. Finally, you can set the optional execution security context and several other parameters. I will discuss them in detail in Chapter 9.

Natively compiled stored procedures execute as atomic blocks indicated by the BEGIN ATOMIC keyword, which is an "all or nothing" approach. Either all of the statements in the procedure succeed or all of them fail.

When a natively compiled stored procedure is called outside the context of an active transaction, it starts a new transaction and either commits or rolls it back at the end of the execution.

In cases where a procedure is called in the context of an active transaction, SQL Server creates a savepoint at the beginning of the procedure's execution. In case of an error in the procedure, SQL Server rolls back the transaction to the created savepoint. Based on the severity and type of error, the transaction is either going to be able to continue and commit or become doomed and uncommittable.

Even though the dbo.InsertRequestInfo_Memory and dbo.InsertRequestInfo_ NativelyCompiled stored procedures accomplish the same task, their implementation is slightly different. Natively compiled stored procedures have an extensive list of limitations and unsupported T-SQL features. In the previous example, you can see that neither the INSERT statement with multiple VALUES nor CTE were supported.

■ **Note**   I will discuss natively compiled stored procedures, atomic transactions, and supported T-SQL language constructs in greater depth in Chapter 9.

Finally, it is worth mentioning that natively compiled modules can access only memory-optimized tables. It is impossible to query disk-based tables or, as another example, join memory-optimized and disk-based tables together. You have to use interpreted T-SQL and the Interop Engine for such tasks.

In-Memory OLTP in Action: Resolving Latch Contention

Latches are lightweight synchronization objects that SQL Server uses to protect the consistency of internal data structures. Multiple sessions (or, in that context, threads) cannot modify the same object simultaneously.

Consider the situation when multiple sessions try to access the same data page in the buffer pool. While it is safe for the multiple sessions/threads to read the data simultaneously, data modifications must be serialized and have exclusive access to the page. If such a rule is not enforced, multiple threads could update a different part of the data page at once, overwriting each other's changes and making the data inconsistent, which would lead to page corruption.

Latches help to enforce that rule. The threads that need to read data from the page obtain shared (S) latches, which are compatible with each other. Data modification, on the other hand, requires an exclusive (X) latch, which prevents other readers and writers from accessing the data page.

■ **Note**   Even though latches are conceptually similar to locks, there is a subtle difference between them. Locks enforce *logical* consistency of the data. For example, they reduce or prevent concurrency phenomena, such as dirty or phantom reads. Latches, on the other hand, enforce *physical* data consistency, such as preventing corruption of the data page structures.

Usually, latches have a short lifetime and are barely noticeable in the system. However, in busy OLTP systems, with a large number of CPUs and a high rate of simultaneous data modifications, latch contention can become a bottleneck. You can see the sign of such a bottleneck by the large percent of PAGELATCH waits in the wait statistics or by analyzing the sys.dm_os_latch_stats data management view.

In-Memory OLTP can be extremely helpful in addressing latch contention because of its latch-free architecture. It can help to dramatically increase data modification throughput in some scenarios. In this section, you will see one such example.

In my test environment, I used a Microsoft Azure DS15V2 virtual machine with the Enterprise edition of SQL Server 2016 SP1 installed. This virtual machine has 20 cores and 140GB of RAM and disk subsystem that performs 62,500 IOPS.

I created the database shown in Listing 2-1 with 16 data files in the LOGDATA filegroup to minimize allocation maps latch contention. The log file has been placed on the local SSD storage, while data and In-Memory OLTP filegroups share the main disk array. It is worth noting that placing disk-based and In-Memory filegroups on the different arrays in production often leads to better I/O performance. However, it did not affect the test scenarios where I did not mix disk-based and In-Memory OLTP workloads in the same tests.

As the first step, I created a set of disk-based tables that mimics the structure of memory-optimized tables created earlier in the chapter, and I created the stored procedure that inserts data into those tables. Listing 2-5 shows the code to accomplish this.

Listing 2-5. Creating Disk-Based Tables and a Stored Procedure

```
create table dbo.WebRequests_Disk
(
   RequestId int not null identity(1,1),
   RequestTime datetime2(4) not null
      constraint DEF_WebRequests_Disk_RequestTime
      default sysutcdatetime(),
   URL varchar(255) not null,
   RequestType tinyint not null, -- GET/POST/PUT
   ClientIP varchar(15) not null,
   BytesReceived int not null,

   constraint PK_WebRequests_Disk
   primary key nonclustered(RequestID)
   on [LOGDATA]
) on [LOGDATA];

create unique clustered index IDX_WebRequests_Disk_RequestTime_RequestId
on dbo.WebRequests_Disk(RequestTime,RequestId)
on [LOGDATA];

create table dbo.WebRequestHeaders_Disk
(
   RequestId int not null,
   HeaderName varchar(64) not null,
   HeaderValue varchar(256) not null,

   constraint PK_WebRequestHeaders_Disk
   primary key clustered(RequestID,HeaderName)
   on [LOGDATA]
);
```

```
create table dbo.WebRequestParams_Disk
(
   RequestId int not null,
   ParamName varchar(64) not null,
   ParamValue nvarchar(256) not null,

   constraint PK_WebRequestParams_Disk
   primary key clustered(RequestID,ParamName)
   on [LOGDATA]
);
go

create proc dbo.InsertRequestInfo_Disk
(
   @URL varchar(255)
   ,@RequestType tinyint
   ,@ClientIP varchar(15)
   ,@BytesReceived int
   -- Header fields
   ,@Authorization varchar(256)
   ,@UserAgent varchar(256)
   ,@Host varchar(256)
   ,@Connection varchar(256)
   ,@Referer varchar(256)
   -- Parameters.. Just for the demo purposes
   ,@Param1 varchar(64) = null
   ,@Param1Value nvarchar(256) = null
   ,@Param2 varchar(64) = null
   ,@Param2Value nvarchar(256) = null
   ,@Param3 varchar(64) = null
   ,@Param3Value nvarchar(256) = null
   ,@Param4 varchar(64) = null
   ,@Param4Value nvarchar(256) = null
   ,@Param5 varchar(64) = null
   ,@Param5Value nvarchar(256) = null
)
as
begin
   set nocount on
   set xact_abort on

   declare
      @RequestId int
```

```
    begin tran
        insert into dbo.WebRequests_Disk
            (URL,RequestType,ClientIP,BytesReceived)
        values
            (@URL,@RequestType,@ClientIP,@BytesReceived);

        select @RequestId = SCOPE_IDENTITY();

        insert into dbo.WebRequestHeaders_Disk
            (RequestId,HeaderName,HeaderValue)
        values
            (@RequestId,'AUTHORIZATION',@Authorization)
            ,(@RequestId,'USERAGENT',@UserAgent)
            ,(@RequestId,'HOST',@Host)
            ,(@RequestId,'CONNECTION',@Connection)
            ,(@RequestId,'REFERER',@Referer);

        ;with Params(ParamName, ParamValue)
        as
        (
            select ParamName, ParamValue
            from (
                values
                    (@Param1, @Param1Value)
                    ,(@Param2, @Param2Value)
                    ,(@Param3, @Param3Value)
                    ,(@Param4, @Param4Value)
                    ,(@Param5, @Param5Value)
                ) v(ParamName, ParamValue)
            where
                ParamName is not null and
                ParamValue is not null
        )
        insert into dbo.WebRequestParams_Disk
            (RequestID,ParamName,ParamValue)
            select @RequestId, ParamName, ParamValue
                from Params;
    commit
end;
```

In the tests, I compared the insert throughput of disk-based and memory-optimized tables using the dbo.InsertRequestInfo_Disk, dbo.InsertRequestInfo_Memory, and dbo.InsertRequestInfo_NativelyCompiled stored procedures, calling them simultaneously from the multiple sessions in the loop. Each call inserted one row into the dbo.WebRequests table, five rows into the dbo.WebRequestHeaders table, and from one to five rows into the dbo.WebRequestDisks table, which makes nine rows total on average in the single transaction.

21

■ **Note** The test application and scripts are included in the companion materials of the book.

In the case of the `dbo.InsertRequestInfo_Disk` stored procedure and disk-based tables, my test server achieved a maximum throughput of about 4,500 batches/calls per second with 150 concurrent sessions. Figure 2-1 shows several performance counters at the time of the test.

```
\\SQL2016
    Processor Information                          _Total
        % Processor Time                          20.387

SQLServer:Latches
    Average Latch Wait Time (ms)                    2.377
    Latch Waits/sec                            72,594.302
    Total Latch Wait Time (ms)                174,727.498

SQLServer:SQL Statistics
    Batch Requests/sec                          4,507.167
```

Figure 2-1. *Performance counters when data was inserted into disk-based tables (150 concurrent sessions)*

Even though I maxed out the insert throughput, the CPU load on the server was very low, which clearly indicated that the CPU was not the bottleneck during the test. At the same time, the server suffered from the large number of latches, which were used to serialize access to the data pages in the buffer pool. Even though the wait time of each individual latch was relatively low, the total latch wait time was high because of the excessive number of them acquired every second.

A further increase in the number of sessions did not help and, in fact, even slightly reduced the throughput. Figure 2-2 illustrates performance counters with 300 concurrent sessions. As you can see, the average latch wait time has been increasing with the load.

```
\\SQL2016
    Processor Information                          _Total
        % Processor Time                          19.485

SQLServer:Latches
    Average Latch Wait Time (ms)                    4.921
    Latch Waits/sec                            67,330.041
    Total Latch Wait Time (ms)                338,081.355

SQLServer:SQL Statistics
    Batch Requests/sec                          3,841.084
```

Figure 2-2. *Performance counters when data was inserted into disk-based tables (300 concurrent sessions)*

You can confirm that latches were the bottleneck by analyzing the wait statistics collected during the test. Figure 2-3 illustrates the output from the sys.dm_os_wait_ stats view. You can see that latch waits are at the top of the list.

	Wait Type	Wait Count	Wait Time (ms)	Avg Wait Time (ms)	Percent
1	PAGELATCH_EX	3013621	6779076.000	2.0	51.059
2	PAGELATCH_SH	1546503	4663412.000	3.0	35.124
3	WRITELOG	290686	1652691.000	5.0	12.448

Figure 2-3. *Wait statistics collected during the test (insert into disk-based tables)*

The situation changed when I repeated the tests with the dbo.InsertRequestInfo_ Memory stored procedure, which inserted data into memory-optimized tables through the Interop Engine. I maxed out the throughput with 300 concurrent sessions, which doubled the number of sessions from the previous test. In this scenario, SQL Server was able to handle about 74,000 batches/calls per second, which is more than a 16 times increase in the throughput. A further increase in the number of concurrent sessions did not change the throughput; however, the duration of each call linearly increased as more sessions were added.

Figure 2-4 illustrates the performance counters during the test. As you see, there were no latches with memory-optimized tables, and the CPUs were fully utilized.

\\SQL2016

Processor Information	**_Total**
% Processor Time	97.615
SQLServer:Latches	
Average Latch Wait Time (ms)	0.000
Latch Waits/sec	0.000
Total Latch Wait Time (ms)	0.000
SQLServer:SQL Statistics	
Batch Requests/sec	74,028.710

Figure 2-4. *Performance counters when data was inserted into memory-optimized tables through the Interop Engine*

As you can see in Figure 2-5, the only significant wait in the system was WRITELOG, which is related to the transaction log write performance.

	Wait Type	Wait Count	Wait Time (ms)	Avg Wait Time (ms)	Percent
1	WRITELOG	5162084	15969687.000	3.0	99.986

Figure 2-5. *Wait statistics collected during the test (insert into memory-optimized tables through the Interop Engine)*

The natively compiled dbo.InsertRequestInfo_NativelyCompiled stored procedure improved the situation even further. With 400 concurrent sessions, SQL Server was able to handle about 106,000 batches/calls per second, which translates to about 950,000 individual inserts per second.

Figure 2-6 illustrates the performance counters during test execution. Even with the increase in throughput, the natively compiled stored procedure put less load on the CPU than the Interop Engine, and disk performance became the clear bottleneck in this setup.

\\SQL2016	
Processor Information	_Total
% Processor Time	91.565
SQLServer:Latches	
Average Latch Wait Time (ms)	0.000
Latch Waits/sec	0.000
Total Latch Wait Time (ms)	0.000
SQLServer:SQL Statistics	
Batch Requests/sec	106,386.319

Figure 2-6. *Performance counters when data was inserted into memory-optimized tables using natively compiled stored procedure*

Waits in the wait statistics were similar to the previous test, with WRITELOG as the only significant wait in the system (see Figure 2-7).

	Wait Type	Wait Count	Wait Time (ms)	Avg Wait Time (ms)	Percent
1	WRITELOG	7120451	21115668.000	2.0	99.913

Figure 2-7. *Wait statistics collected during the test (insert into memory-optimized tables using natively compiled stored procedure)*

You can confirm that disk performance was the limiting factor in this setup by running the same test with nondurable memory-optimized tables. You can do this by dropping and re-creating the database and creating the same set of memory-optimized tables using the DURABILITY=SCHEMA_ONLY option. No other code changes are required.

Figure 2-8 shows the performance counters collected during the test, with 400 concurrent sessions calling the dbo.InsertRequestInfo_NativelyCompiled stored procedure to insert data into nondurable tables. As you can see, in that scenario, I was able to fully utilize the CPU on the system after I removed the I/O bottleneck, which improved throughput by another 50 percent compared to the durable memory-optimized tables.

```
\\SQL2016
    Processor Information                            _Total
        % Processor Time                            100.000

SQLServer:Latches
    Average Latch Wait Time (ms)                      0.000
    Latch Waits/sec                                   0.000
    Total Latch Wait Time (ms)                        0.000

SQLServer:SQL Statistics
    Batch Requests/sec                          153,785.607
```

Figure 2-8. *Performance counters when data was inserted into nondurable memory-optimized tables using a natively compiled stored procedure*

Finally, it is worth noting that In-Memory OLTP uses different and more efficient logging, which leads to a much smaller transaction log footprint. Figure 2-9 illustrates the log file write statistics collected during one minute of test execution using the sys.dm_io_virtual_file_stats DMF. The order of outputs in the figure corresponds to the order in which the tests were run: disk-based table inserts, inserts into memory-optimized tables through the Interop Engine, and natively compiled stored procedures.

	File Name	Written MB	Writes	IO Count
1	InMemoryOLTP2016_log	635.793	20067	20067

	File Name	Written MB	Writes	IO Count
1	InMemoryOLTP2016_log	4834.148	147347	147347

	File Name	Written MB	Writes	IO Count
1	InMemoryOLTP2016_log	5396.695	141134	141134

Figure 2-9. *Transaction log write statistics during the tests*

As you see, in interop mode In-Memory OLTP inserted more than 16 times more data; however, it used just 7.6 times more space in the transaction log than with disk-based tables. The situation is even better with natively compiled stored procedures. Even though it wrote about 12 percent more to the log, it inserted about 30 percent more data compared to interop mode.

■ **Note**   I will discuss In-Memory OLTP transaction logging in greater depth in Chapter 10.

Obviously, different scenarios will lead to different results, and performance improvements would greatly depend on the hardware, database schema, and use case and workload in the system. However, with OLTP workloads, it is not uncommon to see an improvement of 3 to 5 times when you access memory-optimized tables through the Interop Engine and an improvement of 10 to 40 times with natively compiled stored procedures.

More importantly, In-Memory OLTP allows you to improve the performance of the system by scaling up and upgrading hardware. For example, in this scenario, you can achieve better throughput by adding more CPUs and/or increasing I/O performance. This would be impossible to do with disk-based tables where latch contention becomes a bottleneck.

Summary

The In-Memory OLTP engine is fully integrated into SQL Server and is installed with the product. It is an Enterprise edition feature in SQL Server 2016 RTM; however, it is available in all editions starting with SQL Server 2016 SP1. It is also available in the Premium tiers of Microsoft Azure SQL Database. You should remember, however, about the resource limitations that exist in non-Enterprise editions of SQL Server.

Every database that uses In-Memory OLTP objects should have the separate In-Memory OLTP filegroup created. This filegroup should be placed in the disk array optimized for sequential I/O performance. Microsoft Azure SQL Database does not require or allow you to create that filegroup.

You can create memory-optimized tables with the regular CREATE TABLE statement, marking tables as MEMORY_OPTIMIZED and specifying the table durability option. The data in the tables with SCHEMA_AND_DATA durability is persisted on disk. Tables with SCHEMA_ONLY durability do not persist the data, and they can be used as in-memory temporary tables that provide extremely fast performance.

You can access memory-optimized tables either from interpreted T-SQL through the Interop Engine or from natively compiled modules. Almost all T-SQL features are supported in interpreted mode. Natively compiled modules, on the other hand, have the large set of limitations. Nevertheless, they can introduce significant performance improvements compared to the interop engine.

CHAPTER 3

■ ■ ■

Memory-Optimized Tables

This chapter discusses memory-optimized tables in detail. It shows how memory-optimized tables store their data and how SQL Server accesses them. It covers the format of the data rows in memory-optimized tables and talks about the process of native compilation.

Finally, the chapter provides an overview of the limitations of memory-optimized tables that exist in SQL Server 2016.

Disk-Based vs. Memory-Optimized Tables

Data and index structures in memory-optimized tables are different from those in disk-based tables. In disk-based tables, the data is stored in the 8KB data pages grouped together in eight-page extents on a per-index or per-heap basis. Every page stores the data from one or multiple data rows. Moreover, the data from variable-length or LOB columns can be stored off-row on ROW_OVERFLOW and LOB data pages when it does not fit on one in-row page.

All pages and rows in disk-based tables are referenced by in-file offsets, which are a combination of file_id, data page offset/position in the file, and, in the case of a data row, row offset/position on the data page.

Finally, every nonclustered index stores its own copy of the data from the index key columns, referencing the main row by *row ID*, which is either the clustered index key value or a physical address (offset) of the row in the heap table.

Figures 3-1 and 3-2 illustrate these concepts. They show clustered and nonclustered index B-Trees defined on a table. As you see, pages are linked through in-file offsets. The nonclustered index persists the separate copy of the data and references the clustered index through clustered index key values.

© Dmitri Korotkevitch 2017
D. Korotkevitch, *Expert SQL Server In-Memory OLTP*, DOI 10.1007/978-1-4842-2772-5_3

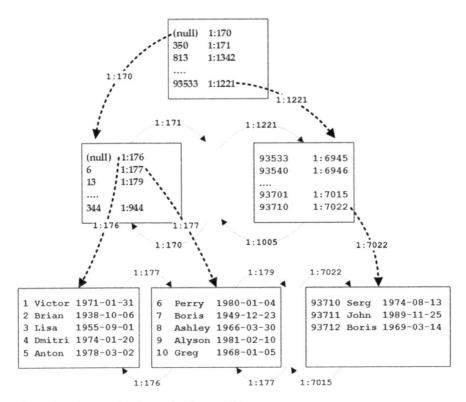

Figure 3-1. *Clustered index on disk-based table*

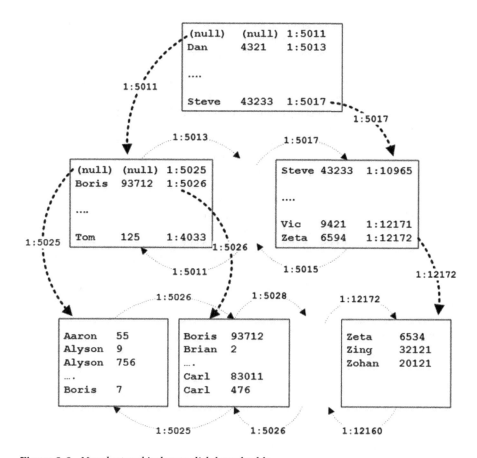

Figure 3-2. Nonclustered index on disk-based table

Every time you need to access the data from the page, SQL Server loads the copy of the page to the memory, caching it in the buffer pool. However, the format and structure of the data page in the buffer pool does not change, and pages there still use in-file offsets to reference each other. The SQL Server component called the *Buffer Manager* manages the buffer pool, and it tracks the data page's in-memory locations, translating in-file offsets to the corresponding memory addresses of the page structures.

Consider the situation when SQL Server needs to scan several data pages in the index. The worker thread requests the page from the Buffer Manager, using file_id and page_id to identify it. The Buffer Manager, in turn, checks whether the page is already cached, reading it from disk when necessary. When the page is read and processed, SQL Server obtains the address of the next page in the index and repeats the process.

It is also entirely possible that SQL Server needs to access multiple pages in order to read a single row. This happens in case of off-row storage and/or when the execution plan uses nonclustered indexes and issues *Key* or *RID Lookup* operations, obtaining the data from the clustered index or heap.

29

The process of locating a page in the buffer pool is very fast; however, it still introduces overhead that affects the performance of the queries. The performance hit is much worse when the data page is not in memory and a physical I/O operation is required.

As you already know, SQL Server protects the internal consistency of the data pages, with latches preventing multiple sessions from modifying the data on the data page simultaneously. Acquiring and managing those latches also adds overhead to the system.

Finally, SQL Server uses locking to protect the transactional consistency of the data acquiring locks on the data row- and page- and object- levels. Those locks may introduce blocking in the system, and they also add the overhead associated with their management.

The In-Memory OLTP engine uses a completely different approach with memory-optimized tables. With the exception of Bw-Trees in nonclustered indexes, which I will discuss in Chapter 5, in-memory objects do not use data pages. Data rows reference each other through the memory pointers. Every row knows the memory address of the next row in the chain, and SQL Server does not need to do any extra steps to locate it.

Every memory-optimized table has at least one index row chain to link rows together; therefore, every table must have at least one index defined. In the case of durable memory-optimized tables, there is the requirement of creating a primary key constraint, which can serve this purpose.

To illustrate the concepts of row chains, let's create the memory-optimized table shown in Listing 3-1.

Listing 3-1. Creating the Memory-Optimized Table

```
create table dbo.People
(
   Name varchar(64) not null
      constraint PK_People
      primary key nonclustered
      hash with (bucket_count = 1024),
   City varchar(64) not null,

   index IDX_City nonclustered hash(City)
   with (bucket_count = 1024),
)
with (memory_optimized = on, durability = schema_only);
```

This table has two hash indexes defined on the Name and City columns. I will not discuss hash indexes in depth in this chapter, but as a general overview, they consist of a hash table, which is an array of hash buckets, each of which contains a memory pointer to the data row. SQL Server applies a hash function to the index key columns, and the result of the function determines to which bucket a row belongs. All rows that have the same hash value and belong to the same bucket are linked together in a row chain; every row has a pointer to the next row in a chain.

■ **Note**   I will discuss hash indexes in detail in Chapter 4.

Figure 3-3 illustrates this. Solid arrows represent pointers in the index on the Name column. Dotted arrows represent pointers in the index on the City column. For simplicity's sake, let's assume that the hash function generates a hash value based on the first letter of the string. Two numbers, displayed in each row, indicate the row lifetime, which I will explain in the next section of this chapter.

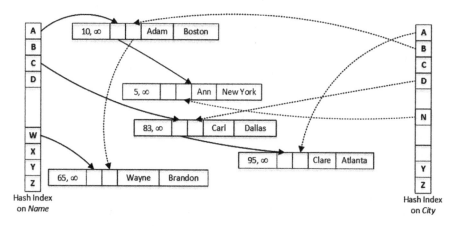

Figure 3-3. *Memory-optimized table with two hash indexes*

In contrast to disk-based tables, indexes on memory-optimized tables are not created as separate data structures but rather *embedded* as pointers in the data rows, which, in a nutshell, makes every index *covering* for in-row columns. The indexes, however, do not cover off-row column data, where data is stored in the separate internal tables. I will discuss them in depth in Chapter 6.

■ **Note**   To be precise, nonclustered indexes and clustered columnstore indexes on memory-optimized tables introduce additional data structures in memory. I will discuss nonclustered indexes in detail in Chapter 5 and clustered columnstore indexes in Chapter 8.

Introduction to Multiversion Concurrency Control

As you already noticed in Figure 3-3, every row in a memory-optimized table has two values, called BeginTs and EndTs, which define the lifetime of the row. A SQL Server instance maintains the *Global Transaction Timestamp* value, which is auto-incremented when the transaction commits and is unique for every committed transaction. BeginTs stores the Global Transaction Timestamp of the transaction that inserted a row, and EndTs stores the timestamp of the transaction that deleted a row. A special value called Infinity is used as EndTs for the rows that have not been deleted.

The rows in memory-optimized tables are never updated. The update operation creates the new version of the row with the new Global Transaction Timestamp set as BeginTs and marks the old version of the row as deleted by populating the EndTs timestamp with the same value.

When a new transaction starts, In-Memory OLTP assigns the *logical start time* for the transaction, which represents the Global Transaction Timestamp value when a transaction starts. It dictates what version of the rows is visible to the transaction. A transaction can see a row *only* when its logical start time (the Global Transaction Timestamp value when the transaction starts) is between the BeginTs and EndTs timestamps of the row.

To illustrate this, let's assume you ran the statement shown in Listing 3-2 and committed the transaction when the Global Transaction Timestamp value was 100.

Listing 3-2. Updating Data in the dbo.People Table

```
update dbo.People
set City = 'Cincinnati'
where Name = 'Ann'
```

Figure 3-4 illustrates the data in the table after an update transaction has been committed. As you can see, you now have two rows with Name='Ann' and different lifetimes. The new row has been appended to the row chain referenced by the hash bucket for the value of A in the index on the Name column. The hash index on the City column did not have any rows referenced by the C bucket; therefore, the new row becomes the first in the row chain referenced from that bucket.

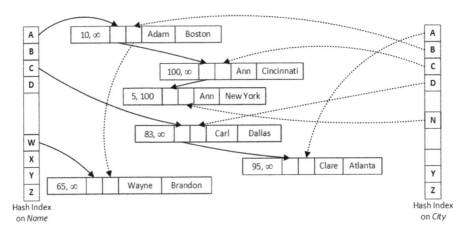

Figure 3-4. *Data in the table after update*

Let's assume you need to run a query that selects all the rows with Name='Ann' in the transaction with the logical start time (Global Transaction Timestamp when the transaction started) of 110. SQL Server calculates the hash value for Ann, which is A, and finds the corresponding bucket in the hash index on the Name column. It follows the pointer from that bucket, which references a row with Name='Adam'. This row has a BeginTs value of 10 and an EndTs value of Infinity; therefore, it is visible to the transaction. However, the Name value does not match the predicate, and the row is ignored.

In the next step, SQL Server follows the pointer from the Adam index pointer array, which references the first Ann row. This row has a BeginTs value of 100 and an EndTs value of Infinity; therefore, it is visible to the transaction and needs to be selected.

As a final step, SQL Server follows the next pointer in the index. Even though the last row also has Name='Ann', it has an EndTs value of 100 and is invisible to the transaction.

As you should have already noticed, this concurrency behavior and data consistency corresponds to the SNAPSHOT transaction isolation level when every transaction *sees* the data as of the time the transaction started. SNAPSHOT is the default transaction isolation level in the In-Memory OLTP Engine, which also supports the REPEATABLE READ and SERIALIZABLE isolation levels. However, the REPEATABLE READ and SERIALIZABLE transactions in In-Memory OLTP behave differently than with disk-based tables. In-Memory OLTP raises an exception and rolls back a transaction if REPEATABLE READ or SERIALIZABLE data consistency rules were violated instead of blocking a transaction as with disk-based tables.

The In-Memory OLTP documentation also indicates that autocommitted (single-statement) transactions can run in the READ COMMITTED isolation level. However, this is a bit misleading. SQL Server promotes and executes such transactions in the SNAPSHOT isolation level and does not require you to explicitly specify the isolation level in your code. Similarly to SNAPSHOT transactions, the autocommitted READ COMMITTED transaction would not *see* the changes committed after the transaction started, which is a different behavior compared to the READ COMMITTED transactions against disk-based tables.

■ **Note**   I will discuss the concurrency model in In-Memory OLTP in Chapter 7.

SQL Server keeps track of the active transactions in the system and detects stale rows when their EndTs of stake rows is older than the logical start time of the *oldest active transaction* in the system. Stale rows are invisible for active transactions in the system, and eventually they are removed from the index row chains and deallocated by the garbage collection process.

■ **Note**   I will cover the garbage collection process in more detail in Chapter 11.

Data Row Format

As you can guess, the format of the data rows in memory-optimized tables is entirely different from disk-based tables and consists of two different sections, the *row header* and the *payload,* as shown in Figure 3-5.

Figure 3-5. *The structure of a data row in a memory-optimized table*

You are already familiar with the BeginTs and EndTs timestamps in the row header. The next element there is StmtId, which references the statement that inserted that row. Every statement in a transaction has a unique 4-byte StmtId value, which works as a *Halloween protection* technique and allows the statement to skip rows it just inserted.

HALLOWEEN PROTECTION

The Halloween effect is a known problem in the relational database world. It was discovered by IBM researchers in 1976 around Halloween, which gave the name to phenomena. In a nutshell, it refers to the situation when the execution of a data modification query is affected by the previous modifications it performed.

You can think of the following statement as a classic example of the Halloween problem:

```
insert into T
    select * from T
```

Without Halloween protection, this query would fall into an infinitive loop, reading the data it just inserted and inserting it over and over again.

With disk-based tables, SQL Server implements Halloween protection by adding *Spool* operators to the execution plan. These operators create a temporary copy of the data before processing it. In this example, all data from the table is cached in the *Table Spool* first, which will work as the source of the data for the insert.

StmtId helps to avoid the Halloween problem in memory-optimized tables. Statements check the StmtId value of the rows and skip those they just inserted.

The next element in the header, the 2-byte `IdxLinkCount`, indicates how many indexes (pointers) reference the row (or, in the other words, in how many index chains this row is participating). SQL Server uses it to detect rows that can be deallocated by the garbage collection process. SQL Server also adds empty 2-byte padding after `IdxLinkCount` to align the row header with 8-byte boundaries.

An array of 8-byte index pointers is the last element of the row header. As you already know, every memory-optimized table should have at least one index to link data rows together. In SQL Server 2016, you can define up to eight indexes per memory-optimized table, including the primary key constraint. This restriction has been removed in SQL Server 2017.

The actual row data is stored in the payload section of the row. The payload format may vary depending on the table schema. SQL Server works with the payload through a DLL that is generated and compiled for the table (more on that in the next section of this chapter).

I would like to reiterate that a key principle of In-Memory OLTP is that payload data is never updated. When a table row needs to be updated, In-Memory OLTP *deletes* the version of the row by setting the `EndTs` timestamp of the original row and inserts the new data row version with the new `BeginTs` value and an `EndTs` value of `Infinity`.

Native Compilation of Memory-Optimized Tables

One of the key differences between the Storage Engine and In-Memory OLTP Engine resides in how engines work with the data rows. The data in disk-based tables is always stored using one of the three predefined formats, which do not depend on the table schema and are controlled by the index data compression option.

As usual, that approach comes with benefits and downsides. It is extremely flexible and allows you to alter a table and mix per- and post-altered versions of the rows together. For example, adding a new nullable column to the table is the metadata-level operation, which does not change existing rows. The Storage Engine analyzes table metadata and different row attributes and handles multiple versions of the rows correctly.

However, such flexibility comes at a cost. Consider the situation when the query needs to access the data from the variable-length column in the row. In this scenario, SQL Server needs to find the offset of the variable-length array section in the row, calculate an offset and length of the column data from that array, and analyze whether the column data is stored in-row or off-row before getting the required data. All of that can lead to the large number of CPU instructions to execute.

The In-Memory OLTP Engine uses a completely opposite approach. SQL Server creates and compiles the separate DLLs for every memory-optimized table in the system. Those DLLs are loaded into the SQL Server address space, and they are responsible for accessing and manipulating the data in the payload section of the row. The In-Memory OLTP Engine is generic and does not know anything about the underlying payload part of the row; all data access is done through those DLLs, which are aware of the data row format and optimized to speed up the data access and data manipulation.

As you can guess, this approach significantly reduces processing overhead; however, it comes at the cost of reduced flexibility. The generated table DLLs require all rows to have the same structure. Table alteration generates the new version of the DLL and, in most cases, will require In-Memory OLTP to re-create all the data rows in the table, transforming them to the new format. I will discuss this in depth in Chapter 10.

This restriction can lead to supportability and performance issues when tables and indexes are defined incorrectly. One such example is the wrong hash index bucket count definition, which can lead to an excessive number of rows in the row chains, which reduces index performance. I will discuss this problem in detail in Chapter 4.

■ **Note**   SQL Server places the source code and compiled DLLs in the XTP subfolder of the SQL Server DATA directory. I will talk about those files and the native compilation process in more detail in Chapter 9.

Memory-Optimized Tables: Surface Area and Limitations

The first release of In-Memory OLTP in SQL Server 2014 had an extensive list of limitations. Fortunately, many of them have been removed in SQL Server 2016.

Let's look at the supported surface area and existing limitations in detail.

Supported Data Types

One of the biggest limitations of In-Memory OLTP in SQL Server 2014 was the inability to support off-row storage. It was impossible to create a table with a row size that exceeded 8,060 bytes or use the (n)varchar(max) and varbinary(max) data types.

Fortunately, this limitation has been removed in the second release of In-Memory OLTP. SQL Server 2016 supports off-row storage and allows data rows to exceed 8,060 bytes. The (n)varchar(max) and varbinary(max) data types are now supported. I would like to reiterate, however, that off-row data is stored in the separate internal tables and can reduce the performance of the system. I will discuss this in detail in Chapter 6.

There are still several data types that are not supported in the SQL Server 2016 release of In-Memory OLTP. They include the following:

- datetimeoffset, rowversion, and sql_variant

- image and (n)text

- CLR-based data types: geography, geometry, and hierarchyid

- User-defined data types

- xml

Even though the list of unsupported data types is not very extensive, those limitations can still complicate In-Memory OLTP migration for existing systems. In some cases, you can store the data from unsupported data types in varbinary(max) column, casting it to the appropriate data type in the code. This approach, however, would require you to use the Interop Engine and would not work with native compilation.

Table Features

The memory-optimized tables have several other requirements and limitations, outlined here:

- Computed columns are not supported in SQL Server 2016. They are supported, however, in SQL Server 2017.

- Sparse columns are not supported.

- IDENTITY columns should have a SEED and INCREMENT value of (1,1).

- Memory-optimized tables cannot participate in FOREIGN KEY constraints with disk-based tables. You can define foreign keys between memory-optimized tables; however, they should always reference primary keys rather than UNIQUE constraints.

- Full-text indexes on memory-optimized tables are not supported.

- Memory-optimized tables cannot be defined as FILETABLE or use FILESTREAM storage.

In SQL Server 2016, every memory-optimized table, durable or nondurable, should have at least one and at most eight indexes. Moreover, the durable memory-optimized table should have a unique primary key constraint defined. This constraint is counted as one of the indexes toward the eight-index limit. The eight-index restriction has been removed in SQL Server 2017.

It is also worth noting that columns participating in the primary key constraint are nonupdatable. You can delete the old and insert the new row as the workaround.

Database-Level Limitations

In-Memory OLTP has several limitations that affect some of the database settings and operations. They include the following:

- You cannot create a database snapshot on databases that use In-Memory OLTP.

- The AUTO_CLOSE database option must be set to OFF.

- CREATE DATABASE FOR ATTACH_REBUILD_LOG is not supported.

- DBCC CHECKDB skips the memory-optimized tables.

- DBCC CHECKTABLE fails if called to check the memory-optimized table.

■ **Note** You can see the full list of limitations at https://docs.microsoft.com/en-us/sql/relational-databases/in-memory-oltp/transact-sql-constructs-not-supported-by-in-memory-oltp.

High Availability Technologies Support

Memory-optimized tables are fully supported in AlwaysOn Failover Clusters and Availability Groups and with Log Shipping. However, in the case of a failover cluster, data from durable memory-optimized tables must be loaded into memory in the case of a failover, which could increase failover time and reduce database availability.

In the case of AlwaysOn Availability Groups, only durable memory-optimized tables are replicated to secondary nodes. You can access and query those tables on the readable secondary nodes if needed.

Data from nondurable memory-optimized tables, on the other hand, is not replicated and will be lost in the case of a failover. You should remember this behavior when you use In-Memory OLTP in Microsoft Azure SQL Database. Transient database failovers in Azure will erase the data from nondurable memory-optimized tables.

Memory-optimized tables can participate in transactional replication. All other replication types, including peer-to-peer replication, are not supported.

In-Memory OLTP is not supported in database mirroring sessions. This does not appear to be a big limitation, however. Database mirroring is a deprecated feature, and you should use AlwaysOn Availability Groups as the replacement for the technology.

SQL Server 2016 Features Support

In-Memory OLTP is fully integrated with many new SQL Server 2016 features. Let's list a few of them.

In-Memory OLTP workloads can be captured by Query Store. It automatically collects queries, plans, and optimization statistics for In-Memory OLTP objects without any additional configuration changes required. However, runtime statistics are not collected by default, and you need to explicitly enable them with the sys.sp_xtp_control_query_exec_stats stored procedure.

Keep in mind that the collection of runtime statistics adds overhead, which can degrade the performance of In-Memory OLTP workloads.

■ **Note** I will talk about In-Memory OLTP Query Store integration in more detail in Chapter 12.

You can use system-versioned temporal tables with memory-optimized tables using disk-based *history* tables to store old row versions. When you enable system versioning in a memory-optimized table, SQL Server creates a staging memory-optimized table and synchronously populates it during UPDATE and DELETE operations. The data from the staging table is asynchronously moved to a disk-based history table by a background process called the *data flush task*. This task wakes up every minute with the light workload and can adjust its schedule to run every five seconds under a heavy workload.

By default, the data flush task moves the data from the staging table when it reaches 8 percent of the size of the *current* memory-optimized table. You can also force data movement manually by calling the sys.sp_xtp_flush_temporal_history stored procedure.

> ■ **Note** You can read more about temporal tables support at `https://docs.microsoft.`
> `com/en-us/sql/relational-databases/tables/system-versioned-temporal-tables-`
> `with-memory-optimized-tables.`

Memory-optimized tables can be configured for row-level security. The configuration process is essentially the same with on-disk tables; however, an inline table-valued function that is used as a security predicate must be natively compiled. I will discuss native compilation in Chapter 9.

> ■ **Note** You can read more about row-level security at `https://docs.microsoft.com/`
> `en-us/sql/relational-databases/security/row-level-security.`

It is also worth noting that starting with SQL Server 2016, the data from memory-optimized tables is encrypted on disk when Transparent Data Encryption (TDE) is enabled in the database. I will discuss how In-Memory OLTP persists data on disk in Chapter 10.

Summary

As the opposite of disk-based tables, where data is stored in 8KB data pages, memory-optimized tables link data rows into the index row chains using regular memory pointers. Every row has multiple pointers, one per index row chain. In SQL Server 2016, every table must have at least one and at most eight indexes defined.

A SQL Server instance maintains the Global Transaction Timestamp value, which is auto-incremented when the transaction commits and is unique for every committed transaction. Every data row has BeginTs and EndTs timestamps that define the row lifetime. A transaction can see a row only when its logical start time (the Global Transaction Timestamp value when the transaction starts) is between the BeginTs and EndTs timestamps of the row.

The row data in memory-optimized tables is never updated. When a table row needs to be updated, In-Memory OLTP creates the new version of the row with a new BeginTs value and *deletes* the old version of the row by populating its EndTs timestamp.

SQL Server generates and compiles native DLLs for every memory-optimized table in the system. Those DLLs are loaded into the SQL Server process, and they are responsible for accessing and manipulating the row data.

The In-Memory OLTP engine is fully supported in AlwaysOn Failover Clusters, Availability Groups, and with Log Shipping. Memory-optimized tables can also participate in transactional replication.

In-Memory OLTP is integrated with many new SQL Server 2016 features. Memory-optimized tables can be configured as system-versioned temporal tables, and they also support row-level security. Query Store can capture optimization and execution statistics for In-Memory OLTP workloads; however, capturing execution statistics introduces noticeable performance overhead to the system.

CHAPTER 4

▓ ▓ ▓

Hash Indexes

This chapter discusses hash indexes, the new type of index introduced in the In-Memory OLTP Engine. It will show their internal structure and explain how SQL Server works with them. You will learn about the most critical property of hash indexes, bucket_count, which defines the number of hash buckets in the index hash array. You will see how incorrect bucket count estimations affect system performance.

Finally, this chapter talks about the SARGability of hash indexes and statistics on memory-optimized tables.

Hashing Overview

Hashing is a widely known concept in computer science that performs the transformation of the data into short, usually fixed-length values. Hashing is often used in scenarios when you need to optimize point-lookup operations that search within a set of large strings or binary data using equality predicates. Hashing significantly reduces an index key size, making the index compact, which, in turn, improves the performance of point-lookup operations.

A properly defined hashing algorithm, often called a *hash function*, provides a relatively random hash distribution. A hash function is always deterministic, which means that the same input always generates the same hash value. However, a hash function does not necessarily guarantee uniqueness, and different input values can generate the same hashes. That situation is called a *collision*, and the chance of it greatly depends on the quality of the hash algorithm and the range of allowed hash keys. For example, a hash function that generates a 2-byte hash has a significantly higher chance of collision compared to a function that generates a 4-byte hash.

Hash tables, often called *hash maps*, are the data structures that store hash keys, mapping them to the original data. The hash keys are assigned to *buckets*, in which the original data can be found. Ideally, each unique hash key is stored in the individual bucket; however, when the number of buckets in the table is not big enough, it is entirely possible that multiple unique hash keys would be placed into the same bucket. Such a situation is called a *hash collision*.

■ **Tip**   The HASHBYTES function allows you to generate hashes in T-SQL using one of the industry-standard algorithms such as MD5, SHA2_512, and a few others. However, the output of the HASHBYTES function is not ideal for point-lookup optimization because of the large size of the output. You can use a CHECKSUM function that generates a 4-byte hash instead.

You can index the hash generated by the CHECKSUM function and use it as the replacement for the indexes on uniqueidentifier columns. It is also useful when you need to perform point-lookup operations on large (greater than 900/1,700 bytes) strings or binary data, which cannot be indexed. I discussed this scenario in Chapter 7 of my book *Pro SQL Server Internals*.

Much Ado About Bucket Count

In the In-Memory OLTP Engine, hash indexes are, in a nutshell, hash tables with buckets implemented as an array of a predefined size. Each bucket contains a pointer to a data row. SQL Server applies a hash function to the index key values, and the result of the function determines to which bucket a row belongs. All rows that have the same hash value and belong to the same bucket are linked together through a chain of index pointers in the data rows.

Figure 4-1 illustrates an example of a memory-optimized table with two hash indexes defined. You saw this diagram in the previous chapter; it's displayed here for reference purposes. Remember that in this example you are assuming that a hash function generates a hash value based on the first letter of the string. Obviously, a real hash function used in In-Memory OLTP is much more random and does not use character-based hashes.

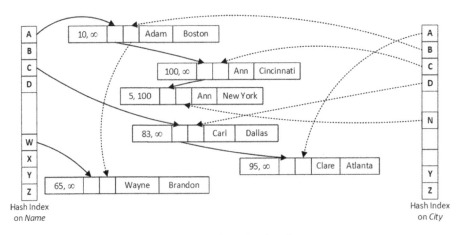

Figure 4-1. *A memory-optimized table with two hash indexes*

The number of buckets is the critical element for hash index performance. An efficient hash function allows you to avoid most collisions during hash key generation; however, you will have collisions in the hash table when the number of buckets is not big enough and SQL Server has to store different hashes together in the same buckets. Those collisions lead to longer row chains; this requires SQL Server to scan more rows through those links during the query processing.

Bucket Count and Performance

Let's consider a hash function that generates a hash based on the first two letters of the string and can return 26 * 26 = 676 different hash keys. This is a purely hypothetical example that I am using just for illustration purposes.

Assuming that the hash table can accommodate all 676 different hash buckets and you have the data shown in Figure 4-2, you will need to traverse at most two rows in the chain when you run a query that looks for a specific value.

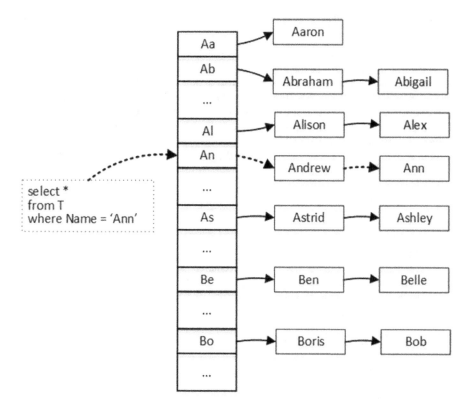

Figure 4-2. *Hash table lookup: 676 buckets*

The dotted arrows in Figure 4-2 illustrate the steps needed to look up the rows for Ann. The process requires you to traverse two rows after you find the right hash bucket in the table.

However, the situation changes if your hash table does not have enough buckets to separate unique hash keys from each other. Figure 4-3 illustrates the situation when a hash table has only 26 buckets and each of them stores multiple different hash keys. Now the same lookup of the Ann row requires you to traverse the chain of nine rows total.

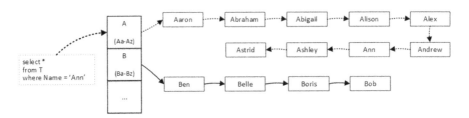

Figure 4-3. *Hash table lookup: 26 buckets*

The same principle applies to the hash indexes where choosing an incorrect number of buckets can lead to serious performance issues.

Let's create two nondurable memory-optimized tables and populate them with 1,000,000 rows each, as shown in Listing 4-1. Both tables have the same schema with a primary key constraint defined as the hash index. The number of buckets in the index is controlled by the bucket_count property. Internally, however, SQL Server rounds the provided value to the next power of 2, so the dbo.HashIndex_HighBucketCount table would have 1,048,576 buckets in the index, and the dbo.HashIndex_LowBucketCount table would have 1,024 buckets.

Listing 4-1. Bucket_count and Performance: Creating Memory-Optimized Tables

```
create table dbo.HashIndex_LowBucketCount
(
    Id int not null
        constraint PK_HashIndex_LowBucketCount
        primary key nonclustered
        hash with (bucket_count=1000),
    Value int not null
)
with (memory_optimized=on, durability=schema_only);

create table dbo.HashIndex_HighBucketCount
(
    Id int not null
        constraint PK_HashIndex_HighBucketCount
        primary key nonclustered
        hash with (bucket_count=1000000),
    Value int not null
)
```

```
with (memory_optimized=on, durability=schema_only);
go

;with N1(C) as (select 0 union all select 0) -- 2 rows
,N2(C) as (select 0 from N1 as t1 cross join N1 as t2) -- 4 rows
,N3(C) as (select 0 from N2 as t1 cross join N2 as t2) -- 16 rows
,N4(C) as (select 0 from N3 as t1 cross join N3 as t2) -- 256 rows
,N5(C) as (select 0 from N4 as t1 cross join N4 as t2) -- 65,536 rows
,N6(C) as (select 0 from N5 as t1 cross join N3 as t2) -- 1,048,576 rows
,Ids(Id) as (select row_number() over (order by (select null)) from N6)
insert into dbo.HashIndex_HighBucketCount(Id, Value)
    select Id, Id
    from ids
    where Id <= 1000000;

;with N1(C) as (select 0 union all select 0) -- 2 rows
,N2(C) as (select 0 from N1 as t1 cross join N1 as t2) -- 4 rows
,N3(C) as (select 0 from N2 as t1 cross join N2 as t2) -- 16 rows
,N4(C) as (select 0 from N3 as t1 cross join N3 as t2) -- 256 rows
,N5(C) as (select 0 from N4 as t1 cross join N4 as t2) -- 65,536 rows
,N6(C) as (select 0 from N5 as t1 cross join N3 as t2) -- 1,048,576 rows
,Ids(Id) as (select row_number() over (order by (select null)) from N6)
insert into dbo.HashIndex_LowBucketCount(Id, Value)
    select Id, Id
    from ids
    where Id <= 1000000;
```

Table 4-1 shows the execution time of the INSERT statements in my test environment. As you can see, inserting data into the dbo.HashIndex_HighBucketCount table is about 35 times faster compared to the dbo.HashIndex_LowBucketCount counterpart.

Table 4-1. *Execution Time of INSERT Statements*

dbo.HashIndex_HighBucketCount (1,048,576 Buckets)	dbo.HashIndex_LowBucketCount (1,024 Buckets)
1,122 ms	39,955 ms

Listing 4-2 shows the query that returns the bucket count and row chains information using the sys.dm_db_xtp_hash_index_stats view. Keep in mind that this view scans the entire table, which is time-consuming when the tables are large.

Listing 4-2. Obtaining Information About Hash Indexes

```
select
    s.name + '.' + t.name as [Table]
    ,i.name as [Index]
    ,stat.total_bucket_count as [Total Buckets]
    ,stat.empty_bucket_count as [Empty Buckets]
```

```
    ,floor(100. * empty_bucket_count / total_bucket_count)
        as [Empty Bucket %]
    ,stat.avg_chain_length as [Avg Chain]
    ,stat.max_chain_length as [Max Chain]
from
    sys.dm_db_xtp_hash_index_stats stat
        join sys.tables t on
            stat.object_id = t.object_id
        join sys.indexes i on
            stat.object_id = i.object_id and
            stat.index_id = i.index_id
        join sys.schemas s on
            t.schema_id = s.schema_id
```

Figure 4-4 shows the output of the query. As you can see, the dbo.HashIndex_
HighBucketCount table has on average one row in the row chains, while the dbo.
HashIndex_LowBucketCount table has almost 1,000 rows per chain. It is worth noting
that even though the hash function used by In-Memory OLTP provides relatively good
random data distribution, some level of hash collision is still present.

	Table	Index	Total Buckets	Empty Buckets	Empty Bucket %	Avg Chain	Max Chain
1	dbo.HashIndex_HighBucketCount	PK_HashIndex_HighBucketCount	1048576	398369	37	1	8
2	dbo.HashIndex_LowBucketCount	PK_HashIndex_LowBucketCount	1024	0	0	976	1035

Figure 4-4. sys.dm_db_xtp_hash_index_stats output

*The incorrect bucket count estimation and long row chains can significantly affect the
performance of both reader and writer queries.* You have already seen the performance
impact for the insert operation. Now let's look at a SELECT query.

Listing 4-3 shows the code that triggers 65,536 Index Seek operations in each
memory-optimized table. I wrote this query in a very inefficient way just to demonstrate
the impact of the long row chains.

Listing 4-3. Bucket_count and Performance: Selecting Data in the Tables

```
declare
    @T table(Id int not null primary key)

;with N1(C) as (select 0 union all select 0) -- 2 rows
,N2(C) as (select 0 from N1 as t1 cross join N1 as t2) -- 4 rows
,N3(C) as (select 0 from N2 as t1 cross join N2 as t2) -- 16 rows
,N4(C) as (select 0 from N3 as t1 cross join N3 as t2) -- 256 rows
,N5(C) as (select 0 from N4 as t1 cross join N4 as t2) -- 65,536 rows
,Ids(Id) as (select row_number() over (order by (select null)) from N5)
insert into @T(Id)
    select Id from Ids;
```

```
select t.id, c.Cnt
from @T t
    cross apply
    (
            select count(*) as Cnt
            from dbo.HashIndex_HighBucketCount h
            where h.Id = t.Id
    ) c;

select t.id, c.Cnt
from @T t
    cross apply
    (
            select count(*) as Cnt
            from dbo.HashIndex_LowBucketCount h
            where h.Id = t.Id
    ) c;
```

You can confirm that the queries traversed the row chains 65,536 times by analyzing the execution plan shown in Figure 4-5.

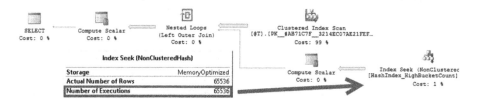

Figure 4-5. *Execution plan of the queries*

Table 4-2 shows the queries' execution time in my environment where the query against the dbo.HashIndex_LowBucketCount table was about 20 times slower.

Table 4-2. *Execution Time of SELECT Statements*

dbo.HashIndex_HighBucketCount (1,048,576 Buckets)	dbo.HashIndex_LowBucketCount (1,024 Buckets)
301 ms	6,259 ms

While you can clearly see that underestimation of the bucket counts can degrade system performance, overestimation is not good either. First, every bucket uses 8 bytes to store the memory pointer, and a large number of unused buckets is a waste of system memory. For example, defining the index with bucket_count=100000000 will introduce 134,217,728 buckets, which will require 128MB of RAM. This does not seem much in the scope of a single index; however, it could become an issue as the number of indexes increases.

47

Moreover, SQL Server needs to scan all buckets in the index when it performs an Index Scan operation, and extra buckets add some overhead to the process. Listing 4-4 shows the queries that demonstrate this kind of overhead.

Listing 4-4. Bucket_count and Performance: Index Scan Queries

```
select count(*)
from dbo.HashIndex_HighBucketCount
    with (index= PK_HashIndex_HighBucketCount)
option (maxdop 1);

select count(*)
from dbo.HashIndex_LowBucketCount
    with (index= PK_HashIndex_LowBucketCount)
option (maxdop 1);
```

Table 4-3 shows the execution time in my environment. As you see, the overhead of scanning extra buckets is not significant; however, it still exists.

Table 4-3. *Execution Time of SELECT Statements (Empty Buckets Overhead)*

dbo.HashIndex_HighBucketCount (1,048,576 Buckets)	dbo.HashIndex_LowBucketCount (1,024 Buckets)
51 ms	62 ms

It is also worth noting that in the majority of cases, SQL Server 2016 will not scan the hash index but rather scan the table heap with the Table Scan operator. I will discuss this in more detail in Chapter 6.

Choosing the Right Bucket Count

Choosing the right number of buckets in a hash index is a tricky but important subject. To make matters worse, you have to make the right decision at the design stage; the only way to change the bucket_count value once a table is created is by altering the table, which creates the new table object in the background.

In an ideal situation, you should have the number of buckets that would exceed the cardinality (the number of unique keys) of the index. Obviously, you should take future system growth and projected workload changes into consideration. It is not a good idea to create an index based on the current data cardinality if you expect the system to handle much more data in the future.

■ **Note**   Microsoft suggests setting bucket_count to be between one and two times the number of distinct values in the index. You can read more at https://docs.microsoft. com/en-us/sql/relational-databases/in-memory-oltp/hash-indexes-for-memory-optimized-tables#configuring_bucket_count.

Low-cardinality columns with a large number of duplicated values are usually bad candidates for hash indexes. The same data values generate the same hash; therefore, rows will be linked to long row chains. Obviously, there are always exceptions, and you should analyze the queries and workload in your system, taking into consideration the data modification overhead introduced by the long row chains.

In existing indexes, you can analyze the output of the sys.dm_db_xpt_hash_index_stats view and code from Listing 4-2 to determine whether the number of buckets in the index is sufficient. If the number of empty buckets is less than 10 percent of the total number of buckets in the index, the bucket count is likely to be too low. Ideally, at least 33 percent of the buckets in the index should be empty.

With all that being said, it is often better to err on the side of caution and overestimate rather than underestimate the number. Even though overestimation impacts the performance of the Index Scan operation, this impact is much lower compared to the one introduced by long row chains. Obviously, you need to remember that every bucket uses 8 bytes of memory whether it is empty or not.

■ **Note** I will discuss In-Memory OLTP index design considerations and choices between hash indexes and nonclustered indexes in the next chapter.

Hash Indexes and SARGability

In the database world, predicates are treated as SARGable (Search ARGument Able) when they allow the Database Engine to utilize Index Seek operations during query execution.

Hash indexes have different SARGability rules than B-Tree indexes defined on disk-based tables. They are efficient only in the case of a *point-lookup equality search*, which allows SQL Server to calculate the corresponding hash value of the index key (or keys) and find a bucket that references the desired chain of rows. SQL Server is unable to use Index Seek operations with hash indexes in any other scenario, for example, with <, >, and BETWEEN predicates. Evaluation of those predicates requires comparison of the index key values, which cannot be done based on hash values.

In the case of composite hash indexes, SQL Server calculates the hash value for the combined value of all key columns. A hash value calculated on a subset of the key columns would be different, and therefore, a query should have equality predicates on all key columns for the index to be useful.

This behavior is different from indexes on disk-based tables. Consider the situation where you defined an index on (LastName, FirstName) columns. In the case of disk-based tables, that index can be used for an Index Seek operation, regardless of whether the predicate on the FirstName column is specified in the where clause of a query. Alternatively, a composite hash index on a memory-optimized table requires queries to have equality predicates on both LastName and FirstName in order to calculate a hash value that allows for choosing the right hash bucket in the index.

Let's create disk-based and memory-optimized tables with composite indexes on the (LastName, FirstName) columns, populating them with the same data as in Listing 4-5.

Listing 4-5. Composite Hash Index: Test Tables Creation

```
create table dbo.CustomersOnDisk
(
    CustomerId int not null identity(1,1),
    FirstName varchar(64) not null,
    LastName varchar(64) not null,
    Placeholder char(100) null,

    constraint PK_CustomersOnDisk
    primary key clustered(CustomerId)
);

create nonclustered index IDX_CustomersOnDisk_LastName_FirstName
on dbo.CustomersOnDisk(LastName, FirstName)
go

create table dbo.CustomersMemoryOptimized
(
    CustomerId int not null identity(1,1)
        constraint PK_CustomersMemoryOptimized
        primary key nonclustered
        hash with (bucket_count = 32768),
    FirstName varchar(64) not null,
    LastName varchar(64) not null,
    Placeholder char(100) null,

    index IDX_CustomersMemoryOptimized_LastName_FirstName
    nonclustered hash(LastName, FirstName)
    with (bucket_count = 1024),
)
with (memory_optimized = on, durability = schema_only)
go

-- Inserting cross-joined data for all first and last names 50 times
-- using GO 50 command in Management Studio
;with FirstNames(FirstName)
as
(
    select Names.Name
    from
    (
        values('Andrew'),('Andy'),('Anton'),('Ashley'),('Boris'),
        ('Brian'),('Cristopher'),('Cathy'),('Daniel'),('Donny'),
        ('Edward'),('Eddy'),('Emy'),('Frank'),('George'),('Harry'),
        ('Henry'),('Ida'),('John'),('Jimmy'),('Jenny'),('Jack'),
        ('Kathy'),('Kim'),('Larry'),('Mary'),('Max'),('Nancy'),
        ('Olivia'),('Paul'),('Peter'),('Patrick'),('Robert'),
```

```
        ('Ron'),('Steve'),('Shawn'),('Tom'),('Timothy'),
        ('Uri'),('Vincent')
    ) Names(Name)
)
,LastNames(LastName)
as
(
    select Names.Name
    from
    (
        values('Smith'),('Johnson'),('Williams'),('Jones'),('Brown'),
            ('Davis'),('Miller'),('Wilson'),('Moore'),('Taylor'),
            ('Anderson'),('Jackson'),('White'),('Harris')
    ) Names(Name)
)
insert into dbo.CustomersOnDisk(LastName, FirstName)
    select LastName, FirstName
    from FirstNames cross join LastNames
go 50

insert into dbo.CustomersMemoryOptimized(LastName, FirstName)
    select LastName, FirstName
    from dbo.CustomersOnDisk;
```

For the first test, let's run SELECT statements against both tables, specifying both LastName and FirstName as predicates in the queries, as shown in Listing 4-6.

Listing 4-6. Composite Hash Index: Selecting Data Using Both Index Columns as Predicates

```
select CustomerId, FirstName, LastName
from dbo.CustomersOnDisk
where FirstName = 'Paul' and LastName = 'White';

select CustomerId, FirstName, LastName
from dbo.CustomersMemoryOptimized
where FirstName = 'Paul' and LastName = 'White';
```

As you can see in Figure 4-6, SQL Server is able to use an Index Seek operation in both cases.

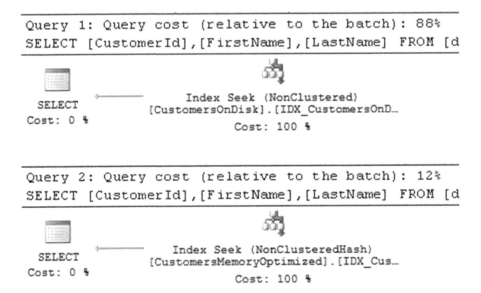

```
Query 1: Query cost (relative to the batch): 88%
SELECT [CustomerId],[FirstName],[LastName] FROM [d
```

SELECT
Cost: 0 %

Index Seek (NonClustered)
[CustomersOnDisk].[IDX_CustomersOnD...
Cost: 100 %

```
Query 2: Query cost (relative to the batch): 12%
SELECT [CustomerId],[FirstName],[LastName] FROM [d
```

SELECT
Cost: 0 %

Index Seek (NonClusteredHash)
[CustomersMemoryOptimized].[IDX_Cus...
Cost: 100 %

Figure 4-6. *Composite hash index: execution plans when queries use both index columns as predicates*

In the next step, let's check what happens if you remove the filter by FirstName from the queries. Listing 4-7 shows the code.

Listing 4-7. Composite Hash Index: Selecting Data Using the Leftmost Index Column Only

```
select CustomerId, FirstName, LastName
from dbo.CustomersOnDisk
where LastName = 'White';

select CustomerId, FirstName, LastName
from dbo.CustomersMemoryOptimized
where LastName = 'White';
```

In the case of the disk-based index, SQL Server is still able to utilize an Index Seek operation. This is not the case for the composite hash index defined on the memory-optimized table. You can see the execution plans for the queries in Figure 4-7.

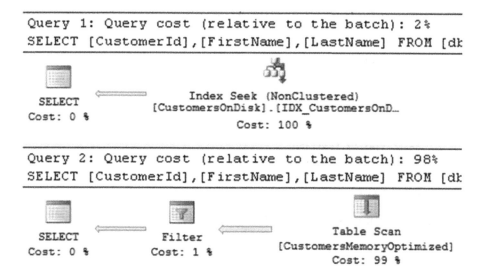

```
Query 1: Query cost (relative to the batch): 2%
SELECT [CustomerId],[FirstName],[LastName] FROM [dk
```

SELECT
Cost: 0 %

Index Seek (NonClustered)
[CustomersOnDisk].[IDX_CustomersOnD...
Cost: 100 %

```
Query 2: Query cost (relative to the batch): 98%
SELECT [CustomerId],[FirstName],[LastName] FROM [dk
```

SELECT
Cost: 0 %

Filter
Cost: 1 %

Table Scan
[CustomersMemoryOptimized]
Cost: 99 %

Figure 4-7. *Composite hash index: execution plans when queries use the leftmost index column only*

Statistics on Memory-Optimized Tables

SQL Server 2016 creates and automatically updates index- and column-level statistics on memory-optimized tables. However, the tables created under database compatibility levels lower than 130 (SQL Server 2016) would have the statistics NORECOMPUTE option enabled, which prevents automatic statistics updates.

This situation may happen in two cases: either when memory-optimized tables were created in SQL Server 2014 and later migrated to SQL Server 2016 or when SQL Server 2016 databases run under a lower compatibility level than 130.

Let's look at this behavior and run the code from Listing 4-8. This code changes the database compatibility level to 120 and creates the table dbo.Stats120. As the next step, it switches the compatibility level back to 130 and creates another table, dbo.Stats130. Finally, the code looks at the statistics properties for the table indexes.

Listing 4-8. *Statistics NORECOMPUTE and Compatibility Level*

```
alter database current set compatibility_level=120;
go

create table dbo.Stats120
(
    Id int not null
        constraint PK_Stats120
        primary key nonclustered
        hash with (bucket_count=1024),
    Value int not null
)
```

53

```
with (memory_optimized=on, durability=schema_only);
go

alter database current set compatibility_level=130;
go

create table dbo.Stats130
(
    Id int not null
        constraint PK_Stats130
        primary key nonclustered
        hash with (bucket_count=1024),
    Value int not null
)
with (memory_optimized=on, durability=schema_only);
go

select
    sc.name + '.' + t.name as [Table]
    ,s.name as [Statistics]
    ,s.no_recompute
from
    sys.stats s join sys.tables t on
        s.object_id = t.object_id
    join sys.schemas sc on
        t.schema_id = sc.schema_id
where
    t.name like 'Stats%';
```

As you can see in Figure 4-8, the dbo.Stats120.PK_Stats120 statistics has the NORECOMPUTE option enabled, which will prevent automatic statistics update for the statistics. This is not the case for the dbo.Stats130.PK_Stats130 statistics, which has been created under a database compatibility level of 130.

	Table	Statistics	no_recompute
1	dbo.Stats120	PK_Stats120	1
2	dbo.Stats130	PK_Stats130	0

Figure 4-8. Statistics NORECOMPUTE option

You can change the value of the NORECOMPUTE option and enable automatic statistics update by manually updating the affected statistics with an UPDATE STATISTICS statement. *It is worth repeating that the statistics NORECOMPUTE option is controlled by the database compatibility level at the time of table creation rather than by the automatic statistics update setting.* Statistics with the NORECOMPUTE=OFF option will be updated automatically regardless of the compatibility level, assuming the Auto Update Statistics database option is enabled.

You should manually update all statistics on memory-optimized tables and enable automatic statistics update after you migrate the database from SQL Server 2014. You can achieve that by running the code shown in Listing 4-9. It generates UPDATE STATISTICS commands for all statistics with the NORECOMPUTE=ON option and runs them using dynamic SQL.

Listing 4-9. Updating All Statistics with NORECOMPUTE=ON

```
declare
    @SQL nvarchar(max)

select
    @SQL = convert(nvarchar(max),
    (
        select
            N'update statistics ' as [text()]
            ,sc.name + N'.' + t.name as [text()]
            ,N'(' + s.name + N'); ' as [text()]
        from
            sys.stats s join sys.tables t on
                s.object_id = t.object_id
            join sys.schemas sc on
                t.schema_id = sc.schema_id
        where
            t.is_memory_optimized = 1 and
            s.no_recompute = 1
        for xml path('')
    ));

exec sp_executesql @SQL;
```

Missing or inaccurate statistics on memory-optimized tables can have a somewhat smaller impact compared to disk-based tables. Indexes on memory-optimized tables reference the actual data rows and, in the nutshell, are covering the queries. In-Memory OLTP does not require Key Lookup operations to access the row data regardless of which index is chosen. Nevertheless, incorrect cardinality estimations could affect the size of the query memory grant and the choice of join type when a query is running through the Interop Engine. All of that may lead to suboptimal execution plans and bad performance.

There is another, less obvious issue. Inaccurate statistics can introduce suboptimal execution plans with the nested loop joins when SQL Server chooses inner and outer inputs for the operator. As you know, the nested loop join algorithm processes the inner input for every row from the outer input, and it is more efficient to put smaller input on the outer side. Listing 4-10 shows the algorithm for the inner nested loop join as a reference.

Listing 4-10. Inner Nested Loop Join Algorithm

```
for each row R1 in outer table
    for each row R2 in inner table
        if R1 joins with R2
            return join (R1, R2)
```

Missing statistics can lead to a situation where SQL Server chooses the inner and outer inputs incorrectly, which can lead to highly inefficient plans.

Let's create two tables under a database compatibility level of 120, populating them with some data, as shown in Listing 4-11. As you know, statistics will be created with the NORECOMPUTE=ON option, which prevents automatic statistics update.

Listing 4-11. Missing Statistics and Inefficient Execution Plans: Table Creation

```
alter database current set compatibility_level=120;
go

create table dbo.T1
(
    ID int not null identity(1,1)
        primary key nonclustered hash
        with (bucket_count = 8192),
    T1Col int not null,
    Placeholder char(100) not null
        constraint DEF_T1_Placeholder
        default('1'),

    index IDX_T1Col
    nonclustered hash(T1Col)
    with (bucket_count = 1024)
)
with (memory_optimized = on, durability = schema_only);

create table dbo.T2
(
    ID int not null identity(1,1)
        primary key nonclustered hash
        with (bucket_count = 8192),
    T2Col int not null,
    Placeholder char(100) not null
        constraint DEF_T2_Placeholder
        default('2'),

    index IDX_T2Col
    nonclustered hash(T2Col)
    with (bucket_count = 1024)
)
with (memory_optimized = on, durability = schema_only);

;with N1(C) as (select 0 union all select 0) -- 2 rows
,N2(C) as (select 0 from N1 as t1 cross join N1 as t2) -- 4 rows
,N3(C) as (select 0 from N2 as t1 cross join N2 as t2) -- 16 rows
,N4(C) as (select 0 from N3 as t1 cross join N3 as t2) -- 256 rows
,N5(C) as (select 0 from N4 as t1 cross join N3 as t2) -- 4,096 rows
```

```
,Ids(Id) as (select row_number() over (order by (select null)) from N5)
insert into dbo.T1(T1Col)
    select 1 from Ids;

insert into dbo.T2(T2Col)
    select -1 from dbo.T1;

update dbo.T1 set T1Col = 2 where ID = 4096;
update dbo.T2 set T2Col = -2 where ID = 1;
```

The data in both tables is distributed unevenly. You can confirm this by running the query in Listing 4-12. Figure 4-9 illustrates the data distribution in the tables.

Listing 4-12. Missing Statistics and Inefficient Execution Plans: Checking Data Distribution in the Tables

```
select 'T1' as [Table], T1Col as [Value], count(*) as [Count]
from dbo.T1
group by T1Col

union all

select 'T2' as [Table], T2Col as [Value], count(*) as [Count]
from dbo.T2
group by T2Col;
```

	Table	Value	Count
1	T1	1	4095
2	T1	2	1
3	T2	-2	1
4	T2	-1	4095

Figure 4-9. *Missing statistics and inefficient execution plans: data distribution*

As the next step, let's run two queries that join the data from the tables, as shown in Listing 4-13. Both queries will return just a single row.

Listing 4-13. Missing Statistics and Inefficient Execution Plans: Test Queries

```
select *
from dbo.T1 t1 join dbo.T2 t2 on
    t1.ID = t2.ID
where
```

```
    t1.T1Col = 2 and
    t2.T2Col = -1;

select *
from dbo.T1 t1 join dbo.T2 t2 on
    t1.ID = t2.ID
where
    t1.T1Col = 1 and
    t2.T2Col = -2
```

As you can see in Figure 4-10, SQL Server generates identical execution plans for both queries using the dbo.T1 table in the outer part of the join. This plan is very efficient for the first query; there is only one row with T1Col = 2. Therefore, SQL Server had to perform an inner input lookup just once. Unfortunately, this is not the case for the second query, which leads to 4,095 Index Seek operations on the dbo.T2 table.

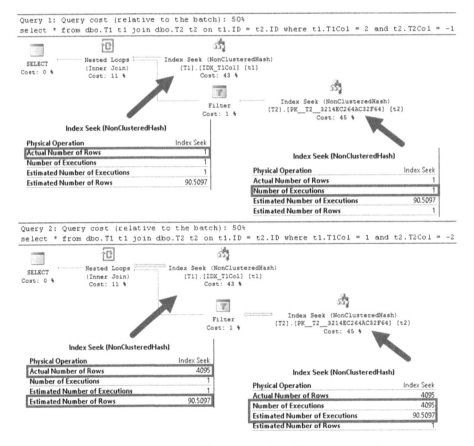

Figure 4-10. *Missing statistics and inefficient execution plans: execution plans*

Let's update the statistics on both tables, as shown in Listing 4-14.

Listing 4-14. Missing Statistics and Inefficient Execution Plans: Updating Statistics

```
update statistics dbo.T1;
update statistics dbo.T2;

dbcc show_statistics('dbo.T1','IDX_T1Col');
dbcc show_statistics('dbo.T2','IDX_T2Col');
```

Figure 4-11 illustrates that the statistics have been updated.

	Name	Updated	Rows	Rows Sampled	Steps	Density	Average key length	String Index	Filter Expression	Unfiltered Rows
1	IDX_T1Col	Dec 20 2016 9:00PM	4096	4096	2	0	4	NO	NULL	4096

	All density	Average Length	Columns
1	0.5	4	T1Col

	RANGE_HI_KEY	RANGE_ROWS	EQ_ROWS	DISTINCT_RANGE_ROWS	AVG_RANGE_ROWS
1	1	0	4095	0	1
2	2	0	1	0	1

	Name	Updated	Rows	Rows Sampled	Steps	Density	Average key length	String Index	Filter Expression	Unfiltered Rows
1	IDX_T2Col	Dec 20 2016 9:00PM	4096	4096	2	0	4	NO	NULL	4096

	All density	Average Length	Columns
1	0.5	4	T2Col

	RANGE_HI_KEY	RANGE_ROWS	EQ_ROWS	DISTINCT_RANGE_ROWS	AVG_RANGE_ROWS
1	-2	0	1	0	1
2	-1	0	4095	0	1

Figure 4-11. *Missing statistics and inefficient execution plans: index statistics after update*

Now, if you run the queries from Listing 4-13 again, SQL Server can generate an efficient execution plan for the second query, as shown in Figure 4-12.

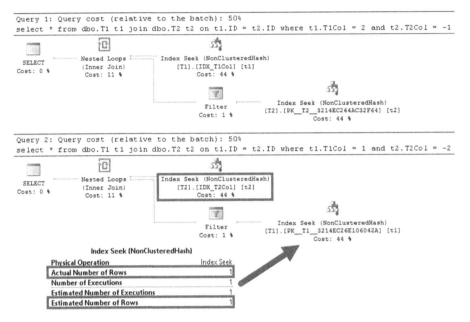

Figure 4-12. *Missing statistics and inefficient execution plans: execution plans after statistics update*

You should remember this behavior when you use natively compiled modules, which have the queries' execution plans embedded into the code. SQL Server does not recompile the modules when the statistics are updated, and you should manually recompile them either by altering them or by using the `sp_recompile` stored procedure when the data distribution has significantly changed.

■ **Note**   I will talk about native compilation and the optimization of natively compiled modules in Chapter 9.

Summary

Hash indexes consist of an array of hash buckets, each of which stores the pointer to the chain of rows with the same index key column hash. Hash indexes help to optimize point-lookup operations when queries search for the rows using equality predicates. In the case of composite hash indexes, the query should have equality predicates on all key columns for the index to be useful.

Choosing the right bucket count is extremely important. Underestimations lead to long row chains, which could seriously degrade the performance of the queries. Overestimations increase memory consumption and decrease the performance of the index scans. Nevertheless, in many cases, it is better to slightly overestimate rather than to underestimate the value.

Low-cardinality columns lead to the long row chains and are usually bad candidates for hash indexes.

You should analyze index cardinality and consider future system growth when choosing the right bucket count. Ideally, you should have at least 33 percent of buckets empty. You can get information about buckets and row chains with the sys.dm_db_xtp_hash_index_stats view.

SQL Server 2016 creates and automatically updates statistics on the indexes on memory-optimized tables; however, statistics created in databases with a compatibility level less than 130 have the NORECOMPUTE=ON option enabled. You should update statistics manually with the UPDATE STATISTICS statement to enable automatic statistics update for such tables.

CHAPTER 5

Nonclustered Indexes

This chapter discusses nonclustered indexes, which is the second type of indexes supported by the In-Memory OLTP Engine. It shows how to define nonclustered indexes, talks about their SARGability rules, and explains their internal structure.

Finally, the chapter discusses several indexing strategies and design considerations for memory-optimized tables.

Working with Nonclustered Indexes

Nonclustered indexes are another type of index supported by the In-Memory OLTP Engine. In contrast to hash indexes, which are optimized to support point-lookup equality searches, nonclustered indexes help you search data based on a range of values. They have a somewhat similar structure to regular indexes on disk-based tables. They are not exactly the same, however, and I will discuss their internal implementation in depth later in this chapter.

TERMINOLOGY ISSUE

Nonclustered indexes were introduced in SQL Server 2014 CTP 2, and the documentation and whitepapers for that version used the term *range indexes* to reference them. However, in the production release of SQL Server 2014, Microsoft changed the terminology to *nonclustered indexes*. Nevertheless, you can still find the term *range indexes* in documentation and in data management views.

That terminology can be confusing because hash indexes are also not clustered. In fact, the concepts of *clustered indexes* cannot be applied to In-Memory OLTP. Data rows are not stored in any particular order in memory.

It is also worth mentioning that the minimal `index_id` value of In-Memory OLTP indexes is 2, which corresponds to nonclustered indexes in disk-based tables.

D. Korotkevitch, *Expert SQL Server In-Memory OLTP*, DOI 10.1007/978-1-4842-2772-5_5

Creating Nonclustered Indexes

Nonclustered indexes are created inline as part of the CREATE TABLE statement. The syntax is similar to hash index creation; however, you should omit the keyword HASH, and you do not need to specify the number of buckets in the index properties.

The code in Listing 5-1 creates a memory-optimized table with two nonclustered indexes, one composite and another on the single column.

Listing 5-1. Creating a Table with Two Nonclustered Indexes

```
create table dbo.Customers
(
    CustomerId int identity(1,1) not null
        constraint PK_Customers
        primary key nonclustered
        hash with (bucket_count=1024),
    FirstName varchar(32) not null,
    LastName varchar(64) not null,
    FullName varchar(97) not null,

    index IDX_LastName_FirstName
    nonclustered(LastName, FirstName),

    index IDX_FullName
    nonclustered(FullName)
)
with (memory_optimized=on, durability=schema_only);
```

Using Nonclustered Indexes

Similar to B-Tree indexes in disk-based tables, the data in nonclustered indexes is sorted according to the value of index key columns. As a result, nonclustered indexes are beneficial in a large number of use cases. They can lead to an Index Seek operation in scenarios when query predicates allow SQL Server to locate and isolate a subset of the index keys for processing. With very few exceptions, the SARGability rules for nonclustered indexes match the rules for indexes defined on disk-based tables.

Listing 5-2 shows several queries against the dbo.Customers table. SQL Server is able to use Index Seek operations with all of them.

Listing 5-2. Queries That Lead to Index Seek Operations

```
-- Point-Lookup specifying all columns in the index
select CustomerId, FirstName, LastName
from dbo.Customers
where LastName = 'White' and FirstName = 'Paul';
```

```
-- Point-lookup using leftmost index column
select CustomerId, FirstName, LastName
from dbo.Customers
where LastName = 'White';

-- Using ">", ">=", "<", "<=" comparison
select CustomerId, FirstName, LastName
from dbo.Customers
where LastName > 'White';

-- Prefix Search
select CustomerId, FirstName, LastName
from dbo.Customers
where LastName like 'Wh%';

-- IN list
select CustomerId, FirstName, LastName
from dbo.Customers
where LastName in ('White','Isakov');
```

Similar to B-Tree indexes, an Index Seek operation is impossible when query predicates do not allow you to isolate a subset of the index keys for processing. Listing 5-3 shows several examples of such queries.

Listing 5-3. Queries That Lead to Index Scan Operations

```
-- Omitting left-most index column(s)
select CustomerId, FirstName, LastName
from dbo.Customers
where FirstName = 'Paul';

-- Substring Search
select CustomerId, FirstName, LastName
from dbo.Customers
where LastName like '%hit%';

-- Functions
select CustomerId, FirstName, LastName
from dbo.Customers
where len(LastName) = 5;
```

As the opposite of B-Tree indexes on disk-based tables, nonclustered indexes are unidirectional, and SQL Server is unable to scan index keys in the opposite order of how they were sorted. You should keep this behavior in mind when you define an index and choose the sorting order for the columns.

Let's illustrate that with an example; we'll create a disk-based table with the same structure as dbo.Customers and populate both tables with the same data. Listing 5-4 shows the code to do this.

Listing 5-4. Nonclustered Indexes and Sorting Order: Disk-Based Table Creation

```
create table dbo.Customers_OnDisk
(
    CustomerId int identity(1,1) not null,
    FirstName varchar(32) not null,
    LastName varchar(64) not null,
    FullName varchar(97) not null,

    constraint PK_Customers_OnDisk
    primary key clustered(CustomerId)
);

create nonclustered index IDX_Customers_OnDisk_LastName_FirstName
on dbo.Customers_OnDisk(LastName, FirstName);

create nonclustered index IDX_Customers_OnDisk_FullName
on dbo.Customers_OnDisk(FullName);
go

;with FirstNames(FirstName)
as
(
    select Names.Name
    from
    (
        values('Andrew'),('Andy'),('Anton'),('Ashley')
        ,('Boris'),('Brian'),('Cristopher'),('Cathy')
        ,('Daniel'),('Don'),('Edward'),('Eddy'),('Emy')
        ,('Frank'),('George'),('Harry'),('Henry'),('Ida')
        ,('John'),('Jimmy'),('Jenny'),('Jack'),('Kathy')
        ,('Kim'),('Larry'),('Mary'),('Max'),('Nancy'),
        ('Olivia'),('Paul'),('Peter'),('Patrick'),('Robert'),
        ('Ron'),('Steve'),('Shawn'),('Tom'),('Timothy'),
        ('Uri'),('Victor')
    ) Names(Name)
)
,LastNames(LastName)
as
```

```
(
    select Names.Name
    from
    (
        values('Smith'),('Johnson'),('Williams'),('Jones')
        ,('Brown'),('Davis'),('Miller'),('Wilson')
        ,('Moore'),('Taylor'),('Anderson'),('Jackson')
        ,('White'),('Isakov')
    ) Names(Name)
)
insert into dbo.Customers(LastName, FirstName, FullName)
    select LastName, FirstName, FirstName + ' ' + LastName
    from FirstNames cross join LastNames;

insert into dbo.Customers_OnDisk(LastName, FirstName, FullName)
    select LastName, FirstName, FullName
    from dbo.Customers;
```

Let's run the queries that select several rows in ascending order, which matches the index sorting order. Listing 5-5 shows the queries.

Listing 5-5. Nonclustered Indexes and Sorting Order: Selecting Data in the Same Order with the Index Key Column

```
select top 3 CustomerId, FirstName, LastName, FullName
from dbo.Customers_OnDisk
order by FullName ASC;

select top 3 CustomerId, FirstName, LastName, FullName
from dbo.Customers
order by FullName ASC;
```

Figure 5-1 shows the execution plans for the queries. SQL Server scans the indexes starting with the lowest key and stops after it reads three rows. The execution plans are similar for both queries with the exception of the required Key Lookup operation with disk-based data. SQL Server uses it to obtain the values of the FirstName and LastName columns from the clustered index of the table. Key Lookup is not required with memory-optimized tables where the index pointers are part of the actual data rows and the indexes are covering all in-row columns in the queries.

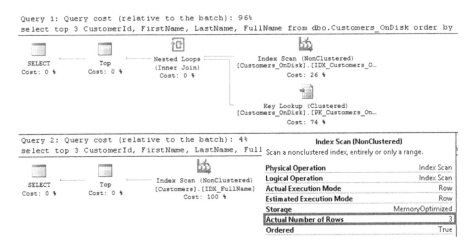

Figure 5-1. *Execution plans when ORDER BY condition matches the index sorting order*

The situation changes if you need to sort the output in descending order, as shown in Listing 5-6.

Listing 5-6. Nonclustered Indexes and Sorting Order: Selecting Data in the Opposite Order with Index Key Column

```
select top 3 CustomerId, FirstName, LastName, FullName
from dbo.Customers_OnDisk
order by FullName DESC;

select top 3 CustomerId, FirstName, LastName, FullName
from dbo.Customers
order by FullName DESC;
```

As you can see in Figure 5-2, SQL Server is able to scan the disk-based table index in the opposite order of how it was defined because of the bidirectional nature of B-Tree indexes. However, this is not the case for memory-optimized tables where indexes are unidirectional. SQL Server decides to scan the table and sort the data afterward.

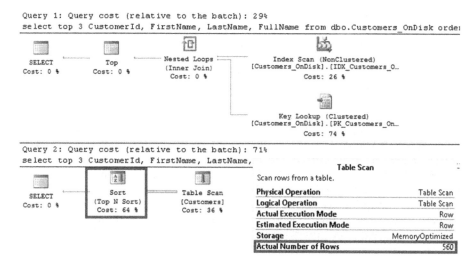

Figure 5-2. *Execution plans when ORDER BY condition is the opposite of the index sorting order*

Finally, index statistics behavior, which I discussed in the previous chapter, still applies to the nonclustered indexes. SQL Server creates statistics at the time of index creation; however, the automatic statistics update behavior depends on the database compatibility level when the tables were created.

Nonclustered Index Internals

Nonclustered indexes use a lock- and latch-free variation of the B-Tree, called a Bw-Tree, which was designed by Microsoft Research in 2011. Let's look at the Bw-Tree structure in detail.

Bw-Tree Overview

Similar to B-Tree, index pages in a Bw-Tree contain a set of ordered index key values. However, Bw-Tree pages do not have a fixed size, and they are unchangeable after they are built. The maximum page size, however, is 8KB.

Rows from a leaf level of the nonclustered index contain the pointers to the data row chains with the same index key values. This works in a similar manner to hash indexes, when multiple rows and/or versions of a row are linked together. Each index in the table adds a pointer to the index pointer array in the row, regardless of its type: hash or nonclustered.

Root and intermediate levels in nonclustered indexes are called *internal pages.*
Similar to B-Tree indexes, internal pages point to the next level in the index. However,
instead of pointing to the actual data page, internal pages use a *logical page ID* (PID),
which is a position (offset) in a separate array-like structure called a *mapping table.* In
turn, each element in the mapping table contains a pointer to the actual index page.
Mapping tables allow In-Memory OLTP to avoid rebuilding internal pages when the
next-level pages they reference need to be changed (more about this later in the chapter).
Only the mapping table pointer is updated in that case.

Figure 5-3 shows an example of a nonclustered index and a mapping table. Each
index row from the internal page stores the *highest* key value on the next-level page and
PID. This is different from a B-Tree index, where intermediate- and root-level index rows
store the *lowest* key value of the next-level page instead. Another difference is that the
pages in a Bw-Tree are not linked in a double-linked list. Each page knows the PID of the
next page on the same level and does not know the PID of the previous page. Even though
it appears as a pointer (arrow) in Figure 5-3, that link is done through the mapping table,
similar to links to pages on the next level.

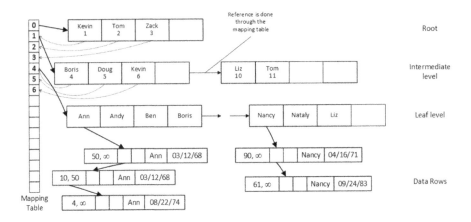

Figure 5-3. *Nonclustered index structure*

Even though a Bw-Tree looks similar to a B-Tree, there is one conceptual difference:
the leaf level of a disk-based B-Tree index consists of separate index rows for each data
row in the index. If multiple data rows have the same key value, the index would have
multiple leaf-level rows with the same index key stored.

Alternatively, in-memory nonclustered indexes store one index row (pointer) to the
row chain that includes all the data rows that have the same key value. Only one index
row (pointer) per key value is stored in the index. You can see this in Figure 5-3, where the
leaf level of the index has single rows for the key values of Ann and Nancy, even though the
row chain includes more than one data row for each value.

▦ **Tip**   You can compare the structure of B-Tree and Bw-Tree indexes by looking at Figures 3-1 and 3-2 from Chapter 3, which show clustered and nonclustered B-Tree indexes on disk-based tables.

Index Pages and Delta Records

As mentioned, pages in nonclustered indexes are unchangeable once they are built. SQL Server builds a new version of the page when it needs to be updated and replaces the page pointer in the mapping table, which avoids changing internal pages that reference an old (obsolete) page.

Every time SQL Server needs to change a leaf-level index page, it creates one or two *delta records* that represent the changes. INSERT and DELETE operations generate a single insert or delete delta record, while an UPDATE operation generates two delta records, deleting old value and inserting new value. Delta records for the same index page are linked through a chain of memory pointers with the last pointer to the actual index page. SQL Server also replaces a pointer in the mapping table with the address of the first delta record in the chain.

Figure 5-4 shows an example of a leaf-level page and delta records if the following actions occurred in this sequence: the R1 index row is updated, the R2 row is deleted, and the R3 row is inserted.

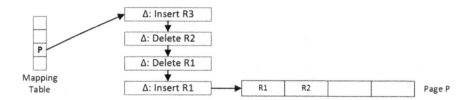

Figure 5-4. *Delta records and nonclustered index leaf page*

▦ **Note**   The internal implementation of the In-Memory OLTP Engine guarantees that multiple sessions cannot simultaneously update memory pointers in the various In-Memory OLTP objects, thereby overwriting each other's changes. I will cover this process in detail in Appendix A.

The internal and leaf pages of nonclustered indexes consist of two areas: a *header* and *data*. The header area includes information about the page such as the following:

- *PID*: The position (offset) in the mapping table

- *Page type*: The type of page, such as leaf, internal, delta, or special

- *Right-page PID*: The position (offset) of the next page in the mapping table

- *Height*: The number of levels from the current page to the leaf level of the index

- *Key values*: The number of key values (index rows) stored on the page

- *Delta record statistics*: The number of delta records and space used by the delta key values

- *Max key value*: The max value of a key on the page

The data area of the page includes either two or three arrays depending on the index key data types. The arrays are as follows:

- *Values*: An array of 8-byte pointers. Internal pages store the PID of next-level pages. Leaf-level pages store pointers to the first row in the row chain with the corresponding key value. It is worth noting that even though the PID requires 4 bytes to store a value, SQL Server uses 8-byte elements to preserve the same page structure between internal and leaf pages.

- *Keys*: An array of key values stored on the page.

- *Offsets*: An array of 2-byte offsets where the individual key values in the keys array start. Offsets are stored only if the keys have variable-length data.

Delta records, in a nutshell, are one-record index data pages. The structure of delta data pages is similar to the structure of internal and leaf pages. However, instead of arrays of values and keys, delta data pages store operation code (insert or delete) and a single key value and pointer to the first data row in a row chain.

Figure 5-5 shows an example of a leaf-level index page with an insert delta record for Bob. The delta record points to the leaf-level index page to which the value Bob logically belongs, and it also has the pointer to the row chain of the data rows with the index key values of Bob. Conceptually, you can think about an *insert* delta record as the leaf-level index row, which is physically separated from the leaf-level index page. A *delete* delta record, on the other hand, indicates that the leaf-level index row has been deleted.

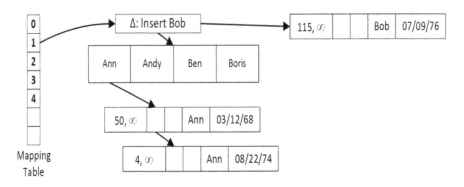

Figure 5-5. *A leaf-level index page with an insert delta record*

SQL Server needs to traverse and analyze all delta records when accessing an index page. As you can guess, a long chain of delta records affects performance. When this is the case, SQL Server consolidates delta records and rebuilds an index page, creating a new one. The newly created page has the same PID and replaces the old page, which is marked for garbage collection. Replacement of the page is accomplished by changing a pointer in the mapping table. SQL Server does not need to change internal pages because they use the mapping table to reference leaf-level pages.

The process of rebuilding is triggered at the moment a new delta record is created for pages that already have 16 delta records in a chain. The action described by the delta record, which triggers the rebuild, is incorporated into the newly created page.

Two other processes can create new or delete existing index pages, in addition to delta records consolidation. The first process, *page splitting*, occurs when a page does not have enough free space to accommodate a new data row. Another process, *page merging*, occurs when a delete operation leaves an index page less than 10 percent from the maximum page size, which is 8KB now, or when an index page contains just a single row.

■ **Note** I will cover the page splitting and page merging processes in depth in Appendix B.

Obtaining Information About Nonclustered Indexes

In addition to the sys.dm_db_xtp_hash_index_stats view, which was discussed in Chapter 4, SQL Server provides two other views to obtain information about indexes on memory-optimized tables. Those views provide the data collected since the memory-optimized tables were loaded into memory, which occurs at database startup.

You can obtain information about index access methods and ghost rows in both hash and nonclustered indexes with the sys.dm_db_xtp_index_stats view. The notable columns in the view are the following:

- xtp_object_id corresponds to the internal ID of the In-Memory OLTP object. This value may change when you alter the table, which rebuilds the table in the background.

- scans_started shows the number of times that row chains in the index were scanned. Because of the nature of the index, every operation, such as SELECT, INSERT, UPDATE, and DELETE, requires SQL Server to scan a row chain and increment this column.

- rows_returned represents the cumulative number of rows returned to the next operator in the execution plan. It does not necessarily match the number of rows returned to a client because further operators in the execution plan can change it.

- rows_touched represents the cumulative number of rows accessed in the index.

- `rows_expired` shows the number of detected stale rows. I will discuss this in greater detail when I talk about the garbage collection process in Chapter 11.

- `rows_expired_removed` returns the number of stale rows that have been unlinked from the index row chains. I will also discuss this in more detail when I talk about garbage collection.

Listing 5-7 shows the query that returns the information about indexes defined on the dbo.Customers table.

Listing 5-7. Querying the sys.dm_db_xtp_index_stats View

```
select
    s.name + '.' + t.name as [table]
    ,i.index_id
    ,i.name as [index]
    ,i.type_desc as [type]
    ,st.scans_started
    ,st.rows_returned
    ,iif(st.scans_started = 0, 0,
        floor(st.rows_returned / st.scans_started))
            as [rows per scan]
from
    sys.dm_db_xtp_index_stats st join sys.tables t on
        st.object_id = t.object_id
    join sys.indexes i on
        st.object_id = i.object_id and
        st.index_id = i.index_id
    join sys.schemas s on
        s.schema_id = t.schema_id
where
    s.name = 'dbo' and t.name = 'Customers'
```

Figure 5-6 illustrates the output of the query. A large number of rows per scan can indicate heavy index scans, which can be the sign of a suboptimal indexing strategy and/or poorly written queries.

	table	index_id	index	type	scans_started	rows_returned	rows per scan
1	dbo.Customers	0	NULL	HEAP	3	1680	560
2	dbo.Customers	4	PK_Customers	NONCLUSTERED HASH	560	0	0
3	dbo.Customers	2	IDX_FullName	NONCLUSTERED	1	3	3
4	dbo.Customers	3	IDX_LastName_FirstName	NONCLUSTERED	7	801	114

Figure 5-6. *Output from the sys.dm_db_xtp_index_stats view*

It is also important to note that the view returns the row for the table heap object (index_id=0). This heap allocates the memory for data rows in the table. In-Memory OLTP accesses this heap at the time of Table Scan operations. I will discuss it in detail in the next chapter.

■ **Note** You can read more about the sys.dm_db_xtp_index_stats view at https://
docs.microsoft.com/en-us/sql/relational-databases/system-dynamic-management-
views/sys-dm-db-xtp-index-stats-transact-sql.

The sys.dm_db_xtp_nonclustered_index_stats view returns information about
nonclustered indexes. It includes information about the total number of pages in the
index along with page splits, merges, and consolidation-related statistics.

Listing 5-8 shows information about nonclustered indexes defined on the dbo.
Customers table. Figure 5-7 shows the output of the query.

Listing 5-8. Querying the sys.dm_db_xtp_nonclustered_index_stats View

```
select
    s.name + '.' + t.name as [table]
    ,i.index_id
    ,i.name as [index]
    ,i.type_desc as [type]
    ,st.delta_pages
    ,st.leaf_pages
    ,st.internal_pages
    ,st.leaf_pages + st.delta_pages + st.internal_pages
            as [total pages]
from
    sys.dm_db_xtp_nonclustered_index_stats st
        join sys.tables t on
            st.object_id = t.object_id
        join sys.indexes i on
            st.object_id = i.object_id and
            st.index_id = i.index_id
        join sys.schemas s on
            s.schema_id = t.schema_id
where
    s.name = 'dbo' and t.name = 'Customers'
```

	table	index_id	index	type	delta_pages	leaf_pages	internal_pages	total pages
1	dbo.Customers	2	IDX_FullName	NONCLUSTERED	16	2	1	19
2	dbo.Customers	3	IDX_LastName_FirstName	NONCLUSTERED	16	2	1	19

Figure 5-7. *Output from the sys.dm_db_xtp_nonclustered_index_stats view*

■ **Note** You can read more about the sys.dm_db_xtp_nonclustered_index_stats view
at https://docs.microsoft.com/en-us/sql/relational-databases/system-dynamic-
management-views/sys-dm-db-xtp-nonclustered-index-stats-transact-sql.

Index Design Considerations

With the exception of the unidirectional nature of Bw-Tree indexes, nonclustered indexes on memory-optimized tables behave similarly to the indexes on disk-based tables. They also cover all in-row columns in the table, which simplifies the indexing process.

There are a couple of aspects of their behavior, however, that I want to mention.

Data Modification Overhead

Indexes on memory-optimized tables introduce data modification overhead similar to indexes on disk-based tables. In-Memory OLTP needs to maintain multiple index row chains along with internal index structures, such as hash and mapping tables and internal and leaf nonclustered index pages.

Let's look at this overhead in detail. The code in Listing 5-9 creates a disk-based table and populates it with 65,536 rows. Next, it creates two memory-optimized tables, with two and eight indexes, respectively.

Listing 5-9. Insert Overhead: Table Creations

```
create table dbo.UpdateOverheadDisk
(
    Id int not null,
    IndexedCol int not null,
    NonIndexedCol int not null,
    Col3 int not null,
    Col4 int not null,
    Col5 int not null,
    Col6 int not null,
    Col7 int not null,
    Col8 int not null,

    constraint PK_UpdateOverheadDisk
    primary key clustered(ID)
);

create nonclustered index IDX_UpdateOverheadDisk_IndexedCol
on dbo.UpdateOverheadDisk(IndexedCol);

;with N1(C) as (select 0 union all select 0) -- 2 rows
,N2(C) as (select 0 from N1 as t1 cross join N1 as t2) -- 4 rows
,N3(C) as (select 0 from N2 as t1 cross join N2 as t2) -- 16 rows
,N4(C) as (select 0 from N3 as t1 cross join N3 as t2) -- 256 rows
,N5(C) as (select 0 from N4 as t1 cross join N4 as t2) -- 65,536 rows
,Ids(Id) as (select row_number() over (order by (select null)) from N5)
insert into dbo.UpdateOverheadDisk(ID,IndexedCol,NonIndexedCol,Col3
,Col4,Col5,Col6,Col7,Col8)
    select Id, Id, Id, Id, Id, Id, Id, Id, Id from Ids;
go
```

```
create table dbo.UpdateOverheadMemory
(
    Id int not null
        constraint PK_UpdateOverheadMemory
        primary key nonclustered
        hash with (bucket_count=2097152),
    IndexedCol int not null,
    NonIndexedCol int not null,
    Col3 int not null,
    Col4 int not null,
    Col5 int not null,
    Col6 int not null,
    Col7 int not null,
    Col8 int not null,

    index IDX_IndexedCol nonclustered(IndexedCol)
)
with (memory_optimized=on, durability=schema_only);

create table dbo.UpdateOverhead8Idx
(
    Id int not null
        constraint PK_UpdateOverhead8Idx
        primary key nonclustered
        hash with (bucket_count=2097152),
    IndexedCol int not null,
    NonIndexedCol int not null,
    Col3 int not null,
    Col4 int not null,
    Col5 int not null,
    Col6 int not null,
    Col7 int not null,
    Col8 int not null,

    index IDX_IndexedCol nonclustered(IndexedCol),
    index IDX_Col3 nonclustered(Col3),
    index IDX_Col4 nonclustered(Col4),
    index IDX_Col5 nonclustered(Col5),
    index IDX_Col6 nonclustered(Col6),
    index IDX_Col7 nonclustered(Col7),
    index IDX_Col8 nonclustered(Col8)
)
with (memory_optimized=on, durability=schema_only);
```

Let's insert the data into both memory-optimized tables using the code from Listing 5-10.

Listing 5-10. Insert Overhead: Inserting Data into Memory-Optimized Tables

```
insert into dbo.UpdateOverheadMemory(ID,IndexedCol,NonIndexedCol,Col3
      ,Col4,Col5,Col6,Col7,Col8)
   select ID,IndexedCol,NonIndexedCol,Col3,Col4,Col5,Col6,Col7,Col8
   from dbo.UpdateOverheadDisk;

insert into dbo.UpdateOverhead8Idx(ID,IndexedCol,NonIndexedCol,Col3
      ,Col4,Col5,Col6,Col7,Col8)
   select ID,IndexedCol,NonIndexedCol,Col3,Col4,Col5,Col6,Col7,Col8
   from dbo.UpdateOverheadDisk;
```

The execution times of the INSERT statements in my environment are 138 ms and 613 ms, respectively. As you can see, maintenance of the six extra indexes in the dbo.UpdateOverhead8Idx table added significant overhead to the operation.

There is also overhead during UPDATE operations; however, it is different compared to disk-based tables. Nonclustered indexes on disk-based tables are the separate data structures that store the copy of the data from the table. SQL Server maintains all those copies; therefore, the update operation modifies all indexes where updated columns were present. There is no overhead, however, when you update the columns that were not present in nonclustered indexes.

In-Memory OLTP, on the other hand, always generates the new row objects regardless of what columns were updated. SQL Server maintains all index row chains, which leads to overhead even when nonindexed columns were modified.

Let's look at an example and perform two updates of the disk-based dbo.UpdateOverheadDisk table, modifying indexed and nonindexed columns there. Both operations change the value of integer fixed-length columns and do not lead to page splits. Listing 5-11 shows the code.

Listing 5-11. Update Overhead: Disk-Based Table Update

```
update dbo.UpdateOverheadDisk
set IndexedCol += 1;

update dbo.UpdateOverheadDisk
set NonIndexedCol += 1;
```

Figure 5-8 illustrates the execution plan and execution time of both statements. As you can see, updating the indexed column forced SQL Server to modify both indexes, and it took significantly longer than updating the nonindexed column.

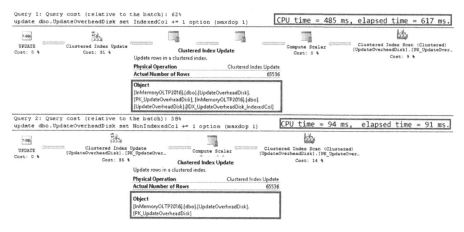

Figure 5-8. *Execution plans and times for disk-based table update*

Listing 5-12 shows the same UPDATE statements for the memory-optimized table. Both statements generated the new data row objects and had to maintain both indexes on the table. That overhead always exists regardless of what columns were updated.

Listing 5-12. Update Overhead: Memory-Optimized Table Update

```
update dbo.UpdateOverheadMemory
set IndexedCol += 1;

update dbo.UpdateOverheadMemory
set NonIndexedCol += 1;
```

Figure 5-9 illustrates the execution plan and execution time of the statements.

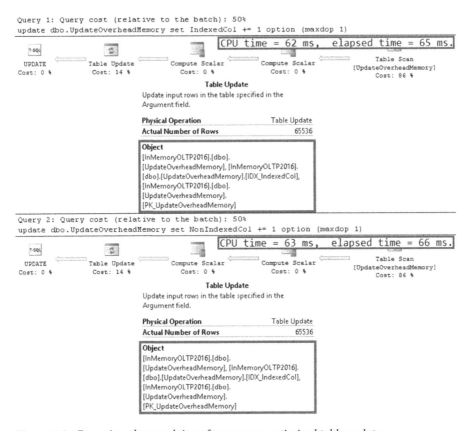

Figure 5-9. *Execution plans and times for memory-optimized table update*

Indexes on memory-optimized tables can also delay the garbage collection. In-Memory OLTP needs to unlink old stale rows from all the index chains, which may take longer when a row is included into the multiple indexes.

■ **Note** I will discuss the garbage collection process in depth in Chapter 11.

As you can see, unnecessary indexes introduce overhead into the system. You should avoid them and create the minimally required set of indexes to support your workload.

Hash Indexes vs. Nonclustered Indexes

As you already know, hash indexes are useful only for point-lookup searches in cases when queries use equality predicates on all index columns. Nonclustered indexes, on the other hand, can be used in a much wider scope, which often makes the choice obvious. You should use nonclustered indexes when your queries benefit from scenarios other than point-lookups.

The situation is less obvious in the case of point-lookups. With the hash indexes, SQL Server can locate the hash bucket, which is the entry point to the data row chain, in a single step by calling the hash function and calculating the hash value. With nonclustered indexes, SQL Server must traverse the Bw-Tree to find a leaf page, and the number of steps depends on the height of the index and the number of delta records there.

Even though nonclustered indexes require more steps to find an entry point to the data row chain, the chain can be smaller compared to hash indexes. Row chains in nonclustered indexes are built based on unique index key values. In hash indexes, row chains are built based on a nonunique hash key and can be larger because of hash collisions, especially when the bucket_count value is insufficient.

Let's compare hash and nonclustered index performance in a point-lookup scenario. Listing 5-13 creates four tables of the same structure. Three of them have hash indexes defined on the Value column using a different bucket_count value. The fourth table has a nonclustered index defined on the same column instead. Finally, the code populates all tables with the same data.

Listing 5-13. Hash and Nonclustered Indexes' Point Lookup Performance: Tables Creation

```
create table dbo.Hash_131072
(
    Id int not null
    constraint PK_Hash_131072
        primary key nonclustered
        hash with (bucket_count=131072),
    Value int not null,

    index IDX_Value hash(Value)
    with (bucket_count=131072)
)
with (memory_optimized=on, durability=schema_only);

create table dbo.Hash_16384
(
    Id int not null
        constraint PK_Hash_16384
        primary key nonclustered
        hash with (bucket_count=16384),
    Value int not null,
```

```
    index IDX_Value hash(Value)
    with (bucket_count=16384)
)
with (memory_optimized=on, durability=schema_only);

create table dbo.Hash_1024
(
    Id int not null
        constraint PK_Hash_1014
        primary key nonclustered
        hash with (bucket_count=1024),
    Value int not null,

    index IDX_Value hash(Value)
    with (bucket_count=1024)
)
with (memory_optimized=on, durability=schema_only);

create table dbo.NonClusteredIdx
(
    Id int not null
        constraint PK_NonClusteredIdx
        primary key nonclustered
        hash with (bucket_count=131072),
    Value int not null,

    index IDX_Value nonclustered(Value)
)
with (memory_optimized=on, durability=schema_only);
go

;with N1(C) as (select 0 union all select 0) -- 2 rows
,N2(C) as (select 0 from N1 as t1 cross join N1 as t2) -- 4 rows
,N3(C) as (select 0 from N2 as t1 cross join N2 as t2) -- 16 rows
,N4(C) as (select 0 from N3 as t1 cross join N3 as t2) -- 256 rows
,N5(C) as (select 0 from N4 as t1 cross join N4 as t2) -- 65,536 rows
,N6(C) as (select 0 from N5 as t1 cross join N1 as t2) -- 131,072 rows
,Ids(Id) as (select row_number() over (order by (select null)) from N6)
insert into dbo.Hash_131072(Id,Value)
    select Id, Id
    from ids
    where Id <= 75000;

insert into dbo.Hash_16384(Id,Value)
    select Id, Value
    from dbo.Hash_131072;
```

```
insert into dbo.Hash_1024(Id,Value)
    select Id, Value
    from dbo.Hash_131072;

insert into dbo.NonClusteredIdx(Id,Value)
    select Id, Value
    from dbo.Hash_131072;
```

Different numbers of buckets led to the different index row chain sizes in the indexes. In this case, the dbo.Hash_131072, dbo.Hash_16384, and dbo.Hash_1024 tables have on average 1, 4, and 73 rows per chain, respectively.

■ **Tip** You can analyze the hash index properties using the sys.dm_db_xtp_hash_index_stats view and the code from Listing 4-2 in Chapter 4.

As the next step, let's compare point-lookup performance using the code from Listing 5-14. This code triggers 75,000 point-lookup selects against each table.

Listing 5-14. Hash and Nonclustered Indexes' Point Lookup Performance: Selecting Data

```
declare
    @T table(Value int not null primary key)

insert into @T(Value)
    select Id from dbo.Hash_131072;

select count(*)
from @T t
    cross apply
    (
        select count(*) as Cnt
        from dbo.Hash_131072 h
        where h.Value = t.Value
    ) c
where c.Cnt > 0;

select count(*)
from @T t
    cross apply
    (
        select count(*) as Cnt
        from dbo.Hash_16384 h
        where h.Value = t.Value
    ) c
where c.Cnt > 0;
```

```
select count(*)
from @T t
    cross apply
    (
        select count(*) as Cnt
        from dbo.Hash_1024 h
        where h.Value = t.Value
    ) c
where c.Cnt > 0;

select count(*)
from @T t
    cross apply
    (
        select count(*) as Cnt
        from dbo.NonClusteredIdx h
        where h.Value = t.Value
    ) c
where c.Cnt > 0;
```

Table 5-1 shows the execution time of the queries in my environment. With a sufficient number of buckets, hash indexes outperform nonclustered indexes. However, an insufficient number of buckets and long row chains significantly degrade their performance, making them less efficient than nonclustered indexes.

***Table 5-1.** Execution Time of Queries*

	Hash_131072	Hash_16384	Hash_1024	NonClusteredIdx
Average Index Row Chain Size	1	4	73	N/A
Execution Time	62 ms	74 ms	129 ms	78 ms

In the end, it all depends on a correct bucket_count estimation. Unfortunately, the volatility of the data makes this task complicated and requires you to factor the future data growth into analysis.

In some cases, when data is relatively static, you can create hash indexes, overestimating the number of buckets there. Consider the catalog entities, for example, the Customers table and the CustomerId and Phone columns in it. Hash indexes on those columns would improve the performance of point-lookup searches and joins. Even though the customer base is growing over time, that growth rate is usually not excessive, and reserving one million empty buckets could be sufficient for a long time. It will use about 8MB of memory per index, which could be acceptable in most cases.

Choosing the hash index for the OrderId column in the Orders table, on the other hand, is more dangerous. Load growth and changes in data retention rules can make the original bucket_count value insufficient. This still can be acceptable if you are planning to monitor the system and can afford the downtime while rebuilding the index; however, nonclustered index would be the safer choice in this scenario.

Memory requirements are another factor to consider. With the hash indexes, memory usage depends on the number of buckets. The amount of memory required for the nonclustered indexes depends on the size of the index key and index cardinality (uniqueness of index key values). For example, if a table has a varchar column with 1,000,000 unique values of 100 bytes each, the nonclustered index on that column would require about 800MB to support a Bw-Tree structure and store key values on internal and leaf index pages. Alternatively, a hash index with 2,097,152 buckets will use just 16MB of memory.

To summarize, for point-lookup and equality joins, create the hash indexes only when you can correctly estimate the number of buckets, factoring future data growth into the analysis. You should also monitor them and can afford the downtime rebuilding the indexes when bucket_count becomes insufficient. Otherwise, use nonclustered indexes, which are the safer choice and do not depend on the bucket count.

Summary

Nonclustered indexes are the second type of indexes supported by the In-Memory OLTP Engine. They have similar SARGability rules, with the B-Tree indexes defined on disk-based tables with exception of the scans in the opposite order to the index sorting order.

Internally, nonclustered indexes use a lock- and latch-free variation of a B-Tree, called a Bw-Tree, which consists of internal and leaf data pages referencing each other through the mapping table. Leaf data pages store one row per each individual key value, with a pointer to the chain of data rows with the same key.

SQL Server never updates index pages. Any changes are referenced through the delta records that correspond to individual INSERT and DELETE operations on the page. SQL Server consolidates the large chains of delta records and performs splitting and merging of the data pages when needed. All of those processes create the new data pages, marking the old ones for garbage collection.

Indexes on memory-optimized tables introduce data modification overhead like indexes on disk-based tables. SQL Server must maintain multiple index row chains when you insert or update the data. You should avoid defining an excessive number of indexes and create a minimally required set of indexes to support the workload.

The performance of hash indexes greatly depends on the bucket_count value. With a correct bucket_count value, hash indexes would outperform nonclustered indexes in point-lookup scenarios. They are a good choice for catalog entities where data is relatively static. Nonclustered indexes, on the other hand, are a good choice in scenarios when point-lookup is not an option and/or when it is hard to estimate the number of buckets in the hash index.

CHAPTER 6

Memory Consumers and Off-Row Storage

This chapter provides an overview of how In-Memory OLTP allocates the memory for different objects and explains how off-row column data is stored. It also illustrates the performance impact of having off-row columns in a table and explains how SQL Server chooses columns that need to be stored off-row.

Varheaps

In-Memory OLTP database objects allocate memory from separate memory heaps called *varheaps*. Varheaps are the data structures that respond to and track memory allocation requests from various database objects, and they can grow and shrink in size when needed. All database objects that consume memory are called *memory consumers*.

Internally, varheaps allocate memory in pages of various size, with 64KB pages being the most common. Each page provides the memory for allocation requests of a predefined size. For example, a varheap can have two 64KB pages; one handles 64-byte allocations, and the other one handles 256-byte allocations.

Let's look at the example shown in Listing 6-1. The code creates the table with the hash index and analyzes the table's memory consumers using the sys.dm_db_xtp_memory_consumers view. As you can guess by the name, this view provides information about memory consumers in the database. You will look at several memory-optimized table-related consumers in this and the next chapter, and I will discuss this view in detail in Chapter 12.

Listing 6-1. Analyzing Varheaps: Table Creation

```
create table dbo.Varheaps
(
    Col varchar(8000) not null
        constraint PK_Varheaps
        primary key nonclustered hash
        with (bucket_count=16384)
)
with (memory_optimized = on, durability = schema_only);
```

```
select
    i.name as [Index], i.index_id, c.memory_consumer_id
    ,c.memory_consumer_type_desc as [mc type]
    ,c.memory_consumer_desc as [description], c.allocation_count as [allocs]
    ,c.allocated_bytes, c.used_bytes
from
    sys.dm_db_xtp_memory_consumers c
        left outer join sys.indexes i on
            c.object_id = i.object_id and c.index_id = i.index_id
where
    c.object_id = object_id('dbo.Varheaps');
```

As you can see in Figure 6-1, the table has two memory consumers/varheaps. The first varheap with type HASH provides memory for the hash table in the hash index. The hash index has 16,384 buckets and uses 131,072 bytes of memory, which was allocated at table creation time. The second varheap with type VARHEAP and the description "Table heap" is providing the memory for the data rows. It did not allocate any memory because the table was empty.

	Index	index_id	memory_consumer_id	mc type	description	allocs	allocated_bytes	used_bytes
1	PK_Varheaps	2	194	HASH	Hash index	1	131072	131072
2	NULL	NULL	193	VARHEAP	Table heap	0	0	0

Figure 6-1. Memory consumers after table creation

Let's insert a row into the table with the INSERT INTO dbo.Varheaps(Col) VALUES('a') statement. If you check the memory consumers with the SELECT statement from Listing 6-1 again, you would see the results shown in Figure 6-2. As you can see, the table varheap allocated one 64KB memory page and provided 40 bytes to store the data row object.

	Index	index_id	memory_consumer_id	mc type	description	allocs	allocated_bytes	used_bytes
1	PK_Varheaps	2	194	HASH	Hash index	1	131072	131072
2	NULL	NULL	193	VARHEAP	Table heap	1	65536	40

Figure 6-2. Memory consumers after inserting the first row

Let's insert another row of the same size with the INSERT INTO dbo.Varheaps(Col) VALUES('b') statement. Figure 6-3 illustrates the memory consumer state after the second insert. The size of both rows was the same, and, therefore, the table heap provided memory from the same, already allocated, memory page to the second row.

	Index	index_id	memory_consumer_id	mc type	description	allocs	allocated_bytes	used_bytes
1	PK_Varheaps	2	194	HASH	Hash index	1	131072	131072
2	NULL	NULL	193	VARHEAP	Table heap	2	65536	80

Figure 6-3. Memory consumers after inserting the second row

Finally, let's insert another row of a different size using the INSERT INTO dbo. Varheaps(Col) VALUES('ccccc') statement. This row requires allocation of a different size, and the table varheap allocated another 64KB memory page to handle those allocations. Figure 6-4 illustrates that.

	Index	index_id	memory_consumer_id	mc type	description	allocs	allocated_bytes	used_bytes
1	PK_Varheaps	2	196	HASH	Hash index	1	131072	131072
2	NULL	NULL	195	VARHEAP	Table heap	3	131072	128

Figure 6-4. Memory consumers after inserting the third row

Obviously, it is inefficient to allocate the separate memory pages for every possible allocation size request. In some cases, the varheap provides the memory from a page that serves allocations of the greater size. For example, a 62-byte memory allocation could come from a page that serves 64-byte allocations. The page would still reserve and use 64 bytes of memory for this allocation even though the memory consumer requested a smaller memory allocation.

Let's see that in action and run the code in Listing 6-2. It inserts the data rows with Col values varying from 2 to 8,000 characters.

Listing 6-2. Analyzing Varheaps: Inserting Rows of Various Sizes

```
declare
    @I int = 2
while @I <= 8000
begin
    insert into dbo.Varheaps(Col) values(replicate('0',@I));
    set @I += 1;
end;
```

Figure 6-5 illustrates the state of the varheap. It allocated 39,452,673 bytes, which correspond to 602 64KB memory pages despite that the table stores 8,000 possible combinations of the data row sizes.

	Index	index_id	memory_consumer_id	mc type	description	allocs	allocated_bytes	used_bytes
1	PK_Varheaps	2	196	HASH	Hash index	1	131072	131072
2	NULL	NULL	195	VARHEAP	Table heap	8002	39452672	32969784

Figure 6-5. Memory consumers after populating table with the data

Per-varheap memory consumer separation allows you to track memory usage on a per-object basis. It also helps SQL Server to optimize some internal operations. For example, it allows the garbage collection process to more quickly deallocate the memory when you drop or alter the table.

This architecture also allows SQL Server to perform a Table Scan operation that scans the varheap pages in a very efficient way. Each varheap page serves allocation requests of the same size, and it is easy to calculate the location of each object stored on the page. It makes the Table (Varheap) Scan operation more efficient compared to the Index Scan operation.

In-Row and Off-Row Storage

As you have already seen in this chapter, In-Memory OLTP uses separate varheaps for a hash table in hash indexes and data rows. Let's look what happens when you add the nonclustered (range) index to the picture.

Listing 6-3 creates a table with one hash and one nonclustered index and provides the information about memory consumers afterward. It is using a slightly modified version of the SELECT statement you ran before, utilizing another view, sys.memory_optimized_tables_internal_attributes. This view returns the information about internal structures that are used by some table columns and indexes.

Listing 6-3. Analyzing Memory Consumers: In-Row Storage

```
create table dbo.MemoryConsumers
(
    ID int not null
        constraint PK_MemoryConsumers
        primary key nonclustered hash with (bucket_count=1024),
    Name varchar(256) not null,
    index IDX_Name nonclustered(Name)
)
with (memory_optimized=on, durability=schema_only);

select
    i.name as [Index], i.index_id, a.xtp_object_id, a.type_desc, a.minor_id
    ,c.memory_consumer_id, c.memory_consumer_type_desc as [mc type]
    ,c.memory_consumer_desc as [description], c.allocation_count as [allocs]
    ,c.allocated_bytes, c.used_bytes
from
    sys.dm_db_xtp_memory_consumers c join
        sys.memory_optimized_tables_internal_attributes a on
            a.object_id = c.object_id and a.xtp_object_id = c.xtp_object_id
    left outer join sys.indexes i on
            c.object_id = i.object_id and
            c.index_id = i.index_id and
            a.minor_id = 0
where
    c.object_id = object_id('dbo.MemoryConsumers');
```

Figure 6-6 shows the output of the query. The xtp_object_id column represents the internal In-Memory OLTP object_id, which is different from the SQL Server object_id. The type of USER_TABLE indicates that the varheap belongs to the main table object.

	index	index_id	xtp_object_id	type_desc	minor_id	memory_consumer_id	mc type	description	allocs	allocated_bytes	used_bytes
1	IDX_Name	2	-2147483641	USER_TABLE	0	281	VARHEAP	Range index heap	2	131072	152
2	PK_MemoryConsumers	3	-2147483641	USER_TABLE	0	280	HASH	Hash index	1	8192	8192
3	NULL	NULL	-2147483641	USER_TABLE	0	279	VARHEAP	Table heap	0	0	0

Figure 6-6. *Memory consumer information (in-row storage)*

As you can see in Figure 6-6, the table has three memory consumers that have the same `xtp_object_id` value as the main table. The range index heap stores internal and leaf pages of nonclustered index. The hash index heap stores the hash table of the index. Finally, the table heap stores actual table rows. Figure 6-7 illustrates that.

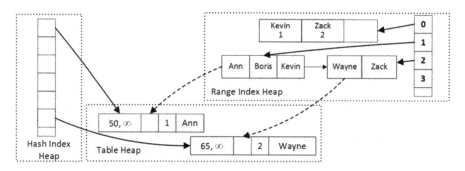

Figure 6-7. *Table memory consumers*

Let's alter the table and add off-row storage columns, as shown in Listing 6-4. RowOverflowCol pushes the size of the row beyond 8,060 bytes, and it will be stored off-row.

Listing 6-4. Adding Off-Row Columns

```
alter table dbo.MemoryConsumers add
    RowOverflowCol varchar(8000),
    LOBCol varchar(max);
```

Now, if you get the list of memory consumers using the query from Listing 6-3 again, you would see the output shown in Figure 6-8. It is worth noting that the `xtp_object_id` column of the USER_TABLE objects has changed because the ALTER TABLE operation rebuilt the table and created the new table object internally.

	Index	index_id	xtp_object_id	type_desc	minor_id	memory_consumer_id	mc type	description	allocs	allocated_bytes	used_bytes
1	IDX_Name	2	-2147483585	USER_TABLE	0	243	VARHEAP	Range index heap	2	131072	152
2	PK_MemoryConsumers	3	-2147483585	USER_TABLE	0	242	HASH	Hash index	1	8192	8192
3	NULL	NULL	-2147483585	USER_TABLE	0	241	VARHEAP	Table Heap	0	0	0
4	NULL	NULL	-2147483581	INTERNAL OFF-ROW DATA TABLE	4	240	VARHEAP	Range index heap	2	131072	152
5	NULL	NULL	-2147483581	INTERNAL OFF-ROW DATA TABLE	4	239	VARHEAP	LOB Page Allocator	0	0	0
6	NULL	NULL	-2147483581	INTERNAL OFF-ROW DATA TABLE	4	238	VARHEAP	Table heap	0	0	0
7	NULL	NULL	-2147483582	INTERNAL OFF-ROW DATA TABLE	3	237	VARHEAP	Range index heap	2	131072	152
8	NULL	NULL	-2147483582	INTERNAL OFF-ROW DATA TABLE	3	236	VARHEAP	Table heap	0	0	0

Figure 6-8. *Memory consumers with off-row storage*

As you can see, both off-row columns introduce their own range index heap and table heap memory consumers. In addition, the LOB column adds a LOB page allocator memory consumer (more about that later). The `minor_id` column provides the `column_id` value in the table to which memory consumers belong. Varheaps from both off-row columns have their own `xtp_object_id` values, which indicate that internally those columns are stored as the different objects.

As you can guess from the output, SQL Server stores both row-overflow and LOB columns in the separate internal tables. The rows in those tables consist of an 8-byte artificial primary key implemented as a nonclustered index and off-row column value. The main row references an off-row column through that artificial key, which is generated when a row is created. It is worth repeating that this reference is done though the artificial value rather than the memory pointer.

This approach allows In-Memory OLTP to decouple off-row columns from the main row using a different lifetime for them. For example, if you update the main row data without touching off-row columns, SQL Server would not generate new versions of off-row column rows. Vice versa, when only off-row data is modified, the main row stays intact.

In-Memory OLTP stores LOB data in the memory provided by the LOB page allocator. That consumer is not limited to 8,060-byte row allocations and can allocate a large amount of memory to store the data. The rows in the table heap of LOB columns contain pointers to the row data in the LOB page allocator.

Let's assume that you run several DML statements with the Global Transaction Timestamp values shown in Listing 6-5.

Listing 6-5. Modifying Data in the Table

```
-- Global Transaction Timestamp: 100
insert into dbo.MemoryConsumers(ID, Name, RowOverflowCol, LobCol)
values
(1,'Ann','A1',replicate(convert(varchar(max),'1'),100000))
,(2,'Bob','B1',replicate(convert(varchar(max),'2'),100000));

-- Global Transaction Timestamp: 110
update dbo.MemoryConsumers set RowOverflowCol = 'B2' where ID = 2;

-- Global Transaction Timestamp: 120
update dbo.MemoryConsumers set Name= 'Greg' where ID = 2;

-- Global Transaction Timestamp: 130
update dbo.MemoryConsumers
set LobCol = replicate(convert(varchar(max),'3'),100000)
where ID = 1;

-- Global Transaction Timestamp: 140
delete from dbo.MemoryConsumers where ID = 1;
```

Figure 6-9 illustrates the state of the data and links between the rows. For simplicity's sake, it is omitting the hash table and nonclustered index structures in the main table along with internal pages of nonclustered indexes for off-row columns.

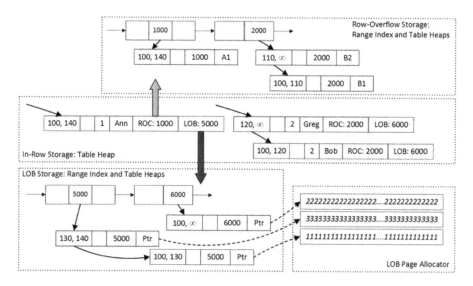

Figure 6-9. *In-row and off-row storage*

SQL Server decides what columns should be stored off-row in the table creation phase based on the table schema. The (n)varchar(max) and varbinary(max) columns are always stored off-row as LOB columns. Moreover, the *largest* non-(max) variable-length column (or columns) will be stored as a row-overflow column (or columns) off-row when the data row size in the table definition exceeds 8,060 bytes.

This behavior is different from disk-based tables where such a decision is made on a per-row basis based on the data row size. With disk-based tables, the data from LOB and large variable-length columns will be stored in-row when it fits into the data page. This is not the case with memory-optimized tables. Off-row columns are always stored off-row regardless of the size of the data. For example, a one-character string in the varchar(max) column will be stored as LOB data off-row even when the total row size is less than 8,060 bytes.

Performance Impact of Off-Row Storage

The decoupling of in-row and off-row data reduces the overhead of creating extra row versions during data modifications. However, it will add additional overhead when you insert and delete the data. SQL Server should create several row objects during the insert stage and update the EndTs value of multiple rows during deletion. It also needs to maintain internal tables for off-row columns.

Let's look at the example and create two tables of a similar schema, as shown in Listing 6-6. One of the tables has 20 varchar(3) columns, while another uses 20 varchar(max) columns. As the next step, you will populate those tables with 100,000 rows with a 1-character value in each column.

Listing 6-6. Off-Row Storage Performance Impact: Insert Operation

```
create table dbo.DataInRow
(
    ID int not null
        constraint PK_DataInRow
        primary key nonclustered hash(ID)
        with (bucket_count = 262144)
    ,Col1 varchar(3) not null
    ,Col2 varchar(3) not null
    ,Col3 varchar(3) not null
    ,Col4 varchar(3) not null
    ,Col5 varchar(3) not null
    ,Col6 varchar(3) not null
    ,Col7 varchar(3) not null
    ,Col8 varchar(3) not null
    ,Col9 varchar(3) not null
    ,Col10 varchar(3) not null
    ,Col11 varchar(3) not null
    ,Col12 varchar(3) not null
    ,Col13 varchar(3) not null
    ,Col14 varchar(3) not null
    ,Col15 varchar(3) not null
    ,Col16 varchar(3) not null
    ,Col17 varchar(3) not null
    ,Col18 varchar(3) not null
    ,Col19 varchar(3) not null
    ,Col20 varchar(3) not null
)
with (memory_optimized = on, durability = schema_only);

create table dbo.DataOffRow
(
    ID int not null
        constraint PK_DataOffRow
        primary key nonclustered hash(ID)
        with (bucket_count = 262144)
    ,Col1 varchar(max) not null
    ,Col2 varchar(max) not null
    ,Col3 varchar(max) not null
    ,Col4 varchar(max) not null
    ,Col5 varchar(max) not null
    ,Col6 varchar(max) not null
    ,Col7 varchar(max) not null
    ,Col8 varchar(max) not null
    ,Col9 varchar(max) not null
    ,Col10 varchar(max) not null
    ,Col11 varchar(max) not null
    ,Col12 varchar(max) not null
```

```
      ,Col13 varchar(max) not null
      ,Col14 varchar(max) not null
      ,Col15 varchar(max) not null
      ,Col16 varchar(max) not null
      ,Col17 varchar(max) not null
      ,Col18 varchar(max) not null
      ,Col19 varchar(max) not null
      ,Col20 varchar(max) not null
)
with (memory_optimized = on, durability = schema_only);

declare
      @Nums table(Num int not null primary key)

;with N1(C) as (select 0 union all select 0) -- 2 rows
,N2(C) as (select 0 from N1 as t1 cross join N1 as t2) -- 4 rows
,N3(C) as (select 0 from N2 as t1 cross join N2 as t2) -- 16 rows
,N4(C) as (select 0 from N3 as t1 cross join N3 as t2) -- 256 rows
,N5(C) as (select 0 from N4 as t1 cross join N4 as t2) -- 65,536 rows
,N6(C) as (select 0 from N5 as t1 cross join N1 as t2) -- 131,072 rows
,Ids(Id) as (select row_number() over (order by (select null)) from N6)
insert into @Nums(Num)
      select Id from Ids where Id <= 100000;

insert into dbo.DataInRow(ID,Col1,Col2,Col3,Col4,Col5,Col6,Col7,Col8,Col9
      ,Col10,Col11,Col12,Col13,Col14,Col15,Col16,Col17,Col18,Col19,Col20)
      select Num,'0','0','0','0','0','0','0','0','0','0','0','0','0'
          ,'0','0','0','0','0','0','0'
      from @Nums;

insert into dbo.DataOffRow(ID,Col1,Col2,Col3,Col4,Col5,Col6,Col7,Col8,Col9
      ,Col10,Col11,Col12,Col13,Col14,Col15,Col16,Col17,Col18,Col19,Col20)
      select Num,'0','0','0','0','0','0','0','0','0','0','0','0','0'
          ,'0','0','0','0','0','0','0'
      from @Nums;
```

Table 6-1 shows the execution times of INSERT statements in my environment. As you can see, the management of multiple internal tables adds considerable performance overhead.

Table 6-1. *Execution Time of INSERT Statements*

dbo.DataInRow Insert Time	dbo.DataOffRow Insert Time
157 ms	8,062 ms

Figure 6-10 illustrates the partial list of memory consumers from both tables. As you already know, each varchar(max) column in the dbo.DataOffRow table will introduce an internal table with three memory consumers.

Index	index_id	xtp_object_id	type_desc	minor_id	memory_consumer_id	mc type	description	allocs	Allocated KB	Used KB
1	PK_DataInRow	2	-2147483581	USER_TABLE	0	217	HASH	Hash index	1	2048	2048
2	NULL	NULL	-2147483581	USER_TABLE	0	216	VARHEAP	Table heap	100000	10240	10156

Index	index_id	xtp_object_id	type_desc	minor_id	memory_consumer_id	mc type	description	allocs	Allocated KB	Used KB
1	PK_DataOffRow	2	-2147483580	USER_TABLE	0	279	HASH	Hash index	1	2048	2048
2	NULL	NULL	-2147483580	USER_TABLE	0	278	VARHEAP	Table heap	100000	19648	19531
3	NULL	NULL	-2147483560	INTERNAL OFF-ROW DATA TABLE	21	277	VARHEAP	Range index heap	400	7808	1673
4	NULL	NULL	-2147483560	INTERNAL OFF-ROW DATA TABLE	21	276	VARHEAP	LOB Page Allocator	100000	3968	3906
5	NULL	NULL	-2147483560	INTERNAL OFF-ROW DATA TABLE	21	275	VARHEAP	Table heap	100000	6336	6250
6	NULL	NULL	-2147483561	INTERNAL OFF-ROW DATA TABLE	20	274	VARHEAP	Range index heap	400	7808	1673
7	NULL	NULL	-2147483561	INTERNAL OFF-ROW DATA TABLE	20	273	VARHEAP	LOB Page Allocator	100000	3968	3906
8	NULL	NULL	-2147483561	INTERNAL OFF-ROW DATA TABLE	20	272	VARHEAP	Table heap	100000	6336	6250
9	NULL	NULL	-2147483562	INTERNAL OFF-ROW DATA TABLE	19	271	VARHEAP	Range index heap	400	7808	1673
10	NULL	NULL	-2147483562	INTERNAL OFF-ROW DATA TABLE	19	270	VARHEAP	LOB Page Allocator	100000	3968	3906
11	NULL	NULL	-2147483562	INTERNAL OFF-ROW DATA TABLE	19	269	VARHEAP	Table heap	100000	6336	6250
12	NULL	NULL	-2147483563	INTERNAL OFF-ROW DATA TABLE	18	268	VARHEAP	Range index heap	400	7808	1673
13	NULL	NULL	-2147483563	INTERNAL OFF-ROW DATA TABLE	18	267	VARHEAP	LOB Page Allocator	100000	3968	3906
..	NULL	NULL	-2147483563	INTERNAL OFF-ROW DATA TABLE	18	266	VARHEAP	Table heap	100000	6336	6250

Figure 6-10. *Memory consumers for the tables*

Listing 6-7 shows the query that calculates the total memory usage for the dbo.DataInRow and dbo.DataOffRow tables, respectively.

Listing 6-7. Off-Row Storage Performance Impact: Memory Usage

```
select
    sum(c.allocated_bytes) / 1024 as [Allocated KB]
    ,sum(c.used_bytes) / 1024 as [Used KB]
from
    sys.dm_db_xtp_memory_consumers c
where
    c.object_id = object_id('dbo.DataInRow');

select
    sum(c.allocated_bytes) / 1024 as [Allocated KB]
    ,sum(c.used_bytes) / 1024 as [Used KB]
from
    sys.dm_db_xtp_memory_consumers c
where
    c.object_id = object_id('dbo.DataOffRow');
```

As you can see in Figure 6-11, the dbo.DataOffRow table uses more than 30 times more memory compared to the dbo.DataInRow table. Every off-row column adds 64+ bytes of overhead to each non-empty value. This overhead consists of the following:

> 32-byte row header and index array in off-row data row

> 8-byte artificial key stored in-row and twice off-row: on the leaf level of nonclustered index and in the off-row data row

> 8-byte pointer on the leaf level index row

> Additional memory to store the nonclustered index structures in off-row column internal table

	Allocated KB	Used KB
1	12288	12204

	Allocated KB	Used KB
1	385664	258182

Figure 6-11. *Table memory usage*

The overhead is even bigger (80+ bytes) in the case of LOB columns that store data in separate varheaps and require two extra pointers per row. Moreover, there is an additional overhead of 32 bytes for every 8KB of LOB data, which may be significant if the stored values are relatively small.

There is another important performance implication. *Indexes defined in the table are not covering the queries that select off-row data.* SQL Server needs to traverse nonclustered indexes on off-row columns to obtain their values. Conceptually, this looks similar to Key Lookup operations in disk-based tables done in the reverse direction, from clustered to nonclustered indexes. Even though the overhead is significantly smaller compared to disk-based tables, it is still overhead you'd like to avoid.

Listing 6-8 shows the code that selects the data from all off-row columns in the table. SQL Server needs to traverse nonclustered indexes in all internal tables to get the data.

Listing 6-8. Off-Row Storage Performance Impact: Select Overhead

```
select count(*)
from dbo.DataInRow
where Col1='0' and Col2='0' and Col3='0' and Col4='0' and Col5='0'
    and Col6='0' and Col7='0' and Col8='0' and Col9='0' and Col10='0'
    and Col11='0' and Col12='0' and Col13='0' and Col14='0' and Col15='0'
    and Col16='0' and Col17='0' and Col18='0' and Col19='0' and Col20='0';

select count(*)
from dbo.DataOffRow
where Col1='0' and Col2='0' and Col3='0' and Col4='0' and Col5='0'
    and Col6='0' and Col7='0' and Col8='0' and Col9='0' and Col10='0'
    and Col11='0' and Col12='0' and Col13='0' and Col14='0' and Col15='0'
    and Col16='0' and Col17='0' and Col18='0' and Col19='0' and Col20='0';
```

Table 6-2 illustrates the execution time in my environment. As you can see, the execution time is almost 20 times slower in the case of off-row data, which corresponds to the number of off-row columns in the table.

Table 6-2. *Execution Time of SELECT Statements*

dbo.DataInRow Select Time	dbo.DataOffRow Select Time
86 ms	1,750 ms

There is overhead during update operations when off-row columns are modified. SQL Server needs to create the new row objects for each affected column.

Similarly, the deletion of the data requires SQL Server to delete the rows in all internal tables. Table 6-3 shows the execution time of DELETE statements that delete all data from both tables.

Table 6-3. *Execution Time of DELETE Statements*

dbo.DataInRow Select Time	dbo.DataOffRow Select Time
32 ms	1,406 ms

You should avoid off-row storage unless you have legitimate reasons to use such columns. It is clearly a bad idea to define text columns as (n)varchar(max) *just in case—* when you do not store a large amount of data there. Do not forget that In-Memory OLTP would use off-row storage based on the table definition rather than the size of the data.

Summary

In-Memory OLTP database objects allocate memory from the separate memory heaps called *varheaps*. Varheaps are the data structures that respond to and track memory allocations from various database objects called *memory consumers*.

There are three most common varheap types related to memory-optimized tables. The hash index varheap allocates memory for a hash table in the hash index. The range index varheap provides memory to nonclustered index pages and the mapping table. Finally, the table heap varheap allocates memory for the data rows.

Every off-row column stores the data in an internal table, which consists of an 8-byte artificial primary key implemented as a nonclustered index along with the column data. Row-overflow columns store the actual value in the column data. LOB columns, on the other hand, store the pointer to another LOB Page Allocator varheap that stores the LOB value. The data row references off-row columns through that artificial 8-byte primary key rather than through the memory pointer.

Even though off-row storage simplifies the migration of the systems to In-Memory OLTP, use it with extreme care. Every off-row value adds 64+ bytes of overhead to every non-empty off-row value. Internal off-row tables introduce a significant performance impact during data modifications. Finally, indexes defined on memory-optimized tables do not cover off-row columns, and queries need to traverse internal tables similarly to Key Lookup operations done on disk-based tables. You should avoid off-row storage unless it is absolutely necessary.

CHAPTER 7

■ ■ ■

Columnstore Indexes

This chapter provides an overview of column-based storage and clustered columnstore indexes that can be defined on memory-optimized tables. It explains their internal structure and discusses several best practices that can improve the performance of data warehouse/reporting and operational analytics queries in the system.

Column-Based Storage Overview

Even though each database system is unique, there are two distinct workload patterns defined in the database world. The first one is online transaction processing (OLTP). OLTP systems usually handle a large number of concurrent transactions from multiple customers. Those transactions are usually small and lightweight and utilize either point-lookup searches or small range scans.

The second type of workload is data warehouse, which includes analysis, reporting, and decision support. These types of use cases use the complex queries that perform aggregations and process a large amount of data. The data in dedicated data warehouse systems is usually static and often updated based on some predefined schedules.

For example, consider a company that sells products to customers. A typical OLTP queries from the company's point-of-sale (POS) system might have the following semantic: *provide a list of orders that were placed by this particular customer this week*. Alternatively, a typical query in a data warehouse system might read as follows: *provide the total number of sales for the year to date, grouping the results by product categories and customer regions*.

There are other differences between data warehouse and OLTP systems. The data in OLTP systems is usually volatile. Such systems serve a large number of requests simultaneously, and they often have a performance SLA associated with the customer-facing queries. Alternatively, the data in data warehouse systems is relatively static and is often updated based on a set schedule, such as at night or on weekends. Those systems usually serve a small number of customers, typically business analysts, managers, and executives who can accept the longer execution time of the queries because of the amount of data that needs to be processed.

To put things into perspective, the response time of the short OLTP queries usually needs to be in the milliseconds range. However, for complex data warehouse queries, a response time in seconds or even minutes is often acceptable.

© Dmitri Korotkevitch 2017
D. Korotkevitch, *Expert SQL Server In-Memory OLTP*, DOI 10.1007/978-1-4842-2772-5_7

Obviously, it is almost impossible to find systems that do not have mixed OLTP and data warehouse workloads. Some degree of reporting and analysis activities is always present in OLTP systems even when companies have a dedicated data warehouse solution implemented. To make matters more complicated, there is another category of tasks called *operational analytics*, which has become popular nowadays. Consider the POS system in which you want to monitor up-to-date sales and dynamically adjust a product's sale price based on its popularity. This requires you to run analytical queries on the recent and volatile OLTP data.

Unfortunately, OLTP and data warehouse systems require different approaches for optimization and performance tuning. They benefit from different database schemas and indexing strategies. For example, data warehouse databases usually have over-normalized star or snowflake database schemas with few huge *facts* and many *dimension* tables. This design does not work efficiently for OLTP queries.

Moreover, OLTP and data warehouse workloads benefit from different storage and processing technologies. This requires some explanation.

Row-Based vs. Column-Based Storage

In SQL Server, classic B-Tree indexes and heaps use row-based storage. All columns that belong to the row are stored together in the single row object. Even though some of the columns can be stored off-row, they are referenced from the main data row structure, and SQL Server accesses them through the main data row. The same applies to memory-optimized tables; the columns in the data rows are grouped into the single in-memory data row objects.

Row-based storage works efficiently for OLTP workloads. OLTP queries usually access a small number of data rows and, in many cases, return a large subset of the columns from the table. Row-based storage allows those queries to access data rows in a single operation, which is especially critical during data modifications when an entire row object is inserted, updated, or deleted.

Data warehouse queries, on the other hand, behave differently. As I already mentioned, the typical data warehouse query joins facts and dimension tables and performs some calculations and aggregations accessing just a subset of a fact table's columns. Listing 7-1 shows an example of such a query in an imaginary POS data warehouse.

Listing 7-1. Typical Query in Data Warehouse Environment

```
select a.ArticleCode, sum(s.Quantity) as [Units Sold]
from dbo.FactSales s join dbo.DimArticles a on
        s.ArticleId = a.ArticleId
    join dbo.DimDates d on
        s.DateId = d.DateId
where d.AnYear = 2017
group by a.ArticleCode
```

As you can see, this query needs to perform a scan of a large amount of data from the fact table; however, it uses just two table columns. With row-based storage, SQL Server accesses rows one by one, loading the entire row into memory, regardless of how many columns from the row are required. Considering that a typical fact table in a large data warehouse environment could store hundreds of gigabytes or even terabytes of data, the query would lead to millions of I/O operations reading a large amount of data from columns that are not required for the query.

With disk-based tables, you can reduce the storage size of the table and, therefore, the number of I/O operations by implementing page compression. However, page compression works in the scope of a single page. All pages will maintain a separate copy of the compression dictionary, which is used for all rows on the page. Different columns in the row store different data, which reduces the possibility of duplicated byte sequences and limits the space saving that can be achieved with the compression.

Obviously, scanning the data from memory-optimized tables does not lead to I/O activity. Nevertheless, it will require traversing a large number of index row chains or scanning many varheap memory pages, and the overhead of row-based storage still exists.

SQL Server addresses those problems with columnstore indexes that store the data on a per-column rather than per-row basis. Figure 7-1 illustrates that approach.

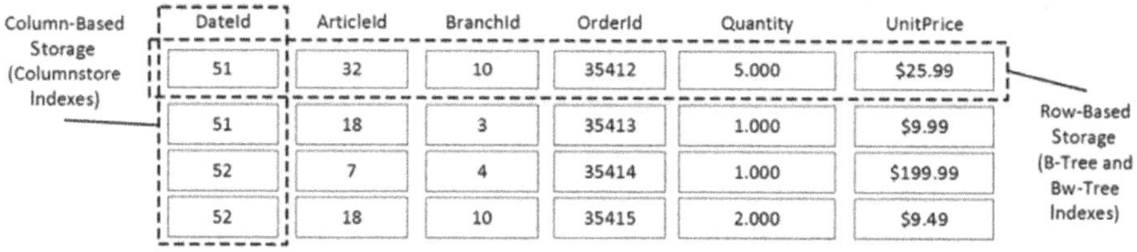

	DateId	ArticleId	BranchId	OrderId	Quantity	UnitPrice
Column-Based Storage (Columnstore Indexes)	51	32	10	35412	5.000	$25.99
	51	18	3	35413	1.000	$9.99
	52	7	4	35414	1.000	$199.99
	52	18	10	35415	2.000	$9.49

Row-Based Storage (B-Tree and Bw-Tree Indexes)

Figure 7-1. *Row-based and column-based storage*

Data in columnstore indexes is heavily compressed using algorithms that provide significant space savings even when compared to page compression. Moreover, SQL Server can skip columns that are not requested by a query reading the data on a per-column basis.

Column-based storage allows SQL Server to implement other query optimization techniques. The most noticeable is *batch mode execution*. In this mode, SQL Server processes data in groups or batches, rather than one row at a time. The size of the batches varies to fit into the CPU cache, which reduces the number of times that the CPU needs to request *external* data from memory. Moreover, the batch approach improves the performance of aggregations, which can be calculated on a per-batch basis rather than on a per-row basis. All of that allows you to achieve orders of magnitude improvement in the performance of data warehouse workload queries.

Columnstore Indexes Overview

Each data column in column-based storage is stored separately in a set of structures called *row groups*. Each row group stores data for up to approximately 1 million, or, to be precise, $2 \wedge 20 = 1,048,576$ rows. SQL Server tries to populate row groups completely during its creation, leaving the last row group partially populated. For example, in the case of 1,500,000 rows, SQL Server creates two row groups with 1,048,576 rows and 451,424 rows, respectively.

After row groups are built, SQL Server combines all the column data on a per-row group basis and encodes and compresses them. The rows within a row group can be rearranged if that helps to achieve a better compression rate. Column data within a row group is called a *segment*. SQL Server also keeps the information about data stored in each segment in segment metadata, for example, minimum and maximum values, and can skip the segments that do not have required data from the processing.

The data row's data can be reconstructed based on the *row locator*, which consists of offsets of the values in the row group's segments. All values with the same offset in the row group (same row locator) belong to the same row. For example, the first values in the segments in a particular row group belong to the first row, the second values belong to the second row, and so forth.

SQL Server uses several methods to encode and compress the data with the goal to replace all values in the data with 64-bit integers. The two most notable algorithms are *dictionary encoding* and *value-based encoding*. With dictionary encoding, SQL Server stores distinct values from the data in a separate structure called a *dictionary*. Every value in a dictionary has a unique ID assigned. SQL Server replaces the actual value in the data with an ID from the dictionary. Figure 7-2 illustrates the main idea of the algorithm.

Original Data	Dmitri	Dmitri	Niko	Victor	Victor	Niko	Niko	Dmitri	Victor

Dictionary	ID	1		2		3	
	Value	Dmitri		Niko		Victor	

Encoded Data	1	1	2	3	3	2	2	1	3

Figure 7-2. Dictionary encoding

The *value-based encoding* is mainly used for numeric and integer data types that do not have enough duplicated values. With this condition, dictionary encoding is inefficient. The purpose of value-based encoding is to convert integer and numeric values to a smaller range of 64-bit integers. This process consists of the following two steps.

In the first step, numeric data types are converted to integers using the minimum positive exponent that allows this conversion. Such an exponent is called *magnitude*. For example, for a set of values such as 0.8, 1.24, and 1.1, the minimum exponent is 2, which represents a multiplier of 100. After this exponent is applied, values would be converted to 80, 124, and 110, respectively. The goal of this process is to convert all numeric values to integers.

Alternatively, for integer data types, SQL Server chooses the smallest negative exponent that can be applied to all values without losing their precision. For example, for the values 1340, 20, and 2,340, that exponent is -1, which represents a divider of 10. After this operation, the values would be converted to 134, 2, and 234, respectively. The goal of such an operation is to reduce the interval between the minimum and maximum values stored in the segment.

During the second step, SQL Server chooses the *base value*, which is the minimum value in the segment, and it subtracts it from all other values. This makes the minimum value in the segment 0.

Figure 7-3 illustrates the process of value-based encoding.

Original Data	Numeric	0.8	1.24	1.1	0.25	9.99	4.99	
	Integer	1340	20	2340	3210	220	3300	
Step 1	Numeric	80	124	110	25	999	499	Exponent: E+2 (value * 100)
	Integer	134	2	234	321	22	330	Exponent: E-1 (value / 10)
Step 2	Numeric	55	99	85	0	974	474	Base: 25 (value - 25)
	Integer	132	0	232	319	20	328	Base: 2 (value - 2)

Figure 7-3. Value-based encoding

Conceptually, each updatable columnstore index includes two additional elements to support data modifications. The first is the *delete bitmap*, which indicates what rows were deleted from a table. The second structure is the *delta store*, which includes newly inserted rows. SQL Server does not update the data in compressed row groups during regular data modifications. Every time you delete a row that is stored in a compressed row group, SQL Server adds information about the deleted row to the delete bitmap. Nothing happens to the original row. It is still stored in a row group. However, SQL Server checks the delete bitmap during query execution, excluding deleted rows from the processing.

Similarly, when you insert data into a columnstore index, it goes into a delta store. Updating a row that is stored in a compressed row group does not change the row data either. Such an update triggers the deletion of a row, which is, in fact, insertion to a delete bitmap and insertion of a new version of a row to a delta store. However, any data modifications of the uncompressed rows in a delta store are done in place in the delta store.

The internal implementation of the delta store and the delete bitmap varies depending on the different technologies. With disk-based tables, both the delta store and delete bitmap are implemented as the set of internal B-Tree tables. Each table partition can have one delete bitmap table and multiple delta store tables, as shown in Figure 7-4. The In-Memory OLTP implementation is a bit different, as you will see later in the chapter.

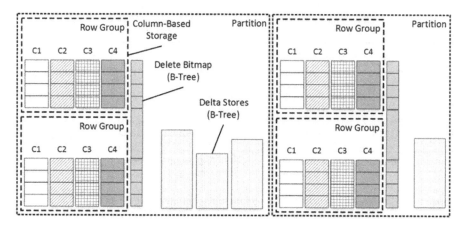

Figure 7-4. Disk-based clustered columnstore index structure

■ **Note** The In-Memory OLTP documentation often references the delta store as the *tail* and the delete bitmap as the *deleted rows table*. In this book, however, I will use classic terminology.

At some point, SQL Server compresses the data in the delta store, creating another compressed row group. Most often it happens when the delta store reaches 1,048,576 rows; however, with disk-based tables, this compression can also be forced by reorganizing the index. With memory-optimized tables, delta store compression is triggered only when the delta store fills up.

Let's look at the In-Memory OLTP implementation of columnstore indexes in detail.

Clustered Columnstore Indexes

Starting with SQL Server 2016, you can create clustered columnstore indexes on memory-optimized tables. Do not be confused by the definition of columnstore indexes as *clustered*, however. As the opposite of disk-based tables, clustered columnstore indexes on memory-optimized tables are separate data structures that keep copies of the data. In this context, *clustered* means that those indexes include all columns from the table.

The memory-optimized tables with clustered columnstore indexes have the hidden column *columnstore RID*, which is used as the row locator in the columnstore index. As with disk-based columnstore indexes, it consists of the row group ID and position of the row in the row group. In-Memory OLTP uses this column as the row locator in the delete bitmap, which is implemented as an internal table with a nonclustered range index.

Memory-optimized columnstore indexes do not have a dedicated delta store. The most recent rows in the memory-optimized table *become* the delta store. When you create a clustered columnstore index, In-Memory OLTP uses another memory consumer for the rows in the delta store. All new row objects from INSERT or UPDATE operations are allocated from this varheap. Figure 7-5 illustrates that.

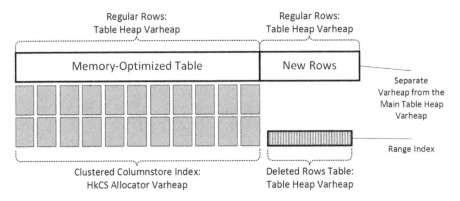

Figure 7-5. Clustered columnstore index on memory-optimized table

The index row chains in the table can link the rows from both, main table heap and the delta store varheaps.

Let's look at an example and create a table with a clustered columnstore index, as shown in Listing 7-2. After the table is created, let's look at the indexes defined on the table using the sys.indexes catalog view.

Listing 7-2. Creating Memory-Optimized Table with Columnstore Index

```
create table dbo.OrderItems
(
    OrderItemID int identity(1,1) not null
        constraint PK_OrderItems
        primary key nonclustered hash
        with (bucket_count = 4194329)
    ,OrderId int not null
    ,ArticleId int not null
    ,SalesPrice money not null
    ,index CCI_OrderItems clustered columnstore
)
with (memory_optimized = on, durability = schema_and_data);

select index_id, name, type, type_desc, compression_delay
from sys.indexes
where object_id = object_id('dbo.OrderItems');
```

As you can see in Figure 7-6, the table has two indexes: a primary key implemented as the hash index and a clustered columnstore index. I would like to reiterate that despite the term *clustered* in the index definition and index_id=1, the clustered columnstore index does not represent the main storage format for the table data. It just indicates that all table columns are included in the index.

	index_id	name	type	type_desc	compression_delay
1	1	CCI_OrderItems	5	CLUSTERED COLUMNSTORE	0
2	2	PK_OrderItems	7	NONCLUSTERED HASH	NULL

Figure 7-6. *Indexes on memory-optimized table*

As the opposite of hash and nonclustered indexes, which are re-created when data is loaded into memory, SQL Server persists columnstore indexes on disk. I will talk about In-Memory OLTP data storage in greater depth in Chapter 10.

Let's populate the table with 3,200,000 rows, as shown in Listing 7-3.

Listing 7-3. Populating the Table with Data and Analyzing Memory Consumers

```
;with N1(C) as (select 0 union all select 0) -- 2 rows
,N2(C) as (select 0 from N1 as t1 cross join N1 as t2) -- 4 rows
,N3(C) as (select 0 from N2 as t1 cross join N2 as t2) -- 16 rows
,N4(C) as (select 0 from N3 as t1 cross join N3 as t2) -- 256 rows
,N5(C) as (select 0 from N4 as t1 cross join N4 as t2) -- 65,536 rows
,N6(C) as (select 0 from N5 as t1 cross join N4 as t2) -- 16,777,316 rows
,Ids(Id) as (select row_number() over (order by (select null)) from N6)
insert into dbo.OrderItems(OrderId, ArticleId, SalesPrice)
    select ID / 3 + 1, ID % 50000, 49.99
    from Ids
    where ID <= 3200000;
```

105

Listing 7-4 shows the code that analyzes memory consumers for the dbo.OrderItems table.

Listing 7-4. Populating the Table with Data and Analyzing Memory Consumers

```
select
    a.xtp_object_id, a.type_desc, a.minor_id
    ,c.memory_consumer_id as [mc id]
    ,c.memory_consumer_type_desc as [mc type]
    ,c.memory_consumer_desc as [description]
    ,c.allocation_count as [allocs]
    ,c.allocated_bytes / 1024 as [Allocated KB]
    ,c.used_bytes / 1024 as [Used KB]
from
    sys.dm_db_xtp_memory_consumers c join
        sys.memory_optimized_tables_internal_attributes a on
            a.object_id = c.object_id and a.xtp_object_id = c.xtp_object_id
where
    c.object_id = object_id('dbo.OrderItems');
```

Figure 7-7 shows the output from Listing 7-4. As you can see, the main table object (the first four rows in the output) has four memory consumers. The HKCS_COMPRESSED consumer stores compressed row groups. The table heap consumer with id=74 is providing memory for the delta store. All new data rows in the table are allocated there. Another table heap with id=75 is the main table heap, and it is storing the rows that were already compressed in the columnstore index. The data has not been compressed yet, and therefore this consumer does not use any memory.

	xtp_object_id	type_desc	minor_id	mc id	mc type	description	allocs	Allocated KB	Used KB
1	-2147483648	USER_TABLE	0	77	HKCS_COMPRESSED	HkCS Allocator	2	16	16
2	-2147483648	USER_TABLE	0	76	HASH	Hash index	1	65536	65536
3	-2147483648	USER_TABLE	0	75	VARHEAP	Table heap	0	0	0
4	-2147483648	USER_TABLE	0	74	VARHEAP	Table heap	3200000	201024	200000
5	-2147483644	ROW_GROUPS_INFO_TABLE	0	73	HASH	Hash index	1	1024	1024
6	-2147483644	ROW_GROUPS_INFO_TABLE	0	72	VARHEAP	Table heap	1	64	0
7	-2147483645	SEGMENTS_TABLE	0	71	HASH	Hash index	1	32768	32768
8	-2147483645	SEGMENTS_TABLE	0	70	HASH	Hash index	1	32768	32768
9	-2147483645	SEGMENTS_TABLE	0	69	VARHEAP	Table heap	0	0	0
10	-2147483646	DICTIONARIES_TABLE	0	68	HASH	Hash index	1	32768	32768
11	-2147483646	DICTIONARIES_TABLE	0	67	VARHEAP	Table heap	0	0	0
12	-2147483647	DELETED_ROWS_TABLE	0	66	VARHEAP	Range index heap	2	128	0
13	-2147483647	DELETED_ROWS_TABLE	0	65	VARHEAP	Table heap	0	0	0

Figure 7-7. *Memory consumers after table has been populated with the data*

Columnstore indexes have several other internal objects.

> DELETED_ROWS_TABLE is an internal table that stores the delete bitmap, which is the information about the deleted rows. It is implemented as a nonclustered (range) index and contains a columnstore locator (RID) of the deleted rows.

ROW_GROUPS_INFO_TABLE stores the information about row groups in columnstore indexes.

SEGMENTS_TABLE stores the information about column segments in the row groups.

DICTIONARIES_TABLE stores columnstore index dictionaries.

There is the background process called the *tuple mover*, which wakes up about every two minutes and estimates the number of rows in the delta store. In the case, when it estimates that the delta store has at least 1,048,576 rows, the tuple mover creates the new row group (or groups) by compressing and encoding the rows from the delta store. During compression, the tuple mover updates the row locator RID column in the rows from the delta store, which generates the new versions of the rows. The memory for the new row objects are allocated from the main table heap.

Finally, the tuple mover deletes (populates the EndTs timestamp) the compressed rows from the delta store, which will be eventually deallocated by the garbage collector process.

Figure 7-8 illustrates the memory consumers after the tuple mover has compressed the data. As you can see, rows have been moved from the delta store to the main table heaps, and compressed data is also stored in the HKCS_COMPRESSED allocator.

	xtp_object_id	type_desc	minor_id	mc id	mc type	description	allocs	Allocated KB	Used KB
1	-2147483648	USER_TABLE	0	77	HKCS_COMPRESSED	HkCS Allocator	2	45248	45248
2	-2147483648	USER_TABLE	0	76	HASH	Hash index	1	65536	65536
3	-2147483648	USER_TABLE	0	75	VARHEAP	Table heap	3143665	222400	221038
4	-2147483648	USER_TABLE	0	74	VARHEAP	Table heap	56406	201024	3525
5	-2147483644	ROW_GROUPS_INFO_TABLE	0	73	HASH	Hash index	1	1024	1024
6	-2147483644	ROW_GROUPS_INFO_TABLE	0	72	VARHEAP	Table heap	4	192	0
7	-2147483645	SEGMENTS_TABLE	0	71	HASH	Hash index	1	32768	32768
8	-2147483645	SEGMENTS_TABLE	0	70	HASH	Hash index	1	32768	32768
9	-2147483645	SEGMENTS_TABLE	0	69	VARHEAP	Table heap	12	192	1
10	-2147483646	DICTIONARIES_TABLE	0	68	HASH	Hash index	1	32768	32768
11	-2147483646	DICTIONARIES_TABLE	0	67	VARHEAP	Table heap	6	192	0
12	-2147483647	DELETED_ROWS_TABLE	0	66	VARHEAP	Range index heap	130	10624	33
13	-2147483647	DELETED_ROWS_TABLE	0	65	VARHEAP	Table heap	0	192	0

Figure 7-8. *Memory consumers after delta store is compressed*

Let's look what happens when you delete some data. Listing 7-5 shows the statement that deletes every 100th row in the table.

Listing 7-5. Deleting 1 Percent of the Rows

```
delete from dbo.OrderItems where OrderItemId % 100 = 0;
```

As I already mentioned, SQL Server does not remove deleted rows from columnstore indexes. The information (RID) of deleted rows is inserted into the delete bitmap, which is displayed as DELETED_ROWS_TABLE in Figure 7-9.

	xtp_object_id	type_desc	minor_id	mc id	mc type	description	allocs	Allocated KB	Used KB
1	-2147483648	USER_TABLE	0	77	HKCS_COMPRESSED	HkCS Allocator	2	45248	45248
2	-2147483648	USER_TABLE	0	76	HASH	Hash index	1	65536	65536
3	-2147483648	USER_TABLE	0	75	VARHEAP	Table heap	3143665	222400	221038
4	-2147483648	USER_TABLE	0	74	VARHEAP	Table heap	56406	201024	3525
5	-2147483644	ROW_GROUPS_INFO_TABLE	0	73	HASH	Hash index	1	1024	1024
6	-2147483644	ROW_GROUPS_INFO_TABLE	0	72	VARHEAP	Table heap	4	192	0
7	-2147483645	SEGMENTS_TABLE	0	71	HASH	Hash index	1	32768	32768
8	-2147483645	SEGMENTS_TABLE	0	70	HASH	Hash index	1	32768	32768
9	-2147483645	SEGMENTS_TABLE	0	69	VARHEAP	Table heap	12	192	1
10	-2147483646	DICTIONARIES_TABLE	0	68	HASH	Hash index	1	32768	32768
11	-2147483646	DICTIONARIES_TABLE	0	67	VARHEAP	Table heap	6	192	0
12	-2147483647	DELETED_ROWS_TABLE	0	66	VARHEAP	Range index	392	15680	574
13	-2147483647	DELETED_ROWS_TABLE	0	65	VARHEAP	Table heap	31439	1664	1473

Figure 7-9. Memory consumers after rows were deleted

You can obtain detailed information about columnstore index row groups from the sys.dm_db_column_store_row_group_physical_stats view, as shown in Listing 7-6.

Listing 7-6. Analyzing Row Groups

```
select row_group_id, state_desc, total_rows, deleted_rows
    ,size_in_bytes, trim_reason_desc
from sys.dm_db_column_store_row_group_physical_stats
where object_id = object_id('dbo.OrderItems')
order by row_group_id
```

Figure 7-10 shows the output of the view. The row group with row_group_id=-1 corresponds to the delta store.

	row_group_id	state_desc	total_rows	deleted_rows	size_in_bytes	trim_reason_desc
1	-1	OPEN	55774	0	NULL	NULL
2	1	COMPRESSED	1048576	10475	9290308	NO_TRIM
3	2	COMPRESSED	1048576	10502	9290308	NO_TRIM
4	3	COMPRESSED	1046513	10462	9274452	STATS_MISMATCH

Figure 7-10. Row group statistics

The trip_reason_desc column indicates why the compressed row group has less than 1,048,476 rows. For memory-optimized tables, it can contain one of the following values:

NO_TRIM indicates that the row group is fully populated.

STATS_MISTMATCH indicates an incorrect estimation of the delta store size.

SPILLOVER indicates that the row group contains leftover rows after all full row groups were created. SQL Server compresses those rows into the smaller row group if there are more than 102,500 rows in the delta store. Otherwise, the rows remain in the delta store, as shown in Figure 7-10.

MEMORY_LIMITATION indicates that the system did not have enough memory to compress all the rows together.

DICTIONARY_SIZE indicates that the dictionary grew too big to compress all the rows together.

Performance Considerations

As you can guess, large delta store and delete bitmaps would add overhead during query execution. SQL Server needs to scan noncompressed rows in the delta store, which is significantly slower compared to compressed row groups. Similarly, a large number of rows in the delete bitmap adds overhead of validation if compressed rows were deleted.

Let's look at this overhead in detail and add 1,500,000 rows to the table using the code from Listing 7-7.

Listing 7-7. Inserting 1.5 Million Rows into Delta Store

```
;with N1(C) as (select 0 union all select 0) -- 2 rows
,N2(C) as (select 0 from N1 as t1 cross join N1 as t2) -- 4 rows
,N3(C) as (select 0 from N2 as t1 cross join N2 as t2) -- 16 rows
,N4(C) as (select 0 from N3 as t1 cross join N3 as t2) -- 256 rows
,N5(C) as (select 0 from N4 as t1 cross join N4 as t2) -- 65,536 rows
,N6(C) as (select 0 from N5 as t1 cross join N4 as t2) -- 16,777,316 rows
,Ids(Id) as (select row_number() over (order by (select null)) from N6)
insert into dbo.OrderItems(OrderId, ArticleId, SalesPrice)
    select 4000000 + ID / 3 + 1, ID % 50000, 49.99
    from Ids
    where ID <= 1500000;
```

If you run the code from Listing 7-6 again after the data was inserted, you would see the output shown in Figure 7-11. The new rows have not been compressed, and they stay in the delta store.

	row_group_id	state_desc	total_rows	deleted_rows	size_in_bytes	trim_reason_desc
1	-1	OPEN	1555774	0	NULL	NULL
2	1	COMPRESSED	1048576	10475	9290308	NO_TRIM
3	2	COMPRESSED	1048576	10502	9290308	NO_TRIM
4	3	COMPRESSED	1046513	10462	9274452	STATS_MISMATCH

Figure 7-11. *Row group status after insert*

If you run the query from Listing 7-6 again after the tuple mover executes, you would see that the new rows have been compressed into two new row groups. Figure 7-12 shows the status of the row groups when it happens.

	row_group_id	state_desc	total_rows	deleted_rows	size_in_bytes	trim_reason_desc
1	-1	OPEN	0	0	NULL	NULL
2	1	COMPRESSED	1048576	10475	9290308	NO_TRIM
3	2	COMPRESSED	1048576	10502	9290308	NO_TRIM
4	3	COMPRESSED	1046513	10462	9274452	STATS_MISMATCH
5	4	COMPRESSED	1048576	0	7892212	NO_TRIM
6	5	COMPRESSED	507198	0	5076476	SPILLOVER

Figure 7-12. *Status of row groups after data is compressed*

Listing 7-8 shows the test query that benefits from the columnstore index. I've executed this query twice, before and after the rows from the delta store were compressed. The execution times in my environment were 343 ms and 160 ms, respectively. As you can see, scanning of large number of uncompressed rows in the delta store affects the performance of the query. It is worth noting, however, that this overhead is significantly smaller compared to the delta store scan in disk-based columnstore indexes because of the in-memory data access and efficiency of varheap scans.

Listing 7-8. Test Query

```
select top 10 ArticleId, avg(SalesPrice)
from dbo.OrderItems
group by ArticleId
order by avg(SalesPrice) desc;
```

As the next step, let's look at the overhead introduced by the large number of deleted rows. Listing 7-9 shows the query, which deletes half the rows from the table. Figure 7-13 illustrates row group statistics after deletion.

Listing 7-9. Deleting 50 Percent of the Data

```
delete from dbo.OrderItems where OrderItemId % 2 = 0;
```

	row_group_id	state_desc	total_rows	deleted_rows	size_in_bytes	trim_reason_desc
1	-1	OPEN	0	0	NULL	NULL
2	1	COMPRESSED	1048576	524271	9290308	NO_TRIM
3	2	COMPRESSED	1048576	524316	9290308	NO_TRIM
4	3	COMPRESSED	1046513	523243	9274452	STATS_MISMATCH
5	4	COMPRESSED	1048576	524288	7892212	NO_TRIM
6	5	COMPRESSED	507198	253321	5076476	SPILLOVER

Figure 7-13. *Status of row groups after data was deleted*

The execution time of the test query from Listing 7-8 in my environment was 516 ms. SQL Server should check whether the RID of compressed rows were present in DELETED_ROWS_TABLE and exclude deleted rows from the processing. All of that added significant overhead during query execution.

There is another implication of the large number of deleted rows and large delete bitmaps. They reduce the amount of memory available to In-Memory OLTP and other SQL Server components.

Unfortunately, it is common to have a large number of deleted rows in memory-optimized columnstore indexes. The data in OLTP systems is usually highly volatile, and data rows may be updated multiple times. If data rows are updated after they were compressed, each obsolete row version would be referenced in the delete bitmap of the index.

Fortunately, it is also common that data rows become static after some time. SQL Server allows you to delay compression of the delta store rows by specifying the COMPRESSION_DELAY columnstore index option. This property indicates how long the rows should stay in the delta store before they can be compressed into row groups. You should set COMPRESSION_DELAY to the value that exceeds the typical post-processing time in the system.

Consider an online shopping cart system as an example. In this scenario, the status of individual orders may be updated multiple times during the fulfillment process. It could be beneficial to set COMPRESSION_DELAY to the value that exceeds the typical fulfillment time and avoid compressing old versions of order rows until the order is fulfilled.

Listing 7-10 shows an example of a table with a columnstore index that has the compression delay set to 1,440 minutes, which is 24 hours. Even though this increases the size of the delta store, it would also prevent compressions of the versions of the rows that have yet to be deleted. As the general rule, it is better to have a slightly larger delta store than increase the size of the delete bitmap.

Listing 7-10. Creating Columnstore Index with Compression Delay

```
create table dbo.OrdersCCI
(
    OrderId int not null
        constraint PK_OrdersCCI
        primary key nonclustered,
    OrderDate datetime2(0) not null,
    OrderNum varchar(32) not null,
    Amount money not null,
    CustomerId int not null,
    OrderStatus tinyint not null,
    FulfillmentDate datetime2(0) not null,
    index CCI_OrdersCCI clustered columnstore
        with (compression_delay=1440)
)
with (memory_optimized=on, durability=schema_and_data);
```

You can monitor the percent of deleted rows in the row groups and fine-tune the index COMPRESSION_DELAY value to minimize it. Unfortunately, changing the property will require you to drop and re-create the columnstore index. This is an offline operation, which will lead to two table rebuilds and can take a significant amount of time and memory in the case of large tables. Neither can you rebuild columnstore indexes, reducing the size of the delete bitmap. Dropping and re-creating the index is the only option available.

There is one case, however, when In-Memory OLTP rebuilds row groups internally. SQL Server decompresses the row groups, moving rows back to the delta store when the row group has 90 percent or more rows deleted.

Listing 7-11 illustrates the code that deletes 99 percent of the data from the table. Figure 7-14 shows the status of the row groups right after deletion.

Listing 7-11. Deleting 99 Percent of the Data

```
delete from dbo.OrderItems where OrderId % 100 < 98;
```

	row_group_id	state_desc	total_rows	deleted_rows	size_in_bytes	trim_reason_desc
1	-1	OPEN	0	0	NULL	NULL
2	1	COMPRESSED	1048576	1038169	9290308	NO_TRIM
3	2	COMPRESSED	1048576	1038066	9290308	NO_TRIM
4	3	COMPRESSED	1046513	1035997	9274452	STATS_MISMATCH
5	4	COMPRESSED	1048576	1038088	7892212	NO_TRIM
6	5	COMPRESSED	507198	502121	5076476	SPILLOVER

Figure 7-14. *Status of row groups after 99 percent of the rows were deleted*

If you look at the row groups after a few minutes, you would see that the tuple mover process moved all nondeleted rows back to the delta store, deallocating all compressed row groups in the system. Figure 7-15 illustrates that condition.

	row_group_id	state_desc	total_rows	deleted_rows	trim_reason_desc	created_time
1	-1	OPEN	46998	0	NULL	NULL

Figure 7-15. *Status of row groups after tuple mover run*

Columnstore Indexes Limitations

There are several limitations related to columnstore indexes. Perhaps the most important is that SQL Server can utilize columnstore indexes only in Query Interop mode. Those indexes are never used from the natively compiled code.

Other important limitations include the following:

> The columnstore index cannot be created if the table uses off-row storage, and, therefore, the row size cannot exceed 8,060 bytes.

> Memory-optimized tables with columnstore indexes cannot be altered. You should drop the index, alter the table, and re-create the index afterward.

> Columnstore indexes on memory-optimized tables cannot be rebuilt or reorganized.

> Archive compression is not supported.

Obviously, the system should have enough memory to accommodate columnstore indexes. Those indexes, however, are heavily compressed and could use just a fraction of the memory used by noncompressed rows.

Catalog and Data Management Views

SQL Server provides several columnstore index-related catalog and data management views.

sys.dm_db_column_store_row_group_physical_stats

The sys.dm_db_column_store_row_group_physical_stats view returns the information about row groups in the columnstore index. You have already seen this view in action in this chapter.

The columns in the output represent the following:

> object_id and index_id provide the information about the object and index to which the row group belongs.
>
> partition_number is the number of partitions in the table. It is always 1 for memory-optimized tables.
>
> row_group_id is the ID of the row group within the partition. The delta store in memory-optimized tables has row_group_id=-1.
>
> delta_store_hobt_id is the hobt_id of the open delta store. It is NULL for memory-optimized tables.
>
> state and state_description show the state of the row group.
>
> total_rows, deleted_rows, and size_in_bytes provide the information about row count and row group size.
>
> trim_reason and trim_reason_desc indicate why a row group has less than 1,048,576 rows.
>
> transition_to_compressed_state provides the reason why a row group was compressed. In memory-optimized tables, the row groups always are compressed by the tuple mover.
>
> generation shows the sequence number in which the row group has been created.

As I already discussed, it is beneficial to monitor the total number of rows and the number of deleted rows in the row groups and fine-tune the COMPRESSION_DELAY index option.

There is another view, called sys.column_store_row_groups, which provides a subset of the columns from the sys.dm_db_column_store_row_group_physical_stats view. The former one was introduced in SQL Server 2014, while the latter one is specific to SQL Server 2016.

sys.column_store_segments

The sys.column_store_segments view returns one row for each column per segment.

Listing 7-12 shows a query that returns information about the CCI_OrderItems columnstore index. There are a couple of things that you should note here. First, the view does not return the object_id or index_id value of the index. This is not a problem because a table can have only one columnstore index defined. However, you need to use the sys.partitions view to obtain the object_id value when it is required.

Second, the column_id value does not match the column_id value in the sys.index_columns view because of the internal columnstore locator (RID) column, which is not exposed there. You need to decrement column_id in sys.column_store_segments by 1 in the joins. This may or may not change in future versions of In-Memory OLTP.

Listing 7-12. Examining the sys.column_store_segments View

```
select
    s.segment_id, s.column_id - 1 as [column_id], c.name as [column]
    ,s.version, s.encoding_type, s.row_count, s.has_nulls, s.magnitude
    ,s.primary_dictionary_id, s.secondary_dictionary_id, s.min_data_id
    ,s.max_data_id, s.null_value
    ,convert(decimal(12,3),s.on_disk_size / 1024.0 / 1024.0)  as [Size MB]
from
    sys.column_store_segments s join sys.partitions p on
        p.partition_id = s.partition_id
    join sys.indexes i on
        p.object_id = i.object_id
    left join sys.index_columns ic on
        i.index_id = ic.index_id and
        i.object_id = ic.object_id and
        s.column_id - 1 = ic.index_column_id
     left join sys.columns c on
        ic.column_id = c.column_id and
        ic.object_id = c.object_id
where
    i.name = 'CCI_OrderItems'
order by
    s.segment_id, s.column_id
```

Figure 7-16 shows the partial output of a query.

	segment_id	column_id	column	version	encoding_type	row_count	has_nulls	magnitude
1	1	1	OrderItemID	1	1	1048576	0	1
2	1	2	OrderId	1	1	1048576	0	1
3	1	3	ArticleId	1	2	1048576	0	-1
4	1	4	SalesPrice	1	2	1048576	0	-1
5	2	1	OrderItemID	1	1	1048576	0	1
6	2	2	OrderId	1	1	1048576	0	1
7	2	3	ArticleId	1	2	1048576	0	-1
8	2	4	SalesPrice	1	2	1048576	0	-1

primary_dictionary_id	secondary_dictionary_id	min_data_id	max_data_id	null_value	Size MB
255	-1	113110	3198641	-1	4.001
255	-1	37704	1066214	-1	2.667
255	2	0	49999	-1	2.001
255	5	499900	499900	-1	0.001
255	-1	40761	3200000	-1	4.001
255	-1	13588	1066667	-1	2.667
255	1	0	49999	-1	2.001
255	4	499900	499900	-1	0.001

Figure 7-16. *sys.column_store_segments output*

The columns in the output represent the following:

column_id is the ID of a column in the index, which you can join with the sys.index_columns view. As I already mentioned, you need to decrement it by 1 in the joins.

partition_id references the partition to which a row group (and, therefore, a segment) belongs. It is always 1 in memory-optimized tables.

segment_id is the ID of the segment, which is basically the ID of a row group. The first segment/row group in a partition has an ID of 1.

version represents a columnstore segment format. SQL Server 2012, 2014, and 2016 return 1 as its value.

encoding_type represents the encoding used for this segment. It can have one of the following four values:

A value-based encoding has encoding_type = 1.

A dictionary encoding of nonstrings has encoding_type = 2.

A dictionary encoding of string values has encoding_type = 3.

No encoding being used has encoding_type = 4.

row_count represents the number of rows in the segment.

has_null indicates whether the data has null values.

magnitude is the magnitude used for value-based encoding. For other encoding types, it returns -1.

min_data_id and max_data_id represent the minimum and maximum values in a column within the segment. SQL Server analyzes those values during query execution and eliminates segments that do not store values that satisfy query predicates. This process works in a similar way to partition elimination in partitioned tables.

null_value represents the value used to indicate nulls.

on_disk_size indicates the size of a segment in bytes.

sys.column_store_dictionaries

The sys.column_store_dictionaries view provides information about the dictionaries used by a columnstore index.

Listing 7-13 shows the code that you can use to examine the list of dictionaries. Similarly to the sys.column_store_segments view, you should decrement column_id by 1 in the joins.

Listing 7-13. Examining the sys.column_store_dictionaries View

```
select
    d.dictionary_id, d.column_id - 1 as [column_id], c.name as [column]
    ,d.version, d.type, d.last_id, d.entry_count
    ,convert(decimal(12,3),d.on_disk_size / 1024.0 / 1024.0)  as [Size MB]
from
    sys.column_store_dictionaries d join sys.partitions p on
        p.partition_id = d.partition_id
    join sys.indexes i on
        p.object_id = i.object_id
    left join sys.index_columns ic on
        i.index_id = ic.index_id and
        i.object_id = ic.object_id and
        d.column_id - 1 = ic.index_column_id
    left join sys.columns c on
        ic.column_id = c.column_id and
        ic.object_id = c.object_id
where
    i.name = 'CCI_OrderItems'
order by
    d.dictionary_id
```

Figure 7-17 illustrates the query output.

	dictionary_id	column_id	column	version	type	last_id	entry_count	Size MB
1	1	3	ArticleId	1	1	50002	50000	0.191
2	2	3	ArticleId	1	1	50002	50000	0.191
3	3	3	ArticleId	1	1	50002	50000	0.191
4	4	4	SalesPrice	1	1	3	1	0.000
5	5	4	SalesPrice	1	1	3	1	0.000
6	6	4	SalesPrice	1	1	3	1	0.000

***Figure 7-17.** sys.column_store_dictionaries output*

The columns in the output represent the following:

column_id is the ID of a column in the index.

dictionary_id is the ID of a dictionary.

version represents a dictionary format. SQL Server 2012, 2014, and 2016 return 1 as its value.

type represents the type of values stored in a dictionary. It can have one of the following three values:

A dictionary that contains int values is specified by type = 1.

A dictionary that contains string values is specified by type = 3.

A dictionary that contains float values is specified by type = 4.

last_id is a last data ID in a dictionary.

entry_count contains the number of entries in a dictionary.

on_disk_size indicates the size of a dictionary in bytes.

Summary

In contrast to B-Tree and Bw-Tree indexes that store data on a per-row basis, columnstore indexes store unsorted and compressed data on a per-column basis. They are beneficial in data warehouse environments where typical queries perform a scan and aggregation of data from large fact tables, selecting just a subset of table columns. With In-Memory OLTP, those indexes help in an operational analytics scenario when systems execute reporting and analytics queries against hot OLTP data.

In-Memory OLTP clustered columnstore indexes are separate data structures from the main data rows. They consist of compressed row groups, a delete bitmap implemented as an internal table with a nonclustered (range) index, and several other internal tables. There is no dedicated delta store; the new versions of the rows are included into the regular data row chain, although they are allocated from a different varheap. The tuple mover process analyzes the number of allocated rows in this varheap and compresses them, moving to the regular table heap once the number reaches 1,048,576 rows.

A large delta store and delete bitmap affects the performance of the queries. You can delay the compression by specifying the COMPRESSION_DELAY index option. It is recommended that you set this value to exceed the typical data post-processing time in the system.

Columnstore indexes have several limitations. They do not support off-row storage, limiting the size of the row to 8,060 bytes. They prevent table alteration, and you should drop and re-create a columnstore index when you need to alter a table. Most importantly, they can be utilized only through the Interop Engine; SQL Server does not use them in natively compiled code.

CHAPTER 8

■ ■ ■

Transaction Processing in In-Memory OLTP

This chapter discusses transaction processing in In-Memory OLTP. It elucidates what isolation levels are supported with native compilation and cross-container transactions, provides an overview of concurrency phenomena encountered in the database systems, and explains how In-Memory OLTP addresses them. Finally, this chapter talks about the lifetime of In-Memory OLTP transactions in detail.

ACID, Transaction Isolation Levels, and Concurrency Phenomena Overview

Transactions are the unit of work that read and modify data in a database and help to enforce the consistency and durability of the data in a system. Every transaction in a properly implemented transaction management system has four characteristics known as *atomicity, consistency, isolation,* and *durability,* often referenced as *ACID.*

- *Atomicity* guarantees that each transaction executes as an "all or nothing" approach. All changes done within a transaction are either committed or rolled back in full. Consider the classic example of transferring money between checking and savings bank accounts. That action consists of two separate operations: decreasing the balance of the checking account and increasing the balance of the savings account. Transaction atomicity guarantees that both operations either succeed or fail together, so a system will never be in the situation that money is deducted from the checking account but never added to the savings account.

- *Consistency* ensures that any database transaction brings the database from one consistent state to another with no defined database rules or constraints violated.

© Dmitri Korotkevitch 2017
D. Korotkevitch, *Expert SQL Server In-Memory OLTP*, DOI 10.1007/978-1-4842-2772-5_8

- *Isolation* ensures that the changes done in the transaction are isolated and invisible to other transactions until the transaction is committed. By the book, transaction isolation should guarantee that the concurrent execution of multiple transactions should bring the system to the same state as if those transactions were executed serially. However, in most database systems, such a requirement is often relaxed and controlled by *transaction isolation levels*.

- *Durability* guarantees that after a transaction is committed, all changes done by the transaction stay permanent and will survive a system crash. SQL Server achieves durability by using *write-ahead logging*, which hardens log records in transaction log synchronously with data modifications.

The isolation requirements are the most complex to implement in multi-user environments. Even though it is possible to completely isolate different transactions from each other, this could lead to a high level of blocking and other concurrency issues in systems with volatile data. SQL Server addresses this situation by introducing several transaction isolation levels that relax isolation requirements at the cost of possible concurrency phenomena related to read data consistency.

- *Dirty reads*: A transaction reads uncommitted (dirty) data from other uncommitted transactions.

- *Nonrepeatable reads*: Subsequent attempts to read the same data from within the same transaction return different results. This data inconsistency issue arises when the other transactions modified, or even deleted, data between the reads done by the affected transaction.

- *Phantom reads*: This phenomenon occurs when subsequent reads within the same transaction return new rows (the ones that the transaction did not read before). This happens when another transaction inserted the new data in between the reads done by the affected transaction.

Table 8-1 shows the data inconsistency issues that are possible for different transaction isolation levels. It is worth mentioning that every isolation level resolves write/write conflicts, preventing multiple active transactions from updating the same rows simultaneously.

Table 8-1. *Transaction Isolation Levels and Concurrency Phenomena*

Isolation Level	Dirty Reads	Nonrepeatable Reads	Phantom Reads
READ UNCOMMITTED	Yes	Yes	Yes
READ COMMITTED	No	Yes	Yes
REPEATABLE READ	No	No	Yes
SERIALIZABLE	No	No	No
SNAPSHOT	No	No	No

With the exception of the SNAPSHOT isolation level, SQL Server uses locking to address concurrency phenomena when dealing with disk-based tables. When a transaction modifies a row, it acquires exclusive (X) locks on the row and holds it until the end of the transaction. That exclusive (X) lock prevents other sessions from accessing uncommitted data until the transaction is completed and the locks are released. This behavior is also known as *pessimistic concurrency*.

Such behavior also means that, in the case of a write/write conflict, the last modification wins. For example, when two transactions are trying to modify the same row, SQL Server blocks one of them until another transaction is committed, allowing blocked transactions to modify the data afterward. No errors or exceptions are raised; however, changes done by the first transaction are overwritten.

In the case of disk-based tables and pessimistic concurrency, transaction isolation levels control how a session acquires and releases shared (S) locks when reading the data. Table 8-2 demonstrates that behavior.

Table 8-2. *Transaction Isolation Levels and Shared (S) Locks Behavior with Disk-Based Tables*

Isolation Level	Shared (S) Locks Behavior	Comments
READ UNCOMMITTED	(S) locks not acquired	The transaction can see uncommitted changes from the other sessions (dirty reads).
READ COMMITTED	(S) locks acquired and released immediately	The transaction will be blocked when it tries to read uncommitted rows with exclusive (X) locks held by the other sessions (no dirty reads).
REPEATABLE READ	(S) locks acquired and held until end of transaction	Other sessions cannot modify a row after it was read (no non-repeatable reads). However, they can still insert new rows in between reads (phantom reads).
SERIALIZABLE	Range (S) locks acquired and held until end of transaction	Other sessions cannot modify a row after it was read or insert new rows in between rows that were read (no non-repeatable or phantom reads).

The SNAPSHOT isolation level uses a row-versioning model by creating the new version of the row after modification. In this model, all data modifications done by other transactions are invisible to the transaction after it starts.

Though SNAPSHOT isolation is implemented differently in disk-based and memory-optimized tables, logically it behaves the same. A transaction will read a version of the row valid at the time when the transaction started, and sessions do not block each other. However, when two transactions try to update the same data, one of them will be aborted and rolled back to resolve the write/write conflict. This behavior is known as *optimistic concurrency*.

SERIALIZABLE VS. SNAPSHOT ISOLATION LEVELS

While the SERIALIZABLE and SNAPSHOT isolation levels provide the same level of protection against data inconsistency issues, there is a subtle difference in their behavior with disk-based tables. A SNAPSHOT isolation level transaction sees data as of the beginning of a transaction. With the SERIALIZABLE isolation level, the transaction sees data as of the time when the data was accessed for the first time.

Consider the situation when a session is reading data from a disk-based table in the middle of a transaction. If another session changed the data in that table after the transaction started but before data was read, the transaction in the SERIALIZABLE isolation level would see the changes, while the SNAPSHOT transaction would not.

Transaction Isolation Levels in In-Memory OLTP

In-Memory OLTP supports three transaction isolation levels: SNAPSHOT, REPEATABLE READ, and SERIALIZABLE. However, In-Memory OLTP uses a completely different approach to enforce data consistency rules compared to disk-based tables. Rather than block or being blocked by other sessions, In-Memory OLTP validates data consistency at the transaction COMMIT time and throws an exception and rolls back the transaction if rules are violated.

- In the SNAPSHOT isolation level, any changes done by other sessions are invisible to the transaction. A SNAPSHOT transaction always works with a snapshot of the data as of the time when the transaction started. The only validation at the time of the commit is checking for primary key violations, which is called *snapshot validation.*

- In the REPEATABLE READ isolation level, In-Memory OLTP validates that the rows that were read by the transaction have not been modified or deleted by the other transactions. A REPEATABLE READ transaction would not be able to commit if this was the case. That action is called *repeatable read validation*, and it is executed in addition to snapshot validation.

- In the SERIALIZABLE isolation level, SQL Server performs repeatable read validation and also checks for phantom rows that were possibly inserted by the other sessions. This process is called *serializable validation*, and it is executed in addition to snapshot validation.

Let's look at a few examples that demonstrate this behavior. As a first step, shown in Listing 8-1, let's create a memory-optimized table and insert a few rows there.

Listing 8-1. Data Consistency and Transaction Isolation Levels: Table Creation

```
create table dbo.HKData
(
    ID int not null
        constraint PK_HKData
        primary key nonclustered hash with (bucket_count=64),
    Col int not null
)
with (memory_optimized=on, durability=schema_only);

insert into dbo.HKData(ID, Col) values(1,1),(2,2),(3,3),(4,4),(5,5);
```

Table 8-3 shows how concurrency works in the REPEATABLE READ transaction isolation level. It is important to note that SQL Server starts a transaction at the moment of the first data access rather than at the time of the BEGIN TRAN statement. Therefore, the Session 1 transaction starts when the first SELECT operator executes.

Table 8-3. *Concurrency in the REPEATABLE READ Transaction Isolation Level*

Session 1	Session 2	Results

begin tran
  select ID, Col
  from dbo.HKData
    with (repeatableread)		

	update dbo.HKData set Col = -2 where ID = 2	

select ID, Col
  from dbo.HKData
    with (repeatableread)
		Return old version of a row (Col = 2).

commit		Msg 41305, Level 16, State 0, Line 0.
		The current transaction failed to commit because of a repeatable read validation failure.

begin tran
  select ID, Col
  from dbo.HKData
    with (repeatableread)		

	insert into dbo. HKData values(10,10)	

select ID, Col
  from dbo.HKData
    with (repeatableread)
		Does not return a new row (10,10).

commit		Success.

As you can see, with memory-optimized tables, other sessions are able to modify data that is read by the active REPEATABLE READ transaction. This leads to a transaction abort at the time of COMMIT when the repeatable read validation fails. This is completely different behavior than that of disk-based tables, where other sessions are blocked, unable to modify data until the REPEATABLE READ transaction successfully commits.

It is also worth noting that in the case of memory-optimized tables, the REPEATABLE READ isolation level protects you from the *phantom read* phenomenon, which is not the case with disk-based tables. The BeginTs value of the newly inserted rows would exceed the logical start time of the active transaction (more on that later), making them invisible for the transaction.

As a next step, let's repeat these tests in the SERIALIZABLE isolation level. You can see the code and the results of the execution in Table 8-4.

Table 8-4. *Concurrency in the SERIALIZABLE Transaction Isolation Level*

Session 1	Session 2	Results

begin tran
  select ID, Col
  from dbo.HKData
    with (serializable)		

	update dbo. HKData set Col = -2 where ID = 2	

select ID, Col
  from dbo.HKData
    with (serializable)
		Return old version of a row (Col = 2).

commit		Msg 41305, Level 16, State 0, Line 0.
		The current transaction failed to commit because of a repeatable read validation failure.

begin tran
  select ID, Col
  from dbo.HKData
    with (serializable)		

	insert into dbo. HKData values(10,10)	

select ID, Col
  from dbo.HKData
    with (serializable)
		Does not return new row (10,10).

commit		Msg 41325, Level 16, State 0, Line 0.
		The current transaction failed to commit because of a serializable validation failure.

As you can see, the SERIALIZABLE isolation level prevents the session from committing a transaction when another session inserted a new row and violated the serializable validation. Like the REPEATABLE READ isolation level, this behavior is different from that of disk-based tables, where the SERIALIZABLE transaction successfully blocks other sessions until the transaction is completed.

Finally, let's repeat the tests in the SNAPSHOT isolation level. Table 8-5 shows the code and results.

Table 8-5. *Concurrency in the SNAPSHOT Transaction Isolation Level*

Session 1	Session 2	Results

begin tran
  select ID, Col
  from dbo.HKData
    with (snapshot)		

	update dbo.HKData set Col = -2 where ID = 2	
select ID, Col from dbo.HKData with (snapshot)		Return old version of a row (Col = 2).
commit		Success.

begin tran
  select ID, Col
  from dbo.HKData
    with (snapshot)		

	insert into dbo.HKData values(10,10)	
select ID, Col from dbo.HKData with (snapshot)		Does not return new row (10,10).
commit		Success.

The SNAPSHOT isolation level behaves in a similar manner to disk-based tables, and it protects from the nonrepeatable reads and phantom reads phenomena. As you can guess, it does not need to perform repeatable read and serializable validations at the commit stage; therefore, it reduces the load on SQL Server. However, there is still snapshot validation, which checks for primary key violations and is done in any transaction isolation level.

Table 8-6 shows the code that leads to the primary key violation condition. In contrast to disk-based tables, the exception is raised at the commit stage rather than at the time of the second INSERT operation.

Table 8-6. *Primary Key Violation*

Session 1	Session 2	Results

begin tran
  insert into dbo.HKData
  with (snapshot)
    (ID, Col)
  values(100,100)		

	begin tran
	  insert into dbo.HKData
	  with (snapshot)
	    (ID, Col)
	  values(100,100)	

commit		Successfully commit the first session.
	commit	Msg 41325, Level 16, State 1, Line 0.
		The current transaction failed to commit because of a serializable validation failure.

It is worth mentioning that the error number and message are the same with the serializable validation failure even though SQL Server validated the different rule.

Write/write conflicts work the same way regardless of the transaction isolation level in In-Memory OLTP. SQL Server does not allow a transaction to modify a row that has been modified by other uncommitted transactions. Table 8-7 illustrates this behavior. It uses the SNAPSHOT isolation level; however, the behavior does not change with different isolation levels.

Table 8-7. *Write/Write Conflicts in In-Memory OLTP*

Session 1	Session 2	Results

begin tran
  select ID, Col
  from dbo.HKData
    with (snapshot)		

	begin tran
	  update dbo.HKData
	    with (snapshot)
	  set Col = -3
	  where ID = 2
	commit	

update dbo.HKData
  with (snapshot)
  set Col = -2
  where ID = 2
		Msg 41302, Level 16, State 110, Line 1.
		
		The current transaction attempted to update a record that has been updated since this transaction started. The transaction was aborted.
		
		Msg 3998, Level 16, State 1, Line 1.
		
		The uncommittable transaction is detected at the end of the batch. The transaction is rolled back.
		
		The statement has been terminated.

begin tran
  select ID, Col
  from dbo.HKData
    with (snapshot)		

	begin tran
	  update dbo.HKData
	    with (snapshot)
	  set Col = -3
	  where ID = 2	

update dbo.HKData with (snapshot) set Col = -2 where ID = 2		Msg 41302, Level 16, State 110, Line 1. The current transaction attempted to update a record that has been updated since this transaction started. The transaction was aborted. Msg 3998, Level 16, State 1, Line 1. The uncommittable transaction is detected at the end of the batch. The transaction is rolled back. The statement has been terminated.
	commit	Successful commit of Session 2 transaction.

Cross-Container Transactions

Any access to memory-optimized tables from interpreted T-SQL is done through the Query Interop Engine and leads to *cross-container transactions*. You can use different transaction isolation levels for disk-based and memory-optimized tables. However, not all combinations are supported. Table 8-8 illustrates possible combinations for transaction isolation levels in cross-container transactions.

Table 8-8. *Isolation Levels Allowed for Cross-Container Transactions*

Isolation Levels for Disk-Based Tables	Isolation Levels for Memory-Optimized Tables
READ UNCOMMITTED, READ COMMITTED, READ COMMITTED SNAPSHOT	SNAPSHOT, REPEATABLE READ, SERIALIZABLE
REPEATABLE READ, SERIALIZABLE	SNAPSHOT only
SNAPSHOT	Not supported

As you already know, internal implementations of the READ READ and SERIALIZABLE isolation levels are very different for disk-based and memory-optimized tables. Data consistency rules with disk-based tables rely on locking, while In-Memory OLTP uses pre-commit validation. This leads to a situation in cross-container transactions where SQL Server supports only the SNAPSHOT isolation levels for memory-optimized tables, while disk-based tables require REPEATABLE READ or SERIALIZABLE isolation.

Moreover, SQL Server does not allow access to memory-optimized tables when disk-based tables require SNAPSHOT isolation. Cross-container transactions, in a nutshell, consist of two internal transactions: one for disk-based and another one for memory-optimized tables. It is impossible to start both transactions at exactly the same time and guarantee the state of the data at the moment the transaction starts.

As the general guideline, it is recommended that you use the READ COMMITTED/SNAPSHOT combination in cross-container transactions during the regular workload. This combination provides the minimal blocking and least pre-commit overhead and should be acceptable in a large number of use cases. Other combinations are more appropriate during data migrations when it is important to avoid the non-repeatable and phantom reads phenomena.

As you may have already noticed, SQL Server requires you to specify the transaction isolation level with a table hint when you are accessing memory-optimized tables. This does not apply to individual statements that execute outside of the explicitly started (with BEGIN TRAN) transaction. Those statements are called *autocommitted transactions,* and each of them executes in a separate transaction that is active for the duration of the statement execution. Listing 8-2 illustrates the code with three statements. Each of them will run in their own autocommitted transactions.

Listing 8-2. Autocommitted Transactions

```
delete from dbo.HKData;

insert into dbo.HKData(ID, Col) values(1,1),(2,2),(3,3),(4,4),(5,5);

select ID, Col from dbo.HKData;
```

An isolation level hint is not required for statements running in autocommitted transactions. When the hint is omitted, the statement runs in the SNAPSHOT isolation level.

SQL Server allows you to keep a NOLOCK hint while accessing memory-optimized tables from autocommitted transactions. That hint is ignored. A READUNCOMMITTED hint, however, is not supported and triggers an error.

There is the useful database option MEMORY_OPTIMIZED_ELEVATE_TO_SNAPSHOT, which is disabled by default. When this option is enabled, SQL Server allows you to omit the isolation level hint in nonautocommitted transactions. SQL Server uses the SNAPSHOT isolation level, as with autocommitted transactions, if the isolation level hint is not specified when the MEMORY_OPTIMIZED_ELEVATE_TO_SNAPSHOT option is enabled. Consider enabling this option when you port an existing system to In-Memory OLTP and have T-SQL code that accesses tables that become memory-optimized.

Transaction Lifetime

Although I have already discussed a few key elements used by In-Memory OLTP to manage data access and the concurrency model, let's review them here.

- *Global Transaction Timestamp* is an auto-incremented value that uniquely identifies every transaction in the system. SQL Server increments and obtains this value at the transaction commit stage.

- Every row has BeginTs and EndTs timestamps, which correspond to the Global Transaction Timestamp of the transaction that created or deleted this version of a row.

When a new transaction starts, In-Memory OLTP generates a TransactionId value, which uniquely identifies the transaction. Moreover, In-Memory OLTP assigns the *logical start time* for the transaction, which represents the Global Transaction Timestamp value when the transaction starts. It dictates what version of the rows is visible to the transaction. The logical start time should be in between the BeginTs and EndTs values for the row to be visible.

When the transaction issues a COMMIT statement, In-Memory OLTP increments the Global Transaction Timestamp value and assigns it to the transaction *logical end time*. The logical end time will become BeginTs for the rows inserted and EndTs for the rows deleted by the transaction after it is committed.

Figure 8-1 shows the lifetime of a transaction that works with memory-optimized tables.

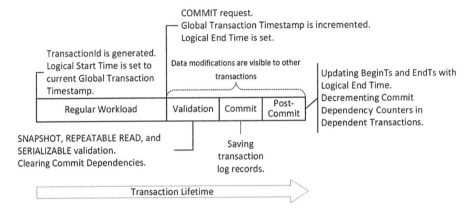

Figure 8-1. Transaction lifetime

When a transaction needs to delete a row, it updates the EndTs timestamp with the TransactionId value. The insert operation creates a new row with the BeginTs value of TransactionId and the EndTs value of Infinity. Finally, the update operation consists of delete and insert operations internally. It is also worth noting that during data modification, transactions raise an error if there are any uncommitted versions of the rows they were modifying. It prevents write/write conflicts when multiple sessions modify the same data.

When the other transaction, called Tx1, encounters uncommitted rows with TransactionId in the BeginTs or EndTs timestamps (TransactionId has a flag that indicates such a condition), it checks the status of the transaction with TransactionId. If that transaction is committing and the logical end time is already set, those uncommitted rows may become visible for the Tx1 transaction, which leads to a situation called *commit dependency*. Tx1 is not blocked; however, it does not return data to the client nor commit until the original transaction on which it has a commit dependency commits itself. I will talk about commit dependencies shortly.

Let's look at the transaction lifetime in detail. Figure 8-2 shows the data rows after you create and populate the dbo.HKData table in Listing 8-1, assuming that the rows were created by a transaction with a Global Transaction Timestamp value of 5. (The hash index structure is omitted for simplicity's sake.)

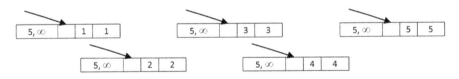

Figure 8-2. Data in the dbo.HKData table after insert

Let's assume you have a transaction that started at the time when the Global Transaction Timestamp value was 9 and TransactionId generated as -8. (I am using a negative value for TransactionId to illustrate the difference between two types of timestamps in the figures.)

Let's assume that the transaction performs the operations shown in Listing 8-3. The explicit transaction has already started, and the BEGIN TRAN statement is not included in the listing. All three statements are executing in the context of a single active transaction.

Listing 8-3. Data Modification Operations

```
insert into dbo.HKData with (snapshot) (ID, Col) values(10,10);
update dbo.HKData with (snapshot) set Col = -2 where ID = 2;
delete from dbo.HKData with (snapshot) where ID = 4;
```

Figure 8-3 illustrates the state of the data after data modifications. An INSERT statement created a new row, a DELETE statement updated the EndTs value in the row with ID=4, and an UPDATE statement changed the EndTs value of the row with ID=2 and created a new version of the row with the same ID.

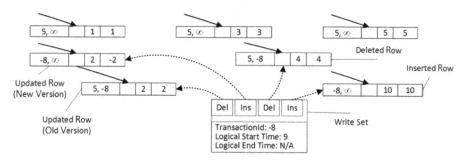

Figure 8-3. *Data in the dbo.HKData table after modifications*

It is important to note that the transaction maintains a *write set*, or pointers to rows that have been inserted and deleted by a transaction, which is used to generate transaction log records.

In addition to the write set, in the REPEATABLE READ and SERIALIZABLE isolation levels, transactions maintain a *read set* of the rows read by a transaction and use it for repeatable read validation. Finally, in the SERIALIZABLE isolation level, transactions maintain a *scan set*, which contains information about predicates used by the queries in the transaction. The scan set is used for serializable validation.

When a COMMIT request is issued, the transaction starts the validation phase. First, it auto-increments the current Global Transaction Timestamp value, which becomes the logical end time of the transaction. Figure 8-4 illustrates this state, assuming that the new Global Transaction Timestamp value is 11. Note that the BeginTs and EndTs timestamps in the rows still have TransactionId at this stage.

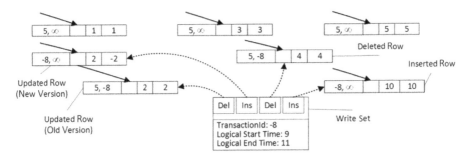

Figure 8-4. *Start of validation phase*

At this moment, the rows modified by transactions become visible to other transactions in the system even though the transaction has yet to be committed, which can lead to commit dependencies. Again, I will talk about them shortly.

As the next step, SQL Server performs several validations based on the isolation level of the transaction, as shown in Table 8-9.

Table 8-9. *Validations Done in the Different Transaction Isolation Levels*

	Snapshot Validation	Repeatable Read Validation	Serializable Validation
	Checking for primary key violations	Checking for nonrepeatable reads	Checking for phantom reads
SNAPSHOT	Yes	No	No
REPEATABLE READ	Yes	Yes	No
SERIALIZABLE	Yes	Yes	Yes

■ **Important**   Repeatable read and serializable validations add overhead to the system. Do not use REPEATABLE READ and SERIALIZABLE isolation levels unless you have a legitimate use case for such data consistency.

After the required rules have been validated, the transaction waits for the commit dependencies to clear and the transaction on which it depends to commit. If those transactions fail to commit for any reason (for example, the validation rules are violated), the dependent transaction is also be rolled back, and an error 41301 is generated.

Figure 8-5 illustrates a commit dependency scenario. Transaction Tx2 can access uncommitted rows from transaction Tx1 during Tx1 validation and commit phases; therefore, Tx2 has a commit dependency on Tx1. After the Tx2 validation phase is completed, Tx2 has to wait for Tx1 to commit and the commit dependency to clear before entering the commit phase.

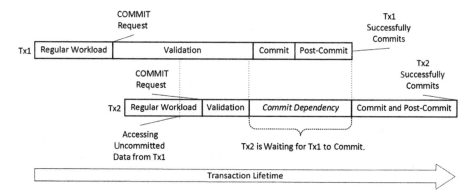

Figure 8-5. *Commit dependency: successful commit*

If Tx1, for example, failed to commit because of serializable validation violation, Tx2 would be rolled back with error 41301, as shown in Figure 8-6.

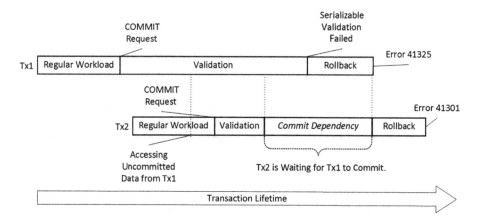

Figure 8-6. *Commit dependency: validation error*

■ **Note** Commit dependency is technically a case of blocking in In-Memory OLTP. However, the validation and commit phases of the transactions are relatively short, and that blocking should not be excessive.

SQL Server allows a maximum of eight commit dependencies on a single transaction. When this number is reached, other transactions that try to take a dependency would fail with error 41839.

■ **Note** You can track commit dependencies using the `dependency_acquiredtx_event` and `waiting_for_dependenciestx_event` extended events.

When all commit dependencies are cleared, the transaction moves to the commit phase, generates one or more log records, and saves them to the transaction log, moving to the post-commit phase afterward. I will talk about transaction logging in more detail in Chapter 10.

At the post-commit phase, the transaction replaces the `BeginTs` and `EndTs` timestamps with the logical end time value and decrements commit dependency counters in the dependent transactions. Figure 8-7 illustrates the final state of the transaction.

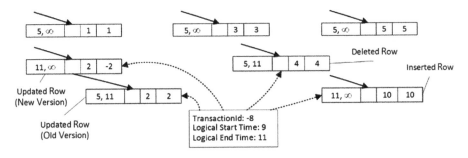

Figure 8-7. *Completed transaction*

Finally, when the transaction is rolled back either because of an explicit `ROLLBACK` command or because of validation violation, In-Memory OLTP resets the `EndTs` timestamp of the deleted rows to *infinity*. The new versions of the rows inserted by the transaction become ghosted. They will be deallocated by the regular garbage collection process, which I will discuss in Chapter 11,

Referential Integrity Enforcement

It is impossible to enforce referential integrity in a *pure* SNAPSHOT isolation level because transactions are completely isolated from each other. Consider the situation when a transaction deletes a row that is referenced by a newly inserted row in another transaction that started after the original one. SNAPSHOT isolation level would prevent transactions to see the changes, which would violate referential integrity.

In-Memory OLTP addresses this problem by maintaining read and/or scan sets in the SNAPSHOT isolation level for the tables and queries that were affected by referential integrity validation. In contrast to REPEATABLE READ and SERIALIZABLE transactions, those sets are maintained only for affected tables rather than for entire transactions. They, however, would include all rows that were read and predicates that were applied during the referential integrity check.

This behavior can lead to issues when the referencing table does not have an index on the foreign key column (or columns). Similar to disk-based tables, SQL Server will have to scan the entire referencing (detail) table when you delete a row in the referenced (master) table. In addition to a performance impact, the transaction will maintain the read set, which includes all rows it read during the scan, regardless of whether those rows referenced a deleted row or not. If any other transactions update or delete any rows from the read set, the original transaction would fail with a *repeatable read rule violation* error.

Let's look at the example and create two tables with the code in Listing 8-4.

Listing 8-4. Referential Integrity Validation: Tables Creation

```
create table dbo.Branches
(
    BranchId int not null
        constraint PK_Branches
        primary key nonclustered hash with (bucket_count = 4)
)
with (memory_optimized = on, durability = schema_only);

create table dbo.Transactions
(
    TransactionId int not null
        constraint PK_Transactions
        primary key nonclustered hash with (bucket_count = 4),
    BranchId int not null
        constraint FK_Transactions_Branches
        foreign key references dbo.Branches(BranchId),
    Amount money not null
)
with (memory_optimized = on, durability = schema_only);

insert into dbo.Branches(BranchId) values(1),(10);
insert into dbo.Transactions(TransactionId,BranchId,Amount)
values(1,1,10),(2,1,20);
```

The dbo.Transactions table has a foreign key constraint referencing the dbo.Branches table. There are no rows, however, referencing the row with BranchId = 10. As the next step, let's run the code shown in Listing 8-5, deleting this row and leaving the transaction active.

Listing 8-5. Referential Integrity Validation: First Session Code

```
begin tran
    delete from dbo.Branches with (snapshot) where BranchId = 10;
```

The DELETE statement would validate the foreign key constraint and would complete successfully. The dbo.Transactions table, however, does not have an index on the BranchId column, and the validation will require you to scan the entire table, as you can see in Figure 8-8.

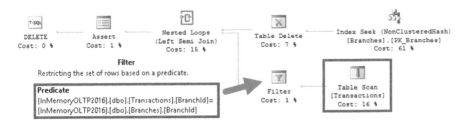

Figure 8-8. *Referential integrity validation: execution plan of DELETE statement*

At this time, all rows from the dbo.Transactions table would be included to the transaction read set. If another session updated one of the rows from the read set with the code shown in Listing 8-6, it would succeed, and the first session would fail to commit with a *repeatable read rule violation* error.

Listing 8-6. Referential Integrity Validation: Second Session Code

```
update dbo.Transactions with (snapshot)
set Amount = 30
where TransactionId = 2;
```

■ **Important**   Similar to disk-based tables, you should always create an index on the foreign key columns in the referencing table to avoid this problem.

Summary

In-Memory OLTP supports three transaction isolation levels, SNAPSHOT, REPEATABLE READ, and SERIALIZABLE. In contrast to disk-based tables, where nonrepeatable and phantom reads are addressed by acquiring and holding the locks, In-Memory OLTP validates data consistency rules at the transaction commit phase. An exception will be raised and the transaction will be rolled back if rules are violated.

Repeatable read and serializable validations add overhead to transaction processing. It is recommended that you use the SNAPSHOT isolation level during a regular workload unless you require REPEATABLE READ or SERIALIZABLE data consistency.

SQL Server performs repeatable read and serializable validations to enforce referential integrity in the system. Always create an index on the foreign key columns in the referencing tables to improve performance and avoid validation errors.

You can use different transaction isolation levels for disk-based and memory-optimized tables in cross-container transactions; however, not all combinations are supported. The recommended practice is to use the READ COMMITTED isolation level for disk-based tables and the SNAPSHOT isolation level for memory-optimized tables.

SQL Server does not require you to specify the transaction isolation level when you access memory-optimized tables through the Interop Engine in autocommitted (single statement) transactions. SQL Server automatically promotes such transactions to the SNAPSHOT isolation level. However, you should specify an isolation level hint when a transaction is explicitly started with the BEGIN TRAN statement. You can avoid this by enabling the MEMORY_OPTIMIZED_ELEVATE_TO_SNAPSHOT database option. This option is useful when you port the existing system to use In-Memory OLTP.

CHAPTER 9

■ ■ ■

In-Memory OLTP Programmability

This chapter focuses on the programmability aspects of the In-Memory OLTP Engine in SQL Server. It describes the process of native compilation, and it provides an overview of the natively compiled modules and T-SQL features that are supported in In-Memory OLTP. Finally, this chapter compares the performance of several use cases that work with the data in memory-optimized tables using natively compiled modules and interpreted T-SQL with the Interop Engine.

Native Compilation Overview

As you already know, memory-optimized tables can be accessed from regular T-SQL code using the Query Interop Engine. This approach is very flexible. As long as you work within the supported feature set, the location of the data is transparent. The code does not need to know, nor does it need to worry about, whether it works with disk-based or with memory-optimized tables.

Unfortunately, this flexibility comes at a cost. T-SQL is an interpreted and CPU-intensive language. Even a simple T-SQL statement requires thousands, and sometimes millions, of CPU instructions to execute. Even though the in-memory data location speeds up data access and eliminates latching and locking contentions, the overhead of T-SQL interpretation sets limits on the level of performance improvements achievable with In-Memory OLTP.

■ **Note** The native compilation does not help in operational analytics scenarios. Columnstore indexes can be utilized only in query interop mode.

In practice, it is common to see a system throughput increase of two to four times when memory-optimized data is accessed through the Interop Engine. To improve performance even further, In-Memory OLTP utilizes native compilation. As a first step, it converts any row-data manipulation and access logic into C code, which is compiled into DLLs and loaded into SQL Server's process memory. These DLLs (one per table) consist of native CPU instructions, and they execute without any further code interpretation overhead of T-SQL statements.

© Dmitri Korotkevitch 2017
D. Korotkevitch, *Expert SQL Server In-Memory OLTP*, DOI 10.1007/978-1-4842-2772-5_9

Consider the simple situation where you need to read the value of a fixed-length column from a data row. In the case of disk-based tables, SQL Server obtains the starting offset and length of the column from the system catalogs, and it performs the required manipulations to convert the sequence of bytes to the required data type. With memory-optimized tables, the DLL already knows the column offset and data type. SQL Server can read data from a predefined offset in a row using a pointer of the correct data type without any further overhead involved. As you can guess, this approach dramatically reduces the number of CPU instructions required for the operation.

On the flip side, this approach brings some limitations. You cannot change the format of a row after the DLL is generated. The compiled code would not know anything about the changes. This problem is more complicated than it seems, and a simple recompilation of the DLL does not address it.

Again, consider the situation where you need to add another nullable column to a table. This is a metadata-level operation for disk-based tables, which does not change the data in existing table rows. T-SQL would be able to detect that column data is not present by analyzing the various data row properties at runtime.

The situation is far more complicated in the case of memory-optimized tables and natively compiled code. It is easy to generate a new version of the DLL that knows about the new data column; however, that is not enough. The DLL needs to handle different versions of rows and different data formats depending on the presence of column data. While this is technically possible, it adds extra logic to the DLL, which leads to additional processing instructions, which slows data access. Moreover, the logic to support multiple data formats remains in the code forever, degrading performance even further with each table alteration.

As you already know, SQL Server addresses it by rebuilding the table in the background. Table alteration generates the new version of the DLL and the new table objects, converting the data rows to the new format. I will talk more about this process in the next chapter.

To reduce the overhead of the T-SQL interpretation even further, the In-Memory OLTP Engine allows you to perform native compilation of T-SQL modules, such as the stored procedures, scalar user-defined functions, and triggers. These modules are compiled in the same way as table-related DLLs and are also loaded into the SQL Server process memory.

Native compilation utilizes both the SQL Server and In-Memory OLTP engines. As a first step, SQL Server parses the T-SQL code and, in the case of T-SQL modules, generates an execution plan using the Query Optimizer. At the end of this stage, SQL Server generates a structure called a *mixed abstract tree* (MAT), which represents metadata, imperative logic, expressions, and query plans. I will discuss how SQL Server optimizes natively compiled modules later in this chapter.

As a next step, In-Memory OLTP transforms MAT to another structure called a *pure imperative tree* (PAT), which is used to generate source code that is compiled and linked into the DLL.

Figure 9-1 illustrates the process of native compilation in SQL Server.

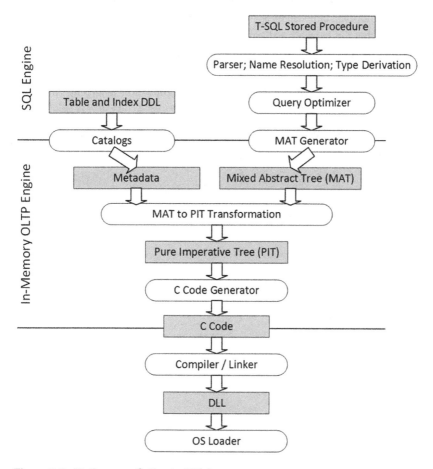

Figure 9-1. *Native compilation in SQL Server*

The code generated for native compilation uses the plain C language and is very efficient. It is hard to read, however. For example, every method is implemented as a single function, which does not call other functions but rather implements its code inline using GOTO as a control flow statement. The intention has never been to generate human-readable code; it is used as the source for native compilation only.

Binary DLL files are not persisted in a database backup. SQL Server re-creates table-related DLLs on database startup and module-related DLLs at the time of the first call. This approach mitigates security risks from hackers, who can substitute DLLs with malicious copies. It is important to remember this behavior because it can add overhead at database startup time and change the execution plans of natively compiled modules after a database restart.

■ **Tip** Natively compiled modules are usually faster than interpreted T-SQL ones. However, their compilation time can be significantly longer compared to T-SQL modules. You should remember this behavior and avoid using extremely short timeouts in natively compiled module calls.

SQL Server places binary DLLs and all other native compilation-related files in an XTP subfolder under the main SQL Server data directory. It groups files on a per-database basis by creating another level of subfolders. Figure 9-2 shows the content of the folder for the database (with an ID of 9), which contains several In-Memory OLTP objects.

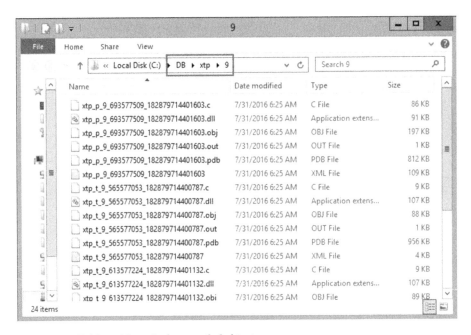

Figure 9-2. *Folder with natively compiled objects*

All the file names start with the prefix xtp_ followed either by a p (stored procedure, scalar function, or trigger) or by a t (table), which indicates the object type. The two last parts of the name include the database and object IDs for the object.

File extensions determine the type of the file, as shown here:

- *.mat.xml files store an XML representation of the MAT structure.

- *.c files are the source file generated by the C code generator.

- *.obj are the object files generated by the C compiler.

- *.pub are symbol files produced by the C compiler.

- *.out are log files from the C compiler.

- *.dll are natively compiled DLLs generated by the C linker. Those files are loaded into SQL Server memory and used by the In-Memory OLTP engine.

■ **Tip**   You can open and analyze the C source code and XML MAT in the text editor application to get a sense of the native compilation process.

Listing 9-1 shows how to obtain a list of natively compiled objects loaded into SQL Server memory. It also returns the list of tables and stored procedures from the database to show the correlation between a DLL file name and object IDs.

Listing 9-1. Obtaining a List of Natively Compiled Objects Loaded into SQL Server Memory

```
select
    s.name + '.' + o.name as [Object Name]
    ,o.object_id
from
    (
        select schema_id, name, object_id
        from sys.tables
        where is_memory_optimized = 1
        union all
        select schema_id, name, object_id
        from sys.procedures
    ) o join sys.schemas s on
        o.schema_id = s.schema_id;

select base_address, file_version, language, description, name
from sys.dm_os_loaded_modules
where description = 'XTP Native DLL';
```

Figure 9-3 illustrates the output of the code.

	Object Name	object_id
1	dbo.WebRequests_Memory	565577053
2	dbo.WebRequestHeaders_Memory	613577224
3	dbo.WebRequestParams_Memory	645577338
4	dbo.InsertRequestInfo_NativelyCompiled	693577509

	base_address	language	description	name
1	0x00007FFFBC550000	67699940	XTP Native DLL	C:\DB\xtp\9\xtp_t_9_565577053_182879714400787.dll
2	0x00007FFFBC520000	67699940	XTP Native DLL	C:\DB\xtp\9\xtp_t_9_613577224_182879714401132.dll
3	0x00007FFFB92E0000	67699940	XTP Native DLL	C:\DB\xtp\9\xtp_t_9_645577338_182879714401367.dll
4	0x00007FFFBC500000	67699940	XTP Native DLL	C:\DB\xtp\9\xtp_p_9_693577509_182879714401603.dll

Figure 9-3. *Natively compiled objects loaded into SQL Server memory*

143

Natively Compiled Modules

Natively compiled modules are the stored procedures, scalar user-defined functions, and triggers that are compiled into native code. They are extremely efficient, and they can provide major performance improvements when working with memory-optimized tables, compared to interpreted T-SQL statements, which access those tables through the query interop component.

■ **Note**   In this chapter, I will reference regular interpreted (non-natively compiled) modules as *T-SQL modules*.

Natively Compiled Stored Procedures

You can create natively compiled stored procedures using the regular CREATE PROCEDURE statement and T-SQL language. However, those procedures have several additional options that need to be specified. Listing 9-2 shows the structure of natively compiled stored procedures along with those options.

Listing 9-2. Natively Compiled Stored Procedure Structure

```
create proc dbo.NativelyCompiledProc
(
    /* Parameters */
    @Param1 int not null = 1
    ,@Param2 int
)
with
    native_compilation    -- Indicates natively compiled SP
    ,schemabinding        -- Required
    ,execute as owner     -- Optional security context
as
-- Natively compiled SPs are executed as atomic blocks
-- (all or nothing)
begin atomic with
(

    transaction isolation level = snapshot  -- Required
    ,language = N'English'                  -- Required
    ,delayed_durability = off               -- Optional
    ,datefirst = 7                          -- Optional
    ,dateformat = 'mdy'                     -- Optional
)
    /* Stored Procedure Body */
end
```

You can define the parameters of natively compiled stored procedures the same way as with T-SQL procedures. However, natively compiled stored procedures allow you to specify whether parameters are required and must be provided at the time of a call using the NOT NULL construct in the definition. SQL Server raises an error if you do not provide their values at the time of the call.

■ **Important** It is recommended that you avoid type conversion and do not use named parameters when you call natively compiled stored procedures. It is more efficient to use the exec Proc value [..,value] calling format rather than the exec Proc @Param=value [..,@Param=value] calling format.

You can detect inefficient parameterization with the hekaton_slow_parameter_parsing extended event.

All natively compiled modules must be schema bound and could have an optional security context specified. It is better to avoid the EXECUTE AS CALLER context because it adds the overhead of per-statement permission checks during the execution.

■ **Note** You can read about execution context at https://docs.microsoft.com/en-us/sql/t-sql/statements/execute-as-clause-transact-sql.

Two other required options include the transaction isolation level and the language setting, which controls a message's language and default date format. Natively compiled modules do not use the runtime SET LANGUAGE session option, relying on the LANGUAGE setting instead.

You can control the date format, first day of the week, and delayed durability of a stored procedure using the DATEFORMAT, DATEFIRST, and DELAYED_DURABILITY settings, respectively.

■ **Note** Delayed durability is a SQL Server feature that controls how SQL Server hardens log records, flushing them from the log buffer to the transaction log. Enabling delayed durability can help to improve transaction throughput in very busy OLTP systems at the cost of a possible small data loss in the event of an unexpected SQL Server shutdown or crash.

You can read more about delayed durability at https://docs.microsoft.com/en-us/sql/relational-databases/logs/control-transaction-durability. You can also read about it in Chapter 30 of my *Pro SQL Server Internals* book.

Natively compiled modules are executed as atomic blocks, which is an "all or nothing" approach; either all statements in the procedure succeed or all of them fail. I will discuss how atomic blocks work later in the chapter.

Natively Compiled Triggers and User-Defined Functions

SQL Server allows you to create natively compiled DML triggers on memory-optimized tables and scalar user-defined functions. As with natively compiled stored procedures, these modules cannot access disk-based objects.

Listing 9-3 shows the code that creates both types of objects.

Listing 9-3. Natively Compiled Trigger and User-Defined Function

```
create trigger NativelyCompiledTrigger on dbo.MemoryOptimizedTable
with native_compilation, schemabinding
after insert
as
begin atomic with
(
    transaction isolation level = snapshot
    ,language = N'English'
)
    if @@rowcount = 0
        return;
    /* Trigger Body */
end
go

create function dbo.NativelyCompiledScalarFunction(@Param1 int not null)
returns int
with native_compilation, schemabinding
as
begin atomic with
(
    transaction isolation level = snapshot
    ,language = N'us_english'
)
    declare
        @Result int = 0
    /* Function Body */
    return @Result;
end
```

As with T-SQL triggers and scalar user-defined functions, you should consider the overhead those modules introduce. You will look at performance overhead of user-defined functions later in the chapter.

You can also mark inline table-valued functions as natively compiled. However, they behave differently than other modules. When you mark those functions as natively compiled, SQL Server just validates that they are using the language constructs supported by native compilation. The functions are not actually compiled but rather embedded into the other natively compiled modules that reference them.

When you call natively compiled inline table-valued functions from T-SQL via Query Interop, SQL Server treats them as the regular T-SQL inline table-valued functions, embedding their statement to the referenced query.

Listing 9-4 illustrates a natively compiled inline table-valued function. As you can guess, you do not need to specify that the function executes as the atomic block.

Listing 9-4. Natively Compiled Inline Table-Valued Function

```
create function dbo.NativeCompiledInlineTVF(@Param datetime)
returns table
with native_compilation, schemabinding
as
return
(
    select count(*) as Result
    from dbo.MemoryOptimizedTable
    where DateCol >= @Param
)
```

You can define the natively compiled module body pretty much the same way as regular T-SQL modules. However, the natively compiled modules support only a limited set of T-SQL constructs. Let's look at the supported features and limitations in different T-SQL areas in detail.

Supported T-SQL Features

One of the biggest limitations of natively compiled modules is that they can access only memory-optimized tables. The only option to join data from memory-optimized and disk-based tables is to use the interpreted T-SQL and the Interop Engine.

There are other limitations you need to remember. Natively compiled code does not support parallelism and always has serial execution plans. Nor can it access and scan the tables with the varheap Table Scan operator. The table scan is implemented as a scan of one of the indexes.

The following T-SQL features and constructs are supported in SQL Server 2016 and can be used with native compilation.

Control Flow

The following control flow options are supported:

- IF and WHILE.

- Assigning a value to a variable with the SELECT and SET operators.

- RETURN.

- TRY/CATCH/THROW (RAISERROR is not supported). It is recommended that you use a single TRY/CATCH block for the entire stored procedure for better performance.

- It is possible to declare variables as NOT NULL as long as they have an initializer as part of the DECLARE statement.

- The nested execution is supported. For example, a natively compiled stored procedure can call another natively compiled procedure or function.

- The CASE statement is not supported in SQL Server 2016. It will be supported, however, in SQL Server 2017.

Operators

The following operators are supported:

- Comparison operators, such as =, <, <=, >, >=, <>, and BETWEEN.

- Unary and binary operators, such as +, -, *, /, and %. Note that + operators are supported for both numbers and strings.

- Bitwise operators, such as &, |, ~, ^.

- Logical operators, such as AND, OR, and NOT.

- IN, BETWEEN, and EXISTS operators.

Query Surface Area

The following query surface area functions are supported:

- SELECT, INSERT, UPDATE, and DELETE operators.

- SELECT DISTINCT operator.

- OUTPUT clause with INSERT, UPDATE, and DELETE operators.

- CROSS JOIN, INNER JOIN, LEFT OUTER JOIN, and RIGHT OUTER JOIN are supported. All joins are implemented as LOOP JOIN internally. Neither MERGE JOIN nor HASH JOIN is supported. Finally, you can use joins only with the SELECT operator.

- Expressions in the SELECT list and the WHERE and HAVING clauses are supported as long as they use supported operators.

- You can use subqueries in FROM and WHERE clauses and scalar subqueries in a SELECT clause.

- IS NULL and IS NOT NULL.

- GROUP BY is supported with the exception of grouping by string or binary data.

- TOP and ORDER BY. However, you cannot use WITH TIES and PERCENT in the TOP clause. Moreover, the TOP operator is limited to 8,192 rows when the TOP <constant> is used, or even a lesser number of rows in the case of joins. You can address this last limitation by using a TOP <variable> approach. However, it is less efficient in terms of performance. It is also worth mentioning that TOP (N) WITH TIES will be supported in SQL Server 2017.

- INDEX, FORCESCAN, FORCESEEK, FORCE ORDER, INNER LOOP JOIN, and OPTIMIZE FOR hints.

Built-in Functions

The following built-in functions are supported:

- All math functions are supported.

- Date/time functions: CURRENT_TIMESTAMP, DATEADD, DATEDIFF, DATEFROMPARTS, DATEPART, DATETIME2FROMPARTS, DATETIMEFROMPARTS, DAY, EOMONTH, GETDATE, GETUTCDATE, MONTH, SMALLDATETIMEFROMPARTS, SYSDATETIME, SYSUTCDATETIME, and YEAR.

- String functions: LEN, LTRIM, RTRIM, and SUBSTRING. SQL Server 2017 will also support TRIM, TRANSLATE, and CONCAT_WS.

- Error functions: ERROR_LINE, ERROR_MESSAGE, ERROR_NUMBER, ERROR_PROCEDURE, ERROR_SEVERITY, and ERROR_STATE.

- Security functions: IS_MEMBER, IS_ROLEMEMBER, IS_SRVROLEMEMBER, ORIGINAL_LOGIN, SESSION_USER, CURRENT_USER, SUSER_ID, SUSER_SID, SUSER_SNAME, SYSTEM_USER, SUSER_NAME, USER, USER_ID, USER_NAME, and CONTEXT_INFO.

- NEWID and NEWSEQUENTIALID.

- CAST and CONVERT. However, it is impossible to convert between a non-Unicode and a Unicode string.

- ISNULL.

- SCOPE_IDENTITY.

- @@SPID.

- You can use @@ROWCOUNT within a natively compiled module; however, its value is reset to 0 at the beginning and end of the module.

Atomic Blocks

Natively compiled modules execute as atomic blocks, which is an "all or nothing" approach; either all statements in the module succeed or all of them fail.

When a natively compiled module is called outside of the context of an active transaction, it starts a new transaction and either commits or rolls it back at the end of the execution.

In cases where a module is called in the context of an active transaction, SQL Server creates a savepoint at the beginning of the module's execution. In the case of an error in the module, SQL Server rolls back the transaction to the created savepoint. Based on the severity and type of the error, the transaction is either going to be able to continue and commit or become doomed and uncommittable.

Let's create a memory-optimized table and natively compiled stored procedure, as shown in Listing 9-5.

Listing 9-5. Atomic Blocks and Transactions: Object Creation

```
create table dbo.MOData
(
    ID int not null
        primary key nonclustered
        hash with (bucket_count=16),
    Value int null
)
with (memory_optimized=on, durability=schema_only);

insert into dbo.MOData(ID, Value)
values(1,1), (2,2);
go

create proc dbo.AtomicBlockDemo
(
    @ID1 int not null
    ,@Value1 bigint not null
    ,@ID2 int
    ,@Value2 bigint
)
with native_compilation, schemabinding, execute as owner
as
begin atomic
with
(
    transaction isolation level = snapshot
    ,language=N'English'
)
    update dbo.MOData set Value = @Value1 where ID = @ID1;

    if @ID2 is not null
        update dbo.MOData set Value = @Value2 where ID = @ID2;
end;
```

At this point, the dbo.MOData table has two rows with the values (1,1) and (2,2). As a first step, let's start the transaction and call a stored procedure twice, as shown in Listing 9-6.

Listing 9-6. Atomic Blocks and Transactions: Calling a Stored Procedure

```
begin tran
    exec dbo.AtomicBlockDemo 1, -1, 2, -2;
    exec dbo.AtomicBlockDemo 1, 0, 2, 999999999999999;
```

The first call of the stored procedure succeeds, while the second call triggers an arithmetic overflow error, as shown here:

```
Msg 8115, Level 16, State 0, Procedure AtomicBlockDemo, Line 49
Arithmetic overflow error converting bigint to data type int.
```

You can check that the transaction is still active and committable with this select: SELECT @@TRANCOUNT as [@@TRANCOUNT], XACT_STATE() as [XACT_STATE()]. It returns the following results:

```
@@TRANCOUNT XACT_STATE()
----------- ------------
1           1
```

If you commit the transaction and check the content of the table, you will see that the data reflects the changes caused by the first stored procedure call. Even though the first update statement from the second call succeeded, SQL Server rolled it back because the natively compiled stored procedure executed as an atomic block. You can see the data in the dbo.MOData table.

```
ID          Value
----------- -----------
1           -1
2           -2
```

As a second example, let's trigger a critical error, which dooms the transaction, making it uncommittable. One such situation is a write/write conflict, when multiple sessions are trying to update the same rows. You can trigger it by executing the code in Listing 9-7 in two different sessions.

Listing 9-7. Atomic Blocks and Transactions: Write/Write Conflict

```
begin tran
    exec dbo.AtomicBlockDemo 1, 0, null, null;
```

When you run the code in the second session, it triggers the following exception:

```
Msg 41302, Level 16, State 110, Procedure AtomicBlockDemo, Line 13
The current transaction attempted to update a record that has been updated
since this transaction started. The transaction was aborted.
Msg 3998, Level 16, State 1, Line 1
Uncommittable transaction is detected at the end of the batch. The
transaction is rolled back.
```

If you check @@TRANCOUNT in the second session, you will see that SQL Server terminates the transaction.

```
@@TRANCOUNT
-----------
0
```

As you can see, when the atomic block executes in the context of the active transaction, severe errors in the atomic block roll back the entire transaction while noncritical errors roll back transaction to the savepoint that corresponds to the beginning of the block.

Finally, it is worth mentioning that atomic blocks are an In-Memory OLTP feature and are not supported in T-SQL stored procedures.

Optimization of Natively Compiled Modules

Interpreted T-SQL stored procedures and other modules are compiled at the time of the first execution. Additionally, they can be recompiled after they are evicted from the plan cache and in a few other cases, such as outdated statistics, changes in database schema, or recompilations, which are explicitly requested in the code.

This behavior is different from natively compiled modules, which are compiled at creation time. They are never automatically recompiled, only with the exception of a SQL Server or database restart. In these cases, recompilation occurs at the time of the first call. It is also worth noting that the DBCC FREEPROCCACHE command does not force recompilation of natively compiled modules.

SQL Server does not sniff parameters at the time of compilation, optimizing statements for UNKNOWN values. It uses memory-optimized table statistics during optimization, which may or may not be up-to-date. The execution plan will not change until the module is recompiled, either explicitly or the after database restart.

Fortunately, cardinality estimation errors have a smaller impact on the performance in the case of natively compiled modules. Contrary to disk-based tables, where such errors can lead to highly inefficient plans because of an incorrect index choice and, therefore, a high number of Key or RID Lookup operations, all indexes in memory-optimized tables reference the same data row and, in a nutshell, are covering indexes for in-row columns. Moreover, errors will not affect the choice of join strategy—the *nested loop* is the only join type supported in natively compiled modules.

Outdated statistics at the time of compilation, however, can still lead to inefficient plans. One such example is a query with multiple predicates on indexed columns. SQL Server needs to know the index's selectivity to choose the most efficient one. Another example is the incorrect choice of inner and outer input for the nested loop join, which you saw in Chapter 4.

It is better to recompile natively compiled modules if the data in the table has significantly changed. You can do it in two different ways—either by altering the module or by using the sp_recompile stored procedure.

The internal implementation and impact of those methods are different. The sp_recompile stored procedure just marks the natively compiled module as obsolete. The first call of the module will trigger the recompilation, similarly to what happens after database startup. *The session that triggers recompilation and all other sessions calling the module during recompilation will be blocked until the compilation is completed.*

The module alteration, on the other hand, works differently. SQL Server recompiles the module in the background, allowing other sessions to use the old version of the code during this time. After compilation is completed, SQL Server waits for all sessions that are running the old code to finish and replaces the code in memory afterward. Even though there is still blocking during the final module replacement phase, there is no blocking during the compilation, which typically takes a significant amount of time. Therefore, module alteration introduces less impact on the workload compared to the sp_recompile call, and it is the recommended approach to alter the modules in busy systems.

■ **Tip** Consider updating the statistics in the tables referenced from natively compiled modules before module recompile or alteration.

Finally, it is worth mentioning that the presence of natively compiled modules requires you to adjust the deployment process in the system. It is common to create all database schema objects, including tables and modules, at the beginning of deployment. While the time of deployment does not matter for T-SQL modules, such a strategy compiles natively compiled modules when the database tables are empty. You should recompile (re-create) natively compiled modules later, after the tables are populated with data and statistics are up-to-date.

Interpreted T-SQL and Memory-Optimized Tables

The Query Interop component provides transparent, memory-optimized table access to interpreted T-SQL code. In interpreted mode, SQL Server treats memory-optimized tables pretty much the same way as disk-based tables. It optimizes queries and caches execution plans, regardless of where the table is located. The same set of operators is used during query execution. From a high level, when the operator's GetRow() method is called, it is routed either to the Storage Engine or to the In-Memory OLTP Engine, depending on the underlying table type.

Most T-SQL features are supported in interpreted mode. There are still a few exceptions, however.

- TRUNCATE TABLE.

- The MERGE operator with memory-optimized table as the target.

- Context connection from CLR code.

- Referencing memory-optimized tables in indexed views. You can reference memory-optimized tables in partitioned views, combining data from memory-optimized and disk-based tables.

- DYNAMIC and KEYSET cursors, which are automatically downgraded to STATIC.

- Cross-database queries and transactions.

- Linked servers.

As you can see, the list of limitations is pretty small. However, the flexibility of query interop access comes at a cost. Natively compiled modules are usually more efficient compared to their interpreted T-SQL counterparts. In some cases, such as joins between memory-optimized and disk-based tables, query interop is the only choice; however, it is usually preferable to use natively compiled modules when possible.

Performance Comparison

Let's run several tests comparing the performance of several use cases that work with memory-optimized tables using natively compiled and T-SQL modules.

Stored Procedures Performance

As the first step, we will compare the performance of T-SQL and natively compiled stored procedures. Let's create two memory-optimized tables using a schema_only durability option to avoid any I/O and transaction logging overhead during the tests. You can see the code in Listing 9-8, which also creates a numbers table and populates it with the values.

Listing 9-8. Creating Test Tables

```
create table dbo.Customers
(
    CustomerId int not null
        primary key nonclustered
        hash with (bucket_count=262144),
    Name nvarchar(255) not null,
    CreatedOn datetime2(0) not null
        constraint DEF_Customers_CreatedOn
        default sysutcdatetime(),
    Placeholder char(200) not null,

    index IDX_Name nonclustered(Name)
)
```

```
with (memory_optimized=on, durability=schema_only);

create table dbo.Orders
(
    OrderId int not null
        primary key nonclustered
        hash with (bucket_count=2097152),
    CustomerId int not null,
    OrderNum varchar(32) not null,
    OrderDate datetime2(0) not null
        constraint DEF_Orders_OrderDate
        default sysutcdatetime(),
    Amount money not null,
    Placeholder char(200) not null,

    index IDX_CustomerId
    nonclustered hash(CustomerId)
    with (bucket_count=262144),

    index IDX_OrderNum nonclustered(OrderNum)
)
with (memory_optimized=on, durability=schema_only);

create table dbo.Numbers
(
    Num int not null
        constraint PK_Numbers
        primary key clustered
);

;with N1(C) as (select 0 union all select 0) -- 2 rows
,N2(C) as (select 0 from N1 as t1 cross join N1 as t2) -- 4 rows
,N3(C) as (select 0 from N2 as t1 cross join N2 as t2) -- 16 rows
,N4(C) as (select 0 from N3 as t1 cross join N3 as t2) -- 256 rows
,N5(C) as (select 0 from N4 as t1 cross join N4 as t2) -- 65,536 rows
,N6(C) as (select 0 from N5 as t1 cross join N3 as t2) -- 1,048,576 rows
,Ids(Id) as (select row_number() over (order by (select null)) from N6)
insert into dbo.Numbers(Num)
    select Id from Ids;
```

As the first step, you will measure the INSERT performance using three
different approaches and batches of different sizes. The first two stored procedures,
InsertCustomers_Row and InsertCustomers_NativelyCompiled, will run INSERT
statements on per-row basis using the Interop Engine and native compilation, respectively.
The third stored procedure, InsertCustomers_Batch, will insert all rows in the single batch
through the Interop Engine. Listing 9-9 shows the implementation of the stored procedures.

Listing 9-9. Inserting Data into the dbo.Customers Table

```
create proc dbo.InsertCustomers_Row
(
    @NumCustomers int
)
as
begin
    set nocount on
    set xact_abort on

    declare
        @I int = 1;

    begin tran
        while @I <= @NumCustomers
        begin
            insert into dbo.Customers(CustomerId,Name,Placeholder)
            values(@I,N'Customer ' + convert(nvarchar(10),@I),'Data');

            set @I += 1;
        end;
    commit
end
go

create proc dbo.InsertCustomers_Batch
(
    @NumCustomers int
)
as
begin
    set nocount on
    set xact_abort on

    if @NumCustomers > 1048576
    begin
        raiserror('@NumCustomers should not exceed 1,048,576',10,1);
        return;
    end;

    begin tran
        insert into dbo.Customers(CustomerId,Name,Placeholder)
            select Num, N'Customer ' + convert(nvarchar(10),Num),'Data'
            from dbo.Numbers
            where Num <= @NumCustomers
    commit
end
go
```

```
create proc dbo.InsertCustomers_NativelyCompiled
(
    @NumCustomers int not null
)
with native_compilation, schemabinding, execute as owner
as
begin atomic with
(
    transaction isolation level = snapshot
    ,language = N'English'
)
    declare
        @I int = 1;

    while @I <= @NumCustomers
    begin
        insert into dbo.Customers(CustomerId,Name,Placeholder)
        values(@I,N'Customer ' + convert(nvarchar(10),@I), 'Data');

        set @I += 1;
    end;
end;
```

Table 9-1 shows the execution time of each stored procedure for the batches of 10,000; 50,000; and 100,000 rows in my environment. As you can see, the natively compiled stored procedure is almost three times faster at row-by-row inserts and about 30 to 40 percent faster compared to batch inserts through the Interop Engine.

Table 9-1. *Execution Times of InsertCustomers Stored Procedures*

	10,000 Rows	50,000 Rows	100,000 Rows
InsertCustomers_Row	77 ms	333 ms	640 ms
InsertCustomers_Batch	40 ms	170 ms	340 ms
InsertCustomers_NativelyCompiled	24 ms	120 ms	222 ms

As the next step, let's compare the performance of UPDATE operations. Listing 9-10 shows a natively compiled stored procedure that updates 50 percent of the rows in the dbo.Customers table.

Listing 9-10. Natively Compiled Stored Procedure That Updates Data in the dbo.
Customers Table

```
create proc dbo.UpdateCustomers
(
    @Placeholder char(100) not null
)
with native_compilation, schemabinding, execute as owner
as
begin atomic with
(
    transaction isolation level = snapshot
    ,language = N'English'
)
    update dbo.Customers
    set Placeholder = @Placeholder
    where CustomerId % 2 = 0;
end;
```

Table 9-2 shows the execution time of the UpdateCustomers stored procedure and
the same UPDATE statement executed through the interop engine. As you see, the natively
compiled stored procedure is almost five times faster than the interop approach.

Table 9-2. *Execution Times of Update Operations*

dbo.UpdateCustomers Natively Compiled Stored Procedure	UPDATE Statement Executed Through Interop Engine
33 ms	154 ms

Finally, let's compare the performance of DELETE operations. Listing 9-11 shows a
natively compiled stored procedure that deletes the data from both tables.

Listing 9-11. Compiled Stored Procedure That Deletes the Data from Both Tables

```
create proc dbo.DeleteCustomersAndOrders
with native_compilation, schemabinding, execute as owner
as
begin atomic with
(
    transaction isolation level = snapshot
    ,language = N'English'
)
    delete from dbo.Orders;
    delete from dbo.Customers;
end;
```

Table 9-3 shows the execution times of the stored procedure and DELETE statements executed through the Interop Engine. In both cases, the dbo.Customers and dbo. Orders tables were populated with the same data, which are 100,000 and 1,000,000 rows, respectively. Again, the natively compiled stored procedure is significantly faster.

Table 9-3. *Execution Times of Delete Operations*

dbo.DeleteCustomersAndOrders Natively Compiled Stored Procedure	DELETE Statements Executed Through Interop Engine
164 ms	690 ms

The performance of SELECT queries, on the other hand, greatly depends on the use case. Natively compiled code works best with OLTP workloads that consist of point-lookup and small range scan operations. However, the Interop Engine could be the better choice for reporting and data warehouse queries. As I already mentioned, natively compiled code does not support parallel execution plans nor does it scan the data using the varheap Table Scan operator. It is entirely possible that data warehouse queries would run faster in interop mode, especially if they have parallel execution plans and/or use columnstore indexes. Moreover, natively compiled code does not support hash and merge joins, which could outperform nested loop joins on large and unsorted inputs with data warehouse workloads.

Scalar User-Defined Function Performance

Even though native compilation could improve the performance of scalar user-defined functions, there is still overhead associated with function invocation.

Let's run a couple tests and compare the performance of interpreted T-SQL and natively compiled scalar functions. Listing 9-12 creates two simple functions that just run an empty WHILE loop without any data access.

Listing 9-12. Natively Compiled vs. Interpreted Function: Function Creation

```
create function dbo.ScalarInterpret(@LoopCnt int)
returns int
as
begin
    declare
        @I int = 0
    while @I < @LoopCnt
        select @I += 1;
    return @I;
end
go
```

```
create function dbo.ScalarNativelyCompiled(@LoopCnt int)
returns int
with native_compilation, schemabinding
as
begin atomic with
(
    transaction isolation level = snapshot
    ,language = N'us_english')
    declare
        @I int = 0
    while @I < @LoopCnt
        select @I += 1;
    return @I;
end
```

In the first test, let's call the functions running 1,000,000 execution loops inside them, as shown in Listing 9-13.

Listing 9-13. Natively Compiled vs. Interpreted Function: Running the Loop Within the Function

```
select dbo.ScalarInterpret(1000000);
select dbo.ScalarNativelyCompiled(1000000);
```

Table 9-4 illustrates the execution time in my environment. As you can see, the natively compiled function is the orders of magnitude faster than the interpreted T-SQL counterpart.

Table 9-4. *Esecution Time When Functions Run 1,000,000-Execution Loop*

Interpreted T-SQL Function	Natively Compiled Function
454 ms	5 ms

Let's run another test and call the functions in the loop, as shown in Listing 9-14. The functions do not execute a WHILE loo internally but rather are invoked 1,000,000 times. Table 9-5 shows the execution time in my environment.

Listing 9-14. Natively Compiled vs. Interpreted Function: Multiple Calls

```
declare
    @Dummy int
    ,@I int = 0

while @I < 1000000
begin
    select @Dummy = dbo.ScalarInterpret(0);
    select @I += 1;
end;
```

```
set @I = 0;
while @I < 1000000
begin
    select @Dummy = dbo.ScalarNativelyCompiled(0);
    select @I += 1;
end;
```

Table 9-5. *Esecution Time of 1,000,000 Function Calls*

Interpreted T-SQL Function	Natively Compiled Function
12,344 ms	11,392 ms

Even though natively compiled functions are significantly faster than interpreted T-SQL functions, the invocation overhead is similar in both cases. You should avoid scalar user-defined functions in your code even when they are natively compiled unless they are absolutely necessary.

Memory-Optimized Table Types and Variables

SQL Server allows you to create memory-optimized table types. Table variables of these types are called *memory-optimized table variables*. In contrast to regular disk-based table variables, memory-optimized table variables live in memory only and do not utilize tempdb.

Memory-optimized table variables provide great performance. They can be used as a replacement for disk-based table variables and, in some cases, temporary tables. Obviously, they have the same set of functional limitations as memory-optimized tables.

Contrary to disk-based table types, you can define indexes on memory-optimized table types; however, similar to disk-based table variables, SQL Server does not maintain statistics on the indexes. Fortunately, as discussed, because of the nature of indexes on memory-optimized tables, cardinality estimation errors yield a much lower negative impact compared to those of disk-based tables.

■ **Note** A statement-level recompile with option (recompile) allows SQL Server to estimate the number of rows in memory-optimized table variables. However, it does not provide SQL Server any information about data distribution there.

SQL Server does not support the inline declaration of memory-optimized table variables. For example, the code shown in Listing 9-15 will not compile, and it will raise an error. The reason behind this limitation is that SQL Server compiles a DLL for every memory-optimized table type, which will not work in the case of inline declaration.

Listing 9-15. (Nonfunctional) Inline Declaration of Memory-Optimized Table Variables

```
declare
    @IDList table
    (
        ID int not null
            primary key nonclustered hash
            with (bucket_count=10000)
    )
    with (memory_optimized=on)
```

```
Msg 319, Level 15, State 1, Line 91
Incorrect syntax near the keyword 'with'. If this statement is a common
table expression, an xmlnamespaces clause or a change tracking context
clause, the previous statement must be terminated with a semicolon.
```

You should define and use a memory-optimized table type instead, as shown in Listing 9-16.

Listing 9-16. Creating a Memory-Optimized Table Type and Memory-Optimized Table Variable

```
create type dbo.mtvIDList as table
(
    ID int not null
        primary key nonclustered hash
        with (bucket_count=16384)
)
with (memory_optimized=on)
go

declare
    @IDList dbo.mtvIDList
```

You can use memory-optimized table variables as table-valued parameters (TVP) in natively compiled and regular T-SQL modules. As with disk-based table-valued parameters, it is an efficient way to pass a batch of rows to a T-SQL routine.

■ **Note**   I will discuss the scenarios of passing a batch of rows to T-SQL routines and using memory-optimized table variables as the replacement of temporary tables in greater detail in Chapter 13.

You can use memory-optimized table variables to imitate row-by-row processing using cursors, which are not supported in natively compiled stored procedures. Listing 9-17 illustrates an example of using a memory-optimized table variable to imitate a static cursor. Obviously, it is better to avoid cursors and use set-based logic if at all possible.

Listing 9-17. Using a Memory-Optimized Table Variable to Imitate a Cursor

```
create type dbo.MODataStage as table
(
    ID int not null
        primary key nonclustered
        hash with (bucket_count=1024),
    Value int null
)
with (memory_optimized=on)
go

create proc dbo.CursorDemo
with native_compilation, schemabinding, execute as owner
as
begin atomic
with
(
    transaction isolation level = snapshot
    ,language=N'English'
)
    declare
        @tblCursor dbo.MODataStage
        ,@ID int = -1
        ,@Value int
        ,@RC int = 1

    /* Staging data in temporary table to imitate STATIC cursor */
    insert into @tblCursor(ID, Value)
        select ID, Value
        from dbo.MOData

    while @RC = 1
    begin
        select top 1 @ID = ID, @Value = Value
        from @tblCursor
        where ID > @ID
        order by ID

        select @RC = @@rowcount
        if @RC = 1
        begin
            /* Row processing */
            update dbo.MOData set Value = Value * 2 where ID = @ID
        end
    end
end
```

Summary

SQL Server uses native compilation to minimize the processing overhead of the interpreted T-SQL language. It generates separate DLLs for every memory-optimized object and loads it into process memory.

SQL Server supports native compilation of regular T-SQL stored procedures, scalar user-defined functions, and triggers. It compiles them into DLLs at creation time or, in the case of a server or database restart, at the time of the first call. SQL Server optimizes natively compiled modules for UNKNOWN values and embeds an execution plan into the code. That plan never changes unless the module is recompiled—either explicitly or after a SQL Server or database restart. You should recompile the module if data distribution has been significantly changed after initial compilation.

You can recompile the module either by altering it or by calling the sp_recompile stored procedure. Altering the module performs recompilation in background, and it introduces less impact on the workload in the busy systems.

While natively compiled modules are incredibly fast, they support a limited set of T-SQL language features. You can avoid such limitations by using interpreted T-SQL code that accesses memory-optimized tables through the Query Interop component of SQL Server. Almost all T-SQL language features are supported in this mode.

Memory-optimized table types and memory-optimized table variables are the in-memory analog of table types and table variables. They live in memory only, and they do not use tempdb. You can use memory-optimized table variables as a staging area for the data and to pass a batch of rows to a T-SQL routine. Memory-optimized table types allow you to create indexes similar to memory-optimized tables.

CHAPTER 10

Data Storage, Logging, and Recovery

This chapter discusses how In-Memory OLTP stores the data from durable memory-optimized tables on disk. It illustrates the concept of checkpoint file pairs used by SQL Server to persist the data, provides an overview of the checkpoint process in In-Memory OLTP, and discusses the recovery of memory-optimized data. It also explains why In-Memory OLTP logging is more efficient compared to disk-based tables.

Finally, this chapter demonstrates how In-Memory OLTP performs table alteration and logs it in the log and checkpoint files.

Data Storage

The data from durable memory-optimized tables is stored separately from disk-based tables. SQL Server uses a streaming mechanism to store it, which is based on the FILESTREAM technology. In-Memory OLTP and FILESTREAM, however, store data separately from each other, and you should have two separate filegroups: one for In-Memory OLTP and another for FILESTREAM data when the database uses both technologies.

There is a conceptual difference between how disk-based data and memory-optimized data are stored. Disk-based tables store the single, most recent version of the row. Multiple updates of the row change the same row object multiple times. Deletion of the row removes it from the database. Finally, it is always possible to locate a data row in a data file when needed.

In-Memory OLTP uses a completely different approach and persists multiple versions of the row on disk. Multiple updates of the data row generate multiple row objects, each of which has a different lifetime. SQL Server appends them to binary files stored in the In-Memory OLTP filegroup, which are called *checkpoint files* or, sometimes, *checkpoint file pairs* (CFP).

It is impossible to predict where a data row is stored in checkpoint files. Nor are there use cases for such an operation. The only purposes these files serve are to provide data durability and to improve the performance of loading data into memory on database startup.

As you can guess by the name, each checkpoint file pair consists of two files: a *data file* and a *delta file*. Each CFP covers operations for a range of Global Transaction Timestamp values, logging operations on the rows that have `BeginTs` values in this range. Every time you insert a row, it is saved into a data file. Every time you delete a row, the information about the deleted row is saved into a delta file. An update generates two operations, `INSERT` and `DELETE`, and it saves this information to both files. You will see how all those operations work in more detail later in the chapter.

Figure 10-1 provides a high-level overview of the structure of checkpoint file pairs.

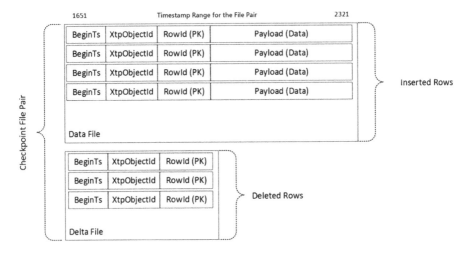

Figure 10-1. *Data in checkpoint files*

As you will remember, memory-optimized tables may include additional internal tables that store data from off-row columns and columnstore index-related structures. Those internal tables are treated as separate objects (the rows in checkpoint files use `xtp_object_id` as the reference), and data from there is stored separately from the main in-row data rows.

The data from LOB columns, such as `(n)varchar(max)` and `varbinary(max)`, is stored in another type of data file, called *large data*. The large data files have a similar structure as the regular data files; however, they can store more than 8,060 bytes in the payload section of the rows. It is worth noting that the data from the row-overflow column tables is stored in the regular data files.

The large data files are also used to store compressed columnstore segments. Compressed segment data is stored in the payload section of the row and referenced by the `segment_id` and `column_id` values. The delete bitmap (the deleted rows table), on the other hand, is stored separately, as the regular table in another checkpoint file pair.

Finally, there is another type of checkpoint file called the *root file*. Root files are generated at each checkpoint event and are used to keep track of checkpoint files in the system.

Figure 10-2 shows an example of a database with 15 checkpoint files in different states. I will cover the states of checkpoint files in detail shortly. This is just an illustration; the actual databases will have at least 17 checkpoint files in various states.

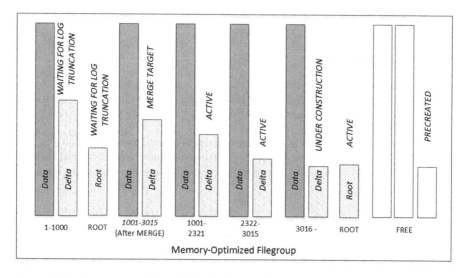

Figure 10-2. *A database with multiple checkpoint file pairs*

Using a separate delta file to log deletions allows SQL Server to avoid modifications in data files and random I/O when rows are deleted. All checkpoint files are append-only. Moreover, when files are closed (again, more on this shortly), they become read-only.

Checkpoint Files States

Each checkpoint file can be in one of several states during its lifetime, as illustrated in Figure 10-3.

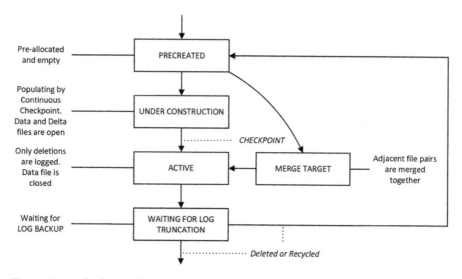

Figure 10-3. *Checkpoint file states*

167

Let's look at all of these states in more detail.

PRECREATED State

When you create the first In-Memory OLTP object in the database, including memory-optimized table types and nondurable memory-optimized tables, SQL Server generates 17 checkpoint files: 1 root and 16 empty files. This is done to minimize wait time when new files are needed.

The initial size of the files is based on the amount of server memory, as shown in Table 10-1. It is possible, however, that SQL Server changes the type of precreated file if needed. For example, a precreated large data file can be converted and used as a regular data file when required.

Table 10-1. *Initial Size of Checkpoint Files*

Server Memory	Data File Size	Large Data File Size	Delta File Size	Root File Size
Less than 16GB	16MB	8MB	8MB	2MB
16GB or more	128MB	64MB	8MB	16MB

SQL Server 2016 RTM supports *large checkpoints*, which is another configuration of checkpoint files and enables it when the server meets the following requirements:

The server has 16 or more logical processors.

The server has 128GB or greater memory.

The server I/O system provides more than 200MB/sec throughput for the database.

In this mode, SQL Server used 1GB/128MB data and delta files and defers the automatic checkpoint process to 12GB of log growth (more on this later). While this configuration may help to improve the performance of the systems with a very high transaction log generation rate, it may lead to a longer recovery time on database startup. This behavior has been disabled in SQL Server 2016 CU1/SQL Server 2016 SP1.

UNDER CONSTRUCTION State and CHECKPOINT Process

As you already know, SQL Server uses the transaction log to persist information about data modifications in the database. Transaction log records can be used to reconstruct any data changes in the event of an unexpected shutdown or crash; however, that process can be time-consuming if a large number of log records need to be replayed.

SQL Server uses *checkpoints* to mitigate that problem. Even though disk-based and In-Memory OLTP checkpoint processes are independent from each other, they do the same thing: they persist the data changes on disk, reducing the database recovery time. The last checkpoint identifies up to which point the data changes have been persisted and which log records need to be replayed.

With disk-based tables, the frequency of checkpoint operations depends on the server-level recovery interval and database-level TARGET_RECOVERY_TIME settings. While such an approach helps SQL Server to improve write performance by batching multiple random I/O writes together, it leads to spikes in I/O activity at the time when the checkpoint occurs.

In contrast, In-Memory OLTP implements *continuous checkpoints*. It continuously scans the transaction log, streaming and appending the changes to checkpoint file pairs in the UNDER CONSTRUCTION state. The new versions of the rows are appended to the data files, and deletions are appended to delta files. The continuous checkpoint also appends information about deletions to CFPs in the ACTIVE state, which I will discuss shortly.

■ **Note** It is worth repeating that the In-Memory OLTP checkpoint relies on transaction log records, which is different from the Storage Engine checkpoint that scans and flushes the dirty data pages from the buffer pool.

In SQL Server 2016, the In-Memory OLTP continuous checkpoint process is multithreaded and significantly more efficient compared to the single-threaded checkpoint in SQL Server 2014. The main work is done by *serializer* threads that scan transaction logs based on about 1MB intervals called *segments*. Those threads process the segments and populate data and delta files based on In-Memory OLTP transaction log records from there.

The segments are identified by *segment log records*, which are generated when a transaction log grows more than 1MB since the last segment log record. Those log records contain information about the range of transactions within the segments. The *controller* thread scans the log identifying the segments and passing them to the serializer threads.

Another thread—*timer tasks*—wakes up on schedule and checks whether the transaction log grew 1.5GB since the last checkpoint event or whether the last checkpoint event occurred more than six hours ago. When this happens, In-Memory OLTP creates another internal transaction that closes the currently opened segment with a special flag that indicates that it should trigger the checkpoint. When this segment is detected by the controller thread, it wakes up another *close* thread, which performs the actual checkpoint operation by converting all UNDER CONSTRUCTION data files to the ACTIVE state and generating another root file with the information about all active files at the time of the checkpoint. It is worth noting that the checkpoint is triggered regardless if the transaction log grew because of disk-based or In-Memory OLTP transactions.

■ **Note** With *large checkpoints* in SQL Server 2016 RTM, checkpoints are triggered based on a 12GB transaction log growth.

ACTIVE State

As already mentioned, the checkpoint event changes the state of all UNDER CONSTRUCTION checkpoint files to ACTIVE. SQL Server does not append new data rows into ACTIVE data files so they become read-only; however, it still appends the information about deleted rows from ACTIVE data files into the ACTIVE delta files.

Consider the situation when the database has two checkpoint file pairs—one in ACTIVE state covering the BeginTs interval between 0 and 1,000 and another one in UNDER CONSTRUCTION state covering the interval starting with a BeginTs value of 1,001. Let's assume you have three data rows in the table stored in the ACTIVE data file. Figure 10-4 illustrates this.

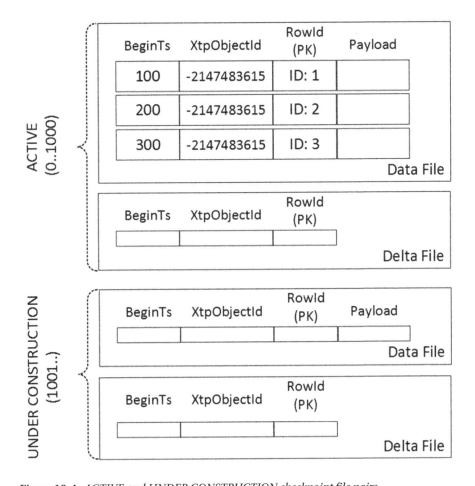

Figure 10-4. ACTIVE and UNDER CONSTRUCTION checkpoint file pairs

Let's assume you have two transactions that modify the data, as shown in Listing 10-1.

Listing 10-1. Modifying the Data in the Table

```
-- Global Transaction Timestamp: 1100
begin tran
    delete from T where RowId = 1;
    update T set Col = 1 where RowId = 3;
    insert into T(RowId) values(4);
commit;

-- Global Transaction Timestamp: 1200
delete from T where RowId = 4;
```

The first transaction with a Global Transaction Timestamp value of 1,100 deletes the row with RowId = 1, which adds the row to the delta file of ACTIVE CFP. It also updates the row with RowId = 2, which adds another row to the ACTIVE delta file, marking deletion of the old version of the row. The new version of the data row is inserted into the UNDER CONSTRUCTION data file along with the row from the INSERT statement.

The second transaction deletes the newly inserted row, which adds the row to the UNDER CONSTRUCTION delta file, as shown in Figure 10-5.

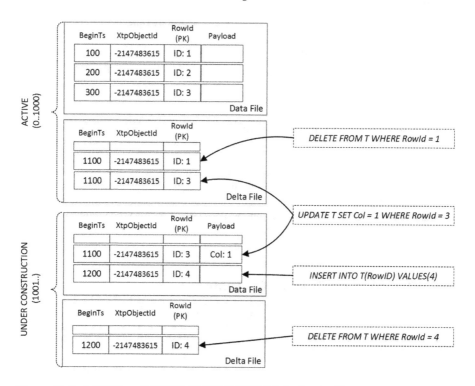

Figure 10-5. *ACTIVE and UNDER CONSTRUCTION checkpoint file pairs after data modifications*

Typically, the combined size of the ACTIVE checkpoint files on disk is about twice the size of the durable memory-optimized tables in memory. However, in some cases, SQL Server may require more space to store memory-optimized data.

MERGE TARGET State and Merge Process

Over time, as data modifications progress, the percent of deleted rows in the ACTIVE checkpoint files increases. This condition adds unnecessary storage overhead and slows down the data-loading process during recovery. SQL Server addresses this situation with a process called *merge*.

A background task called the *Merge Policy Evaluator* periodically analyzes whether adjacent ACTIVE CFPs can be merged in a way that active, nondeleted rows from the merged data files would fit into the new 16MB or 128MB data file. When this happens, SQL Server creates the new CFP in a MERGE TARGET state and populates it with the data from the multiple ACTIVE CFPs, filtering out deleted rows.

Even though the Merge Policy Evaluator can identify multiple possible merges, every CFP can participate in only one of them. Table 10-2 shows several examples of the possible merges.

Table 10-2. Merge Examples

Adjacent Source Files (% Full)	Merge Results
CFP0 (40%), CFP1 (45%), CFP2 (60%)	CFP0 + CFP1 (85%).
CFP0 (10%), CFP1 (15%), CFP2 (70%), CFP3 (10%)	CFP0 + CFP1 + CFP2 (95%).
CFP0 (55%), CFP1 (50%)	No merge is done.

Once the merge process is complete and the checkpoint has occurred, the MERGE TARGET CFP is transitioned to ACTIVE and former ACTIVE CFPs to WAITING FOR LOG TRUNCATION states.

In-Memory OLTP merges LOB-column large data files the same way as the regular data files. However, large data files with columnstore segments and root files are not merged and may transition to a WAITING FOR LOG TRUNCATION state without the need for a merge operation. This transition happens after a new root file is generated at the checkpoint event or when the columnstore index row group has been decompressed after 90 percent of the rows in the group are deleted.

WAITING FOR LOG TRUNCATION State

The data in former ACTIVE and now WAITING FOR LOG TRUNCATION files is no longer needed for database recovery. Former MERGE TARGET and now ACTIVE CFPs can be used for this purpose. However, those WAITING FOR LOG TRUNCATION files are still needed if you want to restore the database from a backup.

The checkpoint files stay in that state until the log truncation point passed their LSNs. In a FULL recovery model, this means that a log backup has been taken, log records were sent to secondary nodes, and other processes that read transaction log have not fallen behind. Obviously, in a SIMPLE recovery model, a log backup is not required, and the log truncation point is controlled by checkpoints.

Once it happens, WAITING FOR LOG TRUNCATION files are no longer needed. They can be either transitioned back to a PRECREATED state or deleted if the system has already enough PRECREATED files.

■ **Note**   You can analyze the state of checkpoint files using the sys.dm_db_xtp_ checkpoint_files view. Appendix C talks about this view in greater depth and shows how checkpoint file states change through their lifetime.

Recovery

As you know, the recovery process may occur during a database or instance restart, failover to another node, or after restoring the database from the backup. SQL Server performs the recovery of disk-based and memory-optimized tables in parallel using ACTIVE data files and transaction logs for In-Memory OLTP data.

At the beginning of the recovery stage, SQL Server locates the most recent root file that contains information about checkpoint files and passes it to the In-Memory OLTP Engine. The Engine obtains the list of all ACTIVE checkpoint file pairs and starts loading data from them. It loads only the nondeleted versions of rows using delta files as the filter. It checks that a row from a data file is not deleted and is not referenced in the delta files. Based on the results of this check, a row is either loaded to memory or discarded.

The process of loading data is highly scalable. SQL Server creates one thread per logical CPU, and each thread processes an individual checkpoint file pair. In a large number of cases, the performance of the I/O subsystem becomes the limiting factor in data-loading performance. This is the reason why you should place checkpoint files on the fast, preferable flash-based, storage.

As the opposite of disk-based tables, indexes on memory-optimized tables are not persisted. As you remember, indexes in In-Memory OLTP are just the memory pointers, and the memory addresses of the rows change after they are reloaded into the memory. Therefore, indexes must be re-created during the recovery stage.

Figure 10-6 illustrates the data-loading process.

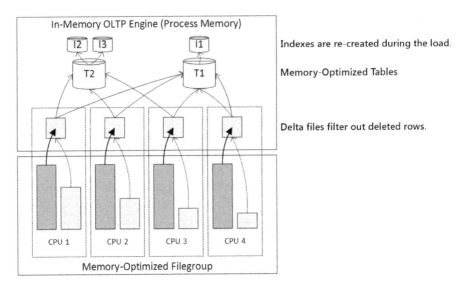

Figure 10-6. *Loading data to memory*

After the data from CFPs has been loaded, SQL Server completes the recovery by applying the changes from the tail of the transaction log, bringing the database back to the state as of the time of crash or shutdown. As you already know, In-Memory OLTP does not log uncommitted changes; therefore, no UNDO stage is required during the recovery.

Finally, it is important to mention the difference in recovery processes during failover in AlwaysOn Availability Groups and Failover Cluster instances. With an AlwaysOn Failover Cluster, failover is conceptually similar to a SQL Server restart. The databases are brought online, and all memory-optimized data needs to be loaded into the memory. AlwaysOn Availability Group nodes, on the other hand, just need to process REDO queue replaying transactions from the unapplied portion of transaction log. The data from memory-optimized tables is already loaded into the memory on all nodes.

You should remember this behavior and consider the memory-optimized data recovery time when you have an availability SLA in your system. This is especially important if you are using failover clusters in the infrastructure. As mentioned, you can reduce this time by placing checkpoint files on the fast storage.

Transaction Logging

As you already know, transaction logging in In-Memory OLTP is more efficient compared to the Storage Engine. Both engines share the same transaction log and perform *write-ahead logging* (WAL); however, the log records format and algorithms are very different.

With disk-based tables, SQL Server generates transaction log records on a per-index basis. For example, when you insert a single row into a table with clustered and nonclustered indexes, it will log insert operations in every individual index separately. Moreover, it will log internal operations, such as extent and page allocations, page splits, and a few others.

All log records are saved in a transaction log and hardened on disk pretty much synchronously at the time when they were created. Even though every database has a cache called *Log Buffer* to batch log writes, that cache is very small, about 60KB. Moreover, some operations, such as COMMIT and CHECKPOINT, flush that cache whether it is full or not.

Finally, SQL Server has to include before-update (UNDO) and after-update (REDO) versions of the row to the log records. The checkpoint process is asynchronous, and it does not check the state of transaction that modified the page. It is entirely possible for the checkpoint to save the dirty data pages from uncommitted transactions, and the UNDO part of the log records are required to roll back the changes.

Transaction logging in In-Memory OLTP addresses these inefficiencies. The first major difference is that In-Memory OLTP generates and saves log records at the time of the transaction COMMIT rather than during each data row modification. Therefore, rolled-back transactions do not generate any log activity.

The format of a log record is also different. Log records do not include any UNDO information. Dirty data from uncommitted transactions will never materialize on disk; therefore, In-Memory OLTP log data does not need to support the UNDO stage of crash recovery or log uncommitted changes.

In-Memory OLTP generates log records based on the transactions write set. All data modifications are combined in one or very few log records based on the write set and inserted rows' size.

Let's examine this behavior and run the code shown in Listing 10-2. It starts a transaction and inserts 500 rows into a memory-optimized table. Then it examines the content of the transaction log using the undocumented sys.fn_dblog system function.

Listing 10-2. Transaction Logging in In-Memory OLTP: Memory-Optimized Table Logging

```
create table dbo.HKData
(
    ID int not null,
    Col int not null,

    constraint PK_HKData
    primary key nonclustered hash(ID)
    with (bucket_count=2048),
)
with (memory_optimized=on, durability=schema_and_data);

declare
    @I int = 1

begin tran
    while @I <= 500
    begin
        insert into dbo.HKData with (snapshot)
            (ID, Col)
        values(@I, @I);
```

```
        set @I += 1
    end
commit
go

select *
from sys.fn_dblog(NULL, NULL)
order by [Current LSN];
```

Figure 10-7 illustrates the content of the transaction log. You can see the single transaction record for the In-Memory OLTP transaction.

	Current LSN	Operation	Context	Transaction ID	LogBlockGeneration	Tag Bits	Log Record Fixed Length	Log Record Length
1	00000022:00000240:0036	LOP_COMMIT_XACT	LCX_NULL	0000:00000317	0	0x0000	80	84
2	00000022:00000240:0035	LOP_HK	LCX_NULL	0000:00000317	0	0x0000	28	9588
3	00000022:00000240:0034	LOP_BEGIN_XACT	LCX_NULL	0000:00000317	0	0x0000	76	144

Figure 10-7. *Transaction log content after the In-Memory OLTP transaction*

Let's repeat this test with a disk-based table of a similar structure. Listing 10-3 shows the code that creates a table and populates it with data.

Listing 10-3. Transaction Logging in In-Memory OLTP: Disk-Based Table Logging

```
create table dbo.DiskData
(
    ID int not null,
    Col int not null,

    constraint PK_DiskData
    primary key nonclustered(ID)
);

declare
    @I int = 1

begin tran
    while @I <= 500
    begin
        insert into dbo.DiskData(ID, Col)
        values(@I, @I);

        set @I += 1;
    end
commit
```

As you can see in Figure 10-8, the same transaction generated more than 1,700 log records.

	Current LSN	Operation	Context	Transaction ID	LogBlockGen ▲
1	00000022:00000530:0014	LOP_COMMIT_XACT	LCX_NULL	0000:0000033f	0
2	00000022:00000530:0013	LOP_INSERT_ROWS	LCX_INDEX_LEAF	0000:0000033f	0
3	00000022:00000530:0012	LOP_INSERT_ROWS	LCX_HEAP	0000:0000033f	0
4	00000022:00000530:0011	LOP_INSERT_ROWS	LCX_INDEX_LEAF	0000:0000033f	0
5	00000022:00000530:0010	LOP_INSERT_ROWS	LCX_HEAP	0000:0000033f	0
6	00000022:00000530:000f	LOP_INSERT_ROWS	LCX_INDEX_LEAF	0000:0000033f	0
7	00000022:00000530:000e	LOP_INSERT_ROWS	LCX_HEAP	0000:0000033f	0
8	00000022:00000530:000d	LOP_INSERT_ROWS	LCX_INDEX_LEAF	000:0000033f	0
9	00000022:00000530:000c	LOP_INSERT_ROWS	LCX_HEAP	0000:0000033f	0
10	00000022:00000530:000b	LOP_INSERT_ROWS	LCX_INDEX_LEAF	0000:0000033f	

Query executed successfully.   SQL2016 (13.0 RTM)   SQL2016\Administrator ...   InMemoryOLTP2016   00:00:00   1782 rows

Figure 10-8. Transaction log content after disk-based table modification

You can use another undocumented function, sys.fn_dblog_xtp, to examine the logical content of an In-Memory OLTP log record. Listing 10-4 shows the code that utilizes this function. You should use the LSN of the LSN_HK log record from the Listing 10-2 output as the parameter of the function.

Listing 10-4. Analyzing an In-Memory OLTP Log Record

```
select [Current LSN], xtp_object_id, operation_desc
    ,tx_end_timestamp, total_size
from sys.fn_dblog_xtp(null, null)
-- <Use LSN of LOP_HK operation from result of sys.fn_dblog>
where [Current LSN] = '00000022:00000240:0035';
```

Figure 10-9 shows the output of that code.

	Current LSN	xtp_object_id	operation_desc	tx_end_timestamp	total_size	(▲
1	00000022:00000240:0035	NULL	HK_LOP_BEGIN_TX	20	17	
2	00000022:00000240:0035	2147483649	HK_LOP_INSERT_ROW	20	19	
3	00000022:00000240:0035	2147483649	HK_LOP_INSERT_ROW	20	19	
4	00000022:00000240:0035	2147483649	HK_LOP_INSERT_ROW	20	19	
5	00000022:00000240:0035	2147483649	HK_LOP_INSERT_ROW	20	19	
6	00000022:00000240:0035	2147483649	HK_LOP_INSERT_ROW	20	19	
7	00000022:00000240:0035	2147483649	HK_LOP_INSERT_ROW	20	19	
8	00000022:00000240:0035	2147483649	HK_LOP_INSERT_ROW	20	19	
9	00000022:00000240:0035	2147483649	HK_LOP_INSERT_ROW	20	19	
10	00000022:00000240:0035	2147483649	HK_LOP_INSERT_ROW	20	

Query executed successfully.   SQL2016 (13.0 RTM)   SQL2016\Administrator ...   InMemoryOLTP2016   00:00:00   502 rows

Figure 10-9. In-Memory OLTP transaction log record details

Finally, it is worth stating again that any data modification on nondurable tables (DURABILITY=SCHEMA_ONLY) is not logged in the transaction log or is its data persisted on disk.

Table Alteration

As you already know, SQL Server 2016 supports table alteration using the ALTER TABLE statement. This is an offline operation that blocks access to the table during execution. SQL Server generates and compiles the new version of the table DLL and loads it into the process memory.

The ALTER TABLE statement runs in two different modes depending on what changes are required.

Metadata-only alteration: With metadata-only alteration, In-Memory OLTP does not modify the structure of the data rows. This may occur when you add or remove DEFAULT, CHECK, and FOREIGN KEY constraints and/or enable or disable the system versioning (temporal tables) for memory-optimized tables.

Regular alteration: That type of alteration requires In-Memory OLTP to change the format of the data rows or internal table objects. It occurs when you add or remove columns and indexes, change column data types, and modify the bucket_count value of the hash indexes, as well as in other cases that require transformation of the data.

During *metadata-only* alteration, SQL Server updates the table metadata and creates, drops, or flushes system-versioning-related objects to disk if needed. The data rows are not re-created, but adding CHECK or FOREIGN KEY constraints may require In-Memory OLTP to scan all the data from the table to validate the constraint.

Regular alteration, on the other hand, will require In-Memory OLTP to re-create the table. This occurs when you need to change the data row format and/or indexing in the table. In this case, SQL Server creates another table object with a different xtp_object_id value and copies the data from the old to the new objects, transforming it during the process. Obviously, the system needs to have enough memory to accommodate both copies of the data.

Let's look at the example and create two tables, obtaining xtp_object_id values for them. Listing 10-5 shows the code that performs this.

Listing 10-5. Creating Two Tables and Obtaining xtp_object_id Values

```
create table dbo.TableA
(
    Col1 int not null
        constraint PK_TableA
        primary key nonclustered hash
        with (bucket_count=1024),
)
with (memory_optimized=on, durability=schema_and_data);
```

```
create table dbo.TableB
(
    Col1 int not null
        constraint PK_TableB
        primary key nonclustered hash
        with (bucket_count=1024),
)
with (memory_optimized=on, durability=schema_and_data);

select
    'dbo.TableA' as [Table]
    ,c.index_id, a.xtp_object_id, a.type_desc, a.minor_id
    ,c.memory_consumer_id, c.memory_consumer_type_desc as [mc type]
from
    sys.dm_db_xtp_memory_consumers c join
        sys.memory_optimized_tables_internal_attributes a on
            a.object_id = c.object_id and
            a.xtp_object_id = c.xtp_object_id
where
    c.object_id = object_id('dbo.TableA');

select
    'dbo.TableB' as [Table]
    ,c.index_id, a.xtp_object_id, a.type_desc, a.minor_id
    ,c.memory_consumer_id, c.memory_consumer_type_desc as [mc type]
from
    sys.dm_db_xtp_memory_consumers c join
        sys.memory_optimized_tables_internal_attributes a on
            a.object_id = c.object_id and
            a.xtp_object_id = c.xtp_object_id
where
    c.object_id = object_id('dbo.TableB');
```

Figure 10-10 illustrates the output of the code.

	Table	index_id	xtp_object_id	type_desc	minor_id	memory_consumer_id	mc type
1	dbo.TableA	2	-2147483636	USER_TABLE	0	123	HASH
2	dbo.TableA	NULL	-2147483636	USER_TABLE	0	122	VARHEAP

	Table	index_id	xtp_object_id	type_desc	minor_id	memory_consumer_id	mc type
1	dbo.TableB	2	-2147483635	USER_TABLE	0	125	HASH
2	dbo.TableB	NULL	-2147483635	USER_TABLE	0	124	VARHEAP

Figure 10-10. *Xtp_object_id values after table creation*

As the next step, let's alter two tables, as shown in Listing 10-6. The code adds a CHECK constraint to dbo.TableA and also adds a new column to dbo.TableB. Finally, it queries the xtp_object_id value of the tables again.

Listing 10-6. Altering the Tables

```
alter table dbo.TableA
add constraint CHK_Col1
check (Col1 > 0);

alter table dbo.TableB
add Col2 int null;

select
    'dbo.TableA' as [Table]
    ,c.index_id, a.xtp_object_id, a.type_desc, a.minor_id
    ,c.memory_consumer_id, c.memory_consumer_type_desc as [mc type]
from
    sys.dm_db_xtp_memory_consumers c join
        sys.memory_optimized_tables_internal_attributes a on
            a.object_id = c.object_id and
            a.xtp_object_id = c.xtp_object_id
where
    c.object_id = object_id('dbo.TableA');

select
    'dbo.TableB' as [Table]
    ,c.index_id, a.xtp_object_id, a.type_desc, a.minor_id
    ,c.memory_consumer_id, c.memory_consumer_type_desc as [mc type]
from
    sys.dm_db_xtp_memory_consumers c join
        sys.memory_optimized_tables_internal_attributes a on
            a.object_id = c.object_id and
            a.xtp_object_id = c.xtp_object_id
where
    c.object_id = object_id('dbo.TableB');
```

As you can see in Figure 10-11, adding a CHECK constraint is a metadata-only alteration, which did not change the xtp_object_id value of the table. Adding a new column, on the other hand, required SQL Server to create another table object internally.

	Table	index_id	xtp_object_id	type_desc	minor_id	memory_consumer_id	mc type
1	dbo.TableA	2	-2147483636	USER_TABLE	0	123	HASH
2	dbo.TableA	NULL	-2147483636	USER_TABLE	0	122	VARHEAP

	Table	index_id	xtp_object_id	type_desc	minor_id	memory_consumer_id	mc type
1	dbo.TableB	2	-2147483633	USER_TABLE	0	127	HASH
2	dbo.TableB	NULL	-2147483633	USER_TABLE	0	126	VARHEAP

Figure 10-11. *Xtp_object_id values after alteration*

180

Obviously, SQL Server has to log and persist table alteration events. Moreover, in the case of regular alteration, checkpoint data files may store the data rows in an old, pre-altered format, which is incompatible with the new table schema and DLL. In-Memory OLTP addresses this by applying the technique called *log optimization,* persisting the history of schema changes in an internal *transformation table.* SQL Server uses that table to transform the data rows into the new format during database startup while loading data into the memory.

Let's illustrate it with the example. Listing 10-7 shows the code that creates the table and performs two table alterations adding some data rows to the table in between them.

Listing 10-7. Log Optimization

```
-- Global Transaction Timestamp = 1
-- xtp_object_id = -2147483615
create table dbo.T1
(
    Id int not null
        constraint PK_T1
        primary key nonclustered hash
        with (bucket_count=1024),
    Col1 int not null;
)
with (memory_optimized=on, durability=schema_and_data);

-- Global Transaction Timestamp = 100
insert into dbo.T1(ID,Col1) values(1,1);

-- Global Transaction Timestamp = 200
-- xtp_object_id = -2147483612
alter table dbo.T1 add Col2 varchar(100);

-- Global Transaction Timestamp = 300
insert into dbo.T1(ID,Col1,Col2) values(2,2,'2');

-- Global Transaction Timestamp = 400
-- xtp_object_id = -2147483609
alter table dbo.T1 alter column Col1 money;

-- Global Transaction Timestamp = 500
insert into dbo.T1(ID,Col1,Col2) values(3,3.33,'3');
```

Table 10-3 illustrates the logical structure of the transformation table.

Table 10-3. *Logical Structure of the Transformation Table*

BeginTs	xtp_object_id	Action
200	-2147483612	ADD Coll2 int
400	-2147483609	MODIFY Col1 money

During database startup, In-Memory OLTP reads the rows from checkpoint files and transforms them to the latest schema based on the data from the transformation table. Figure 10-12 illustrates this process.

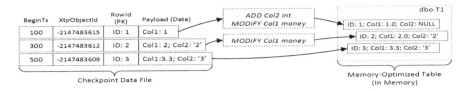

Figure 10-12. *Data row transformation during database startup*

As you can guess, log optimization requires transformation to be *deterministic*. The column values in the rows after the transformation should be the same as after the original alteration. Unfortunately, this is not always possible. Consider the situation when you add a new column to the table either as identity or with the DEFAULT NEWID() WITH VALUES constraint. This modification is *nondeterministic*. It is impossible to predict the values that are generated during alteration and transformation; therefore, log optimization would not work.

When log optimization is impossible, SQL Server uses *naïve logging* and logs the table alteration as the set of individual inserts into the new table, as shown in Listing 10-8. The rows are transformed according to the new table schema during the process.

Listing 10-8. Naïve Logging: Alteration of Table T (Pseudocode)

```
create table NewVersionOfT(..);

insert into NewVersionOfT(..)
    select and transform rows according to the new schema
    from T;

drop table T;
```

In-Memory OLTP treats that INSERT SELECT actions the same way as regular INSERT operations. It logs them in the transaction log, and the continuous checkpoint writes the rows to the checkpoint data files. As you can guess, this approach can introduce significant log overhead, especially in the case of the large tables. *Moreover, table alterations that require naïve logging are single-threaded and can be significantly slower than multithreaded log-optimized alterations.*

Several other cases lead to naïve logging. The most notable is adding new LOB or row-overflow columns to the table. As you will know, off-row columns are stored in the separate internal tables, with the main rows referencing them through the artificial IDs. It is impossible to predict those ID values and use log optimization. Unfortunately, the alteration of off-row columns is also not log-optimized and any changes of off-row columns, including dropping them or bringing them back in-row, will lead to naïve logging.

Finally, SQL Server uses naïve logging with any DEFAULT WITH VALUES constraint that uses system or user-defined functions even when functions are deterministic.

Let's look at the overhead of naïve logging. Listing 10-9 creates the new database and memory-optimized table and populates it with about 8GB of data. Finally, it performs a CHECKPOINT operation making sure that In-Memory OLTP populates checkpoint data files.

Listing 10-9. Naïve Logging Overhead: Object Creation

```
create database [InMemoryOLTP2016_Ch10]
on primary
(
    name = N'Ch10'
    ,filename = N'C:\Data\Ch10.mdf'
),
filegroup HKData CONTAINS MEMORY_OPTIMIZED_DATA
(
    name = N'Ch10_HKData'
    ,filename = N'C:\Data\HKData\Ch10'
)
log on
(
    name = N'Ch10_Log'
    ,filename = N'C:\Data\Ch10_log.ldf'
)
go

create table dbo.AlterLogging
(
    ID int not null
        constraint PK_AlterLogging
        primary key nonclustered,
    IntCol int not null,
    CharCol char(8000) not null
)
with (memory_optimized = on, durability = schema_and_data);

;with N1(C) as (select 0 union all select 0) -- 2 rows
,N2(C) as (select 0 from N1 as t1 cross join N1 as t2) -- 4 rows
,N3(C) as (select 0 from N2 as t1 cross join N2 as t2) -- 16 rows
,N4(C) as (select 0 from N3 as t1 cross join N3 as t2) -- 256 rows
,N5(C) as (select 0 from N4 as t1 cross join N4 as t2) -- 65,536 rows
,N6(C) as (select 0 from N5 as t1 cross join N3 as t2) -- 1,048,576 rows
,Ids(Id) as (select row_number() over (order by (select null)) from N6)
insert into dbo.AlterLogging(Id, IntCol, CharCol)
    select Id, Id, Replicate('0',8000)
    from Ids;

checkpoint;
```

Listing 10-10 shows how to obtain the information about the file size and the used space in transaction log and checkpoint files.

Listing 10-10. Naïve Logging Overhead: Obtaining the Size of Transaction Log and Checkpoint Files

```
select
    convert(decimal(9,3),sum(file_size_in_bytes) / 1024. / 1024)
        as [Checkpoint Files Size MB]
    ,convert(decimal(9,3),sum(file_size_used_in_bytes) / 1024. / 1024)
        as [Checkpoint Files Size Used MB]
from
    sys.dm_db_xtp_checkpoint_files;

select
    name as [FileName]
    ,convert(decimal(9,3),size / 128.)
        as [Log Size MB]
    ,convert(decimal(9,3),fileproperty(name,'SpaceUsed') / 128.)
        as [Log Size Used MB]
from sys.database_files
where name = 'InMemoryOLTP2016_Ch10_log';
```

Figure 10-13 illustrates the size of the transaction log and checkpoint files after the INSERT operation.

	Checkpoint Files Size MB	Checkpoint Files Size Used MB		
1	9425.600	8192.020		

	FileName	Log Size MB	Log Size Used MB
1	InMemoryOLTP2016_Ch10_log	12500.000	12290.820

Figure 10-13. *The size of the log and checkpoint files after INSERT*

As the next step, let's perform a table alteration by adding another int column to the table, as shown in Listing 10-11. As you know, this operation is log optimized, and it took 5.3 seconds in my environment.

Listing 10-11. Naïve Logging Overhead: Altering the Table (Log Optimized Alteration)

```
alter table dbo.AlterLogging add IntCol2 int;
checkpoint;
```

If you ran the queries from Listing 10-10 again, you would see the results shown in Figure 10-14. As you can see, the alteration does not significantly increase the size of the log and checkpoint files.

	Checkpoint Files Size MB	Checkpoint Files Size Used MB	
1	9441.600	8192.039	

	FileName	Log Size MB	Log Size Used MB
1	InMemoryOLTP2016_Ch10_log	12500.000	12291.382

Figure 10-14. *The size of the log and checkpoint files after log-optimized alteration*

Finally, let's run another ALTER TABLE statement adding a LOB column to the table. This operation does not support log optimization, and it requires naïve logging. Listing 10-12 shows the code to perform the action.

Listing 10-12. Naïve Logging Overhead: Altering the Table (Naïve Logging)

```
alter table dbo.AlterLogging add LOBCol varchar(max);
checkpoint;
```

As I already mentioned, a non-log-optimized alteration is the single-threaded process. The operation took 47.1 seconds in my environment, which is about nine times slower than the log-optimized alteration. It also adds significant transaction log overhead and doubles the size of checkpoint files on disk, as shown in Figure 10-15.

	Checkpoint Files Size MB	Checkpoint Files Size Used MB	
1	18179.604	16384.055	

	FileName	Log Size MB	Log Size Used MB
1	InMemoryOLTP2016_Ch10_log	24750.000	24580.859

Figure 10-15. *The size of the log and checkpoint files after naïve logging alteration*

Table alteration overhead is another reason why you should be extremely careful with off-row storage and LOB columns in memory-optimized tables.

You can reduce the impact of table alterations by combining multiple similar schema changes into a single ALTER TABLE statement, as shown in Listing 10-13. Unfortunately, it is impossible to combine different actions in the same ALTER TABLE statement; for example, you cannot add and drop columns simultaneously.

Listing 10-13. Combining Multiple Actions into a Single ALTER TABLE Statement

```
alter table dbo.TableA add
    Col3 int
    ,Col4 int
    ,constraint CHK_Columns_Positive
        check(Col3 > 0 and Col4 > 0);

alter table dbo.TableB drop column Col1, Col2;
```

Finally, SQL Server 2016 SP1 introduces several major performance improvements that can dramatically reduce the time of table alteration. Moreover, adding the columnstore index becomes log optimized, which was not the case in SQL Server 2016 RTM.

Summary

The data from durable memory-optimized tables is placed into a separate filegroup utilizing FILESTREAM technology under the hood. The data is stored in a set of checkpoint files of different types. Data files store the row version data. Delta files store the information about deleted rows. The data from LOB columns and columnstore indexes is stored in large data files. Finally, root files store the information about checkpoint files in the system.

The data in checkpoint files is never updated. A DELETE operation generates the new entry in the delta file. An UPDATE operation stores the new version of the row in the data file, marking the old version as deleted in the delta file. SQL Server utilizes the sequential streaming API to write data to those files without any random I/O involved.

Every checkpoint file pair covers a particular interval of Global Transaction Timestamp values and goes through a set of predefined states. SQL Server stores the new row data in CFPs in the UNDER CONSTRUCTION state. These CFPs are converted to the ACTIVE state at a checkpoint event. Data files of ACTIVE CFPs are closed, and they do not accept the new row versions; however, they still log information about deletions in the delta files.

SQL Server merges the data from the ACTIVE checkpoint file pairs, filtering out deleted rows. After the merge is completed and the source CFPs are backed up, SQL Server either deallocates them or switches them back to the FREE state.

ACTIVE checkpoint file pairs are used during database recovery along with the tail of the log. The In-Memory OLTP recovery process is highly scalable and very fast. Indexes on memory-optimized tables are not persisted on disk and re-created when data is loaded into the memory.

Transaction logging in In-Memory OLTP is more efficient compared to disk-based tables. Transactions are logged at the time of COMMIT based on the transaction write set. Log records are compact and contain information about multiple row-related operations.

There are two types of table alterations in SQL Server 2016. Metadata-only alteration occurs when you add or remove table constraints and/or change system-versioning table properties. SQL Server does not re-create the table object; however, it may scan the data in the table to validate the constraints.

By contrast, a regular alteration re-creates a table object in the background, assigning it a different xtp_object_id value. In the case of deterministic transformations, SQL Server performs log optimization and persists only schema-change information, transforming the rows from checkpoint files on database startup. In the case of nondeterministic transformation, SQL Server uses naïve logging and logs INSERT events for every row from the table.

Table alteration is an offline operation that blocks access to the table during the execution. You can reduce the impact of alteration by combining multiple similar actions into a single ALTER TABLE statement.

■ ■ ■

CHAPTER 11

Garbage Collection

This chapter covers the garbage collection process used in the In-Memory OLTP Engine. It provides an overview of the various components involved in garbage collection and demonstrates how they interact with each other.

Garbage Collection Process Overview

In-Memory OLTP is a row-versioning system. UPDATE operations generate new versions of rows rather than updating row data. DELETE operations do not remove the rows but rather update the EndTs row timestamp. Rows created by aborted transactions are not deallocated immediately, and they stay as part of the index row chains even after rollback.

As you know, every row has two timestamps (BeginTs and EndTs) that indicate row lifetime by specifying when the row was created and when it was deleted. Transactions can see only the versions of rows that were valid when the transaction started. In practice, this means that a row is visible for a transaction only if the transaction *logical start time (the* Global Transaction Timestamp *value at the start of* the *transaction) is* between the BeginTs and EndTs timestamps of the row.

At some point, when the EndTs timestamp of a row is older than the Global Transaction Timestamp of the oldest active transaction in the system, the row *expires*. Expired rows are invisible for active transactions, and eventually they need to be deallocated to reclaim system memory and speed up index chain navigation. This process is called *garbage collection*.

The garbage collection process in In-Memory OLTP has been designed with the following goals:

- *Nonblocking*: The garbage collection process should not block user threads and should produce minimal performance impact on the system.

- *Responsive*: The garbage collection process should react to memory pressure.

- *Cooperative and scalable*: The garbage collection process should not rely on a single system thread to perform memory deallocation and should also utilize regular worker threads during the process.

© Dmitri Korotkevitch 2017
D. Korotkevitch, *Expert SQL Server In-Memory OLTP*, DOI 10.1007/978-1-4842-2772-5_11

The cooperative nature of garbage collection makes it quite different from the typical SQL Server background processes. Even though there is a dedicated system garbage collection thread (one per NUMA node) called the *idle worker thread,* the major part of the work is done by the regular user worker threads. This allows the process to scale and keep up with the workload in the system.

User threads participate in the garbage collection process in two different ways. They unlink old, expired rows from the row chains and perform actual deallocation. These actions are separate from each other, as you will see shortly.

Let's look at the process in detail. Figure 11-1 illustrates the logical structure of a table with two hash indexes on the Name and City columns. You saw this figure in previous chapters; however, in this chapter I've added another element called idxLinkCount, which indicates in how many index chains the rows are participating. It is displayed with an underline in the figure; note that all the rows have a value of 2, which corresponds to the number of indexes in the table.

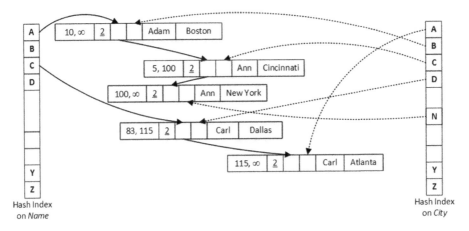

Figure 11-1. *Initial state of the data*

Assume that you have a session that runs two queries, as shown in Listing 11-1, at a time when the Oldest Active Transaction Timestamp is 110 and the Global Transaction Timestamp is 125.

Listing 11-1. First Batch

```
select * from dbo.People where Name = 'Adam';
select * from dbo.People where Name = 'Carl';
```

The first SELECT scanned the Name index row chain for the bucket with the value A and detected the Ann row with an EndTs value of 100. The Oldest Active Transaction Timestamp is 110, so this row is expired and invisible for the active transactions in the system. As result, the user thread unlinked the row from the Name index row chain and decreased the idxLinkCnt value.

I would like to reiterate that this operation has been done by the regular user worker thread rather than the system thread. This illustrates the cooperative nature of garbage collection.

The second SELECT detects the deleted Carl row. However, the EndTs value of this row is greater than the Oldest Active Transaction Timestamp, so this row is still visible for some of the active transactions. Therefore, this row cannot be unlinked from the index chain. Figure 11-2 illustrates the state of the data after the execution of the queries.

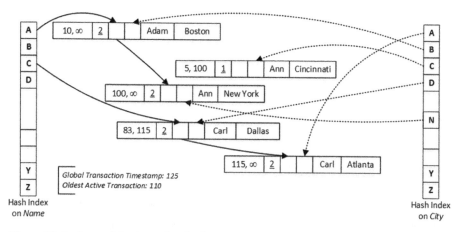

Figure 11-2. *State of the data after the first two queries*

Now, let's assume that some of the active transactions were completed and you ran the second batch of the queries from Listing 11-2 at the time when the Oldest Active Transaction Timestamp was 120 and the Global Transaction Timestamp was 130.

Listing 11-2. Second Batch

```
select * from dbo.People where City = 'Cincinatti';
select * from dbo.People where City = 'Dallas';
```

The first SELECT found the expired Ann row in the City index chain and removed it from there. At this point, the row is not participating in any row chains and, therefore, can be deallocated. However, the row is not deallocated immediately; this is done at a later stage.

The Carl row now is also expired and invisible for the active transactions. The second SELECT removed it from the City index chain; however, it is still present in the Name index chain and cannot be deallocated. Figure 11-3 shows the state of the data at this moment.

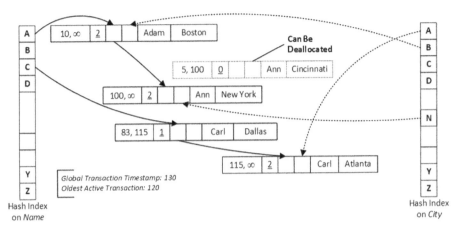

Figure 11-3. *State of the data after the second two queries*

■ **Important** You should remember that the Oldest Active Transaction Timestamp value controls when expired rows can be removed from the index chains and deallocated. Long-running and abandoned transactions can defer garbage collection and lead to a situation when the system runs out of memory because of an excessive number of expired rows.

When the transaction is complete, In-Memory OLTP places the information about it in the queue used by the idle worker thread, which is responsible for garbage collection management. The idle worker thread wakes up every minute or, in case of a heavy load, when the number of completed transactions exceeds the predefined threshold. It analyzes the list of completed transactions and the Oldest Active Transaction Timestamp in the system and separates completed transactions to 16 different queues called *generations*, sorting them based on their Global Transaction Timestamp values.

- *Generation 0* contains the list of transactions that were completed earlier than the current Oldest Active Transaction Timestamp. Rows generated by those transactions are immediately available for the garbage collection. There is no limit on the number of transactions that can be stored there.

- *Generations 1–14* store the list of transactions that were completed after the current Oldest Active Transaction Timestamp. Each generation can hold information up to about 16 transactions. As you can guess, a system can hold up to 224 transactions in generations 1–14 queues.

- *Generation 15* stores the information about the remaining transactions completed after the current Oldest Active Transaction Timestamp. There is no limit on the number of transactions that can be stored there.

Every transaction in the queue exposes its *write set* to the idle worker thread, which builds the set of 16-row *work items* for deallocation. Those work items are distributed across another set of *worker queues*—one queue per scheduler—and then they are picked up and processed by the user threads. The user threads pick up the items and perform deallocation after they complete their work on the other user transactions.

Figure 11-4 illustrates an example of the garbage collection workflow in a system that has an Oldest Active Transaction Timestamp of 10,000.

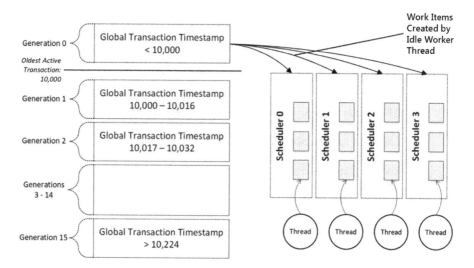

Figure 11-4. *Garbage collection workflow*

The user thread usually picks up the work items from the queue that belong to the same scheduler on which it is running. However, if the queue is empty, the thread checks the queues from the other CPUs that belong to the same NUMA node. Finally, in the case of a heavy load in the system, the thread can pick up a work item from any queue, regardless of the NUMA node to which it belongs.

With the *hot* data and actively used indexes, user threads detect expired rows relatively quickly. However, with rarely used indexes and/or rarely accessed data, there is the possibility that expired rows may not be detected in a timely manner.

This is addressed by the idle worker threads that periodically scan the indexes and detect expired rows there. The idle worker threads can either deallocate those rows immediately or add them to the work items after those rows have been unlinked from all index chains. This process is called a *dusty corners scan* or, sometimes, a *sweep scan*.

As you can see, the garbage collection process in In-Memory OLTP is done asynchronously. Deleted rows and rows from aborted transactions continue to use system memory until they are deallocated. You need to remember this and reserve enough memory in the system to accommodate those rows.

Garbage Collection–Related Data Management Views

SQL Server exposes several data management views that can be used to monitor and analyze the garbage collection process.

- The sys.dm_xtp_gc_stats view provides statistics about the garbage collection process. It includes information about the number of rows examined by the garbage collection subsystem, the number of rows processed by user and idle worker threads, and quite a few other attributes. You can read more about this view at https://docs.microsoft.com/en-us/sql/relational-databases/system-dynamic-management-views/sys-dm-xtp-gc-stats-transact-sql.

- The sys.dm_xtp_gc_queue_stats view provides information about garbage collector worker queues. It provides information about the total number of work items that were enqueued and dequeued, the current queue length, the last time the queue was accessed, and the maximum depth the queue has seen. You can monitor the current queue length, making sure that the garbage collector is keeping up. More information is available at https://docs.microsoft.com/en-us/sql/relational-databases/system-dynamic-management-views/sys-dm-xtp-gc-queue-stats-transact-sql.

- The sys.dm_db_xtp_gc_cycle_stats view provides information about the last (up to 1,024) garbage collection execution cycles including the time and duration of the cycle and the distribution of transactions between generations. You can use this view to find spikes in the garbage collection activity and during long-running transaction troubleshooting. You can read more about this view at https://docs.microsoft.com/en-us/sql/relational-databases/system-dynamic-management-views/sys-dm-db-xtp-gc-cycle-stats-transact-sql.

- Finally, the sys.dm_db_xtp_index_stats view includes several garbage collection–related metrics. The rows_expired column indicates how many rows have expired. The rows_expired_removed value indicates the number of rows unlinked from the index chain. Phantom row columns provide information about rows inserted by aborted transactions. You can read more about this view at https://docs.microsoft.com/en-us/sql/relational-databases/system-dynamic-management-views/sys-dm-db-xtp-index-stats-transact-sql.

Exploring the Garbage Collection Process

Let's examine the garbage collection process and its asynchronous nature. As the first step, create a memory-optimized table and populate it with 65,536 rows, as shown in Listing 11-3.

Listing 11-3. Table Creation

```
create table dbo.GCDemo
(
    ID int not null,
    Placeholder char(8000) not null,

    constraint PK_GCDemo primary key nonclustered(ID)
)
with (memory_optimized=on, durability=schema_only)
go

;with N1(C) as (select 0 union all select 0) -- 2 rows
,N2(C) as (select 0 from N1 as t1 cross join N1 as t2) -- 4 rows
,N3(C) as (select 0 from N2 as t1 cross join N2 as t2) -- 16 rows
,N4(C) as (select 0 from N3 as t1 cross join N3 as t2) -- 256 rows
,N5(C) as (select 0 from N4 as t1 cross join N4 as t2) -- 65,536 rows
,Ids(Id) as (select row_number() over (order by (select null)) from N5)
insert into dbo.GCDemo(Id, Placeholder)
    select Id, Replicate('0',8000)
    from ids;
```

Let's look at the amount of memory used in the table, index statistics, and garbage collection worker queues statistics using the code from Listing 11-4.

Listing 11-4. Analyzing Table Memory Usage, Index, and Worker Queues Statistics

```
select
    convert(decimal(7,2),memory_allocated_for_table_kb / 1024.)
        as [memory allocated for table]
    ,convert(decimal(7,2),memory_used_by_table_kb / 1024.)
        as [memory used by table]
from
    sys.dm_db_xtp_table_memory_stats
where
    object_id = object_id(N'dbo.GCDemo');

select
    s.index_id, i.name, s.rows_touched
    ,s.rows_expired, s.rows_expired_removed
from
    sys.dm_db_xtp_index_stats s left join sys.indexes i on
```

```
        s.object_id = i.object_id and
        s.index_id = i.index_id
where
    s.object_id = object_id(N'dbo.GCDemo');

select
    sum(total_enqueues) as [total enqueues]
    ,sum(total_dequeues) as [total dequeues]
from
    sys.dm_xtp_gc_queue_stats;

select sweep_scans_started, sweep_rows_touched
    ,sweep_rows_expired, sweep_rows_expired_removed
from sys.dm_xtp_gc_stats;
```

Figure 11-5 illustrates the output of the queries. As you can see, the table has about 585MB allocated and 514MB of used space. None of the rows has been deleted or touched (scanned). I also restarted my test server right before the test, so the garbage collection worker queues are empty. As the reminder, the row in the second output with index_id = 0 represents the table varheap.

	memory allocated for table		memory used by table	
1	585.19		514.00	

	index_id	name	rows_touched	rows_expired
1	0	NULL	0	0
2	2	PK_GCDemo	0	0

	total enqueues	total dequeues
1	0	0

	sweep_scans_started	sweep_rows_touched	sweep_rows_expired	sweep_rows_expired_removed
1	0	0	0	0

Figure 11-5. Memory and garbage collection statistics after table creation

Let's run a few queries, analyzing the statistics after each run. As the first step, run a script that deletes 1,500 rows in the individual transactions (see Listing 11-5).

Listing 11-5. Deleting 1,500 Rows from the Table

```
declare
    @I int = 1

while @I <= 1500
begin
    delete from dbo.GCDemo where ID = @I;
    set @I += 1;
end;
```

Now run the code from Listing 11-4 again and look at the output. As you can see in Figure 11-6, index statistics indicate that the deletion statement touched 1,500 rows; however, none of them was marked as expired even though the deletion statements ran in the individual autocommitted transactions.

	memory allocated for table		memory used by table		
1	585.19		514.00		

	index_id	name	rows_touched	rows_expired	rows_expired_removed
1	0	NULL	0	0	0
2	2	PK_GCDemo	1500	0	0

	total enqueues	total dequeues
1	0	0

	sweep_scans_started	sweep_rows_touched	sweep_rows_expired	sweep_rows_expired_removed
1	0	0	0	0

Figure 11-6. Memory and garbage collection statistics after deletion

As the next step, run a SELECT query that scans the entire index, as shown in Listing 11-6. I am forcing the index rather than the table scan by using index hint in the query.

Listing 11-6. Scanning the Table

```
select count(*) from dbo.GCDemo with (index = 2);
```

Figure 11-7 illustrates the statistics after the scan. As you can see, the user thread correctly identified rows as expired and unlinked a majority of them from the index row chains. Some of the expired rows have not been unlinked, though, and they will be processed by either other user threads or the idle worker thread during the sweep scan.

	memory allocated for table		memory used by table		
1	585.19		514.00		

	index_id	name	rows_touched	rows_expired	rows_expired_removed
1	0	NULL	0	0	0
2	2	PK_GCDemo	65536	1500	1406

	total enqueues	total dequeues
1	0	0

	sweep_scans_started	sweep_rows_touched	sweep_rows_expired	sweep_rows_expired_removed
1	0	0	0	0

Figure 11-7. Memory and garbage collection statistics after scan

It is also important to note that none of the work items was enqueued in the garbage collector worker items queues because the idle worker thread has not started yet.

If you look at the statistics again after the idle worker thread execution, you will see the output shown in Figure 11-8. As you can see, the idle worker thread put items into the garbage collection worker queues and deallocated them afterward. You can also see that the sweep scan detected and removed the remaining 94 expired rows from the index row chains.

	memory allocated for table			memory used by table		
1	585.19			502.45		

	index_id	name	rows_touched	rows_expired	rows_expired_removed
1	0	NULL	0	0	0
2	2	PK_GCDemo	65536	1500	1406

	total enqueues	total dequeues
1	94	94

	sweep_scans_started	sweep_rows_touched	sweep_rows_expired	sweep_rows_expired_removed
1	94	282	94	94

Figure 11-8. Memory and garbage collection statistics after the idle worker thread cycle and sweep scan

As I already mentioned, garbage collection is a cooperative process, and in other cases, the items will be deallocated by the user threads rather than the idle worker threads.

The sys.dm_db_xtp_gc_cycle_stats view shows that the garbage collection idle worker threads performed just a handful of cycles (remember, I restarted SQL Server in my test environment before the test) and processed all the completed transactions at once. You can see the partial output from the view in Figure 11-9.

cycle_id	ticks_at_cycle_start	ticks_at_cycle_end	node_id	base_generation	xacts_copied_to_local
1	1553346807	1553346807	2	1	1
2	1553376807	1553376808	2	1489	1499
3	1553376809	1553376809	2	1505	0
4	1553406809	1553406809	2	1505	0
1	1553357863	1553357863	3	1409	0

Figure 11-9. Sys.dm_db_xtp_gc_cycle_stats view after the test

The situation will change if you repeat the entire test, deleting more rows from the table. The garbage collection process will be triggered based on the number of completed transactions in the queue rather than based on the timer.

Figure 11-10 shows the summary statistics from my environment when I repeated the test, deleting 32,768 rows in the individual transactions. Note that the garbage collection process was started at the middle of deletions rather than based on a timer. You can also see that in this test some of the items were deallocated by the user thread during the first SELECT scan.

	Stage	Alloc Memory	Used Memory	Touched	Expired	Removed	Enqueues	Dequeues	Sweep Rows Expired	Sweep Rows Removed
1	Initial	585.19	514.00	0	0	0	0	0	0	0
2	After Deletion	585.19	477.83	0	0	0	2049	289	4612	4612
3	After Scan	585.19	422.84	32768	0	0	2049	729	11638	11638
4	After Delay	585.19	257.44	0	0	0	2050	2050	11640	11640
5	After Second Scan	585.19	257.44	65536	21130	21128	2050	2050	11640	11640

Figure 11-10. Memory and garbage collection statistics during the second set of tests

You can also confirm this by looking at the sys.dm_db_xtp_gc_cycle_stats view output in Figure 11-11. It shows a much higher number of cycles with very short delays in between them.

cycle_id	ticks_at_cycle_start	ticks_at_cycle_end	node_id	base_generation	xacts_copied_to_local
1	1557007790	1557007790	1	1	1
2	1557007834	1557007836	1	2049	2045
3	1557007876	1557007878	1	4097	2048
4	1557007887	1557007888	1	4625	518
5	1557007918	1557007920	1	6145	1526
6	1557007960	1557007961	1	8193	2048
7	1557008001	1557008003	1	10241	2048
8	1557008042	1557008044	1	12289	2045
9	1557008083	1557008085	1	14337	2051

Figure 11-11. Sys.dm_db_xtp_gc_cycle_stats view after the second test

Summary

The garbage collection process in In-Memory OLTP is designed to be nonblocking, cooperative, and scalable. Even though it is managed by a dedicated system thread (the idle worker thread), most of the work is done by the user threads. The idle worker thread (one per NUMA node) wakes up every minute or when the number of completed transactions exceeds an internal threshold.

Deleted rows can be deallocated only after they are expired and their EndTs timestamp is older the than the Oldest Active Transaction Timestamp in the system. Moreover, they need to be removed from all index row chains before deallocation. When the user thread encounters an expired row, the thread may unlink it from the row chain. In-Memory OLTP periodically scans rarely accessed parts of the indexes during its *dusty corners (sweep) scan* and processes expired rows that were missed by the user threads.

User threads provide information about completed transactions to the idle worker threads, which build the list of work items that consist of 16-row batches to deallocate. The work items are distributed between garbage collector worker queues—one queue per scheduler in the system. In turn, user threads pick up one or several items from the worker queues and deallocate them. The work items can also be deallocated by the idle worker threads.

Long-running and uncommitted transactions prevent rows from expiring by *freezing* the Oldest Active Transaction Timestamp in the system. This defers the garbage collection process and can lead to a situation where deleted rows use a large amount of memory.

CHAPTER 12

■ ■ ■

Deployment and Management

This chapter discusses the deployment and management aspects of systems that utilize In-Memory OLTP. It provides a set of guidelines about hardware and server configurations, and it covers In-Memory OLTP–related database administration and management tasks. Finally, this chapter gives an overview of the changes and enhancements in the catalog and data management objects related to In-Memory OLTP.

Hardware Considerations

In-Memory OLTP uses hardware in a different, and often more efficient, way than the SQL Server Storage Engine. It is often possible to achieve high OLTP throughput even with midrange servers. Moreover, In-Memory OLTP is highly scalable, and it is possible to increase transaction throughput by adding more CPUs and memory to the server and more drives to the disk array as the load and amount of data in the system increases.

Obviously, you should not forget that In-Memory OLTP plays in the same sandbox with other SQL Server components, sharing resources with them. Memory becomes one of the most critical resources for which the In-Memory OLTP and Storage Engines compete. The memory used by memory-optimized data is inaccessible to the Storage Engine and, therefore, cannot be used by the buffer pool. It is entirely possible that using In-Memory OLTP on servers with an insufficient amount of memory would degrade the performance of the queries against disk-based tables if an excessive amount of physical I/O was required. You should remember this when designing the system and avoid putting unnecessary data into memory-optimized tables.

■ **Tip** Consider splitting *hot current* and rarely accessed *historical* data between memory-optimized and disk-based tables. I will discuss this scenario in more depth in the next chapter.

Let's discuss the In-Memory OLTP requirements for different hardware components. Obviously, you need to take the workload from other SQL Server components into consideration when you build servers that utilize In-Memory OLTP.

CPU

The number of CPUs in the system greatly depends on the required OLTP throughput. However, as mentioned, it is entirely possible to achieve high transactional throughput even with a midrange server. It is impossible to predict how many CPUs you will need without performing some testing and analysis; however, it is beneficial to use the proper hardware, which will allow you to scale and add more CPUs as load grows.

When possible, you should choose processors with a higher base clock speed. With SQL Server per-core licensing, you can often get a better OLTP performance/cost ratio by using high-end CPUs with fewer cores and higher single-threaded performance compared to slower CPUs with more cores. This is also extremely critical in the case of the Standard Edition of SQL Server, which is limited to the lesser of 4 sockets or 24 cores. You would be unable to scale the CPUs beyond this limit, and faster CPUs will allow you to achieve better transaction throughput in non-Enterprise editions of SQL Server.

Finally, you should have hyperthreading enabled on the servers.

I/O Subsystem

As a general rule, you should place an In-Memory OLTP filegroup on the dedicated disk array optimized for sequential I/O performance. It is better to use Flash-based storage when possible. Even though HDD-based disk arrays can provide *good enough* sequential I/O performance to handle a regular In-Memory OLTP workload, they may become the bottleneck during database startup. As you know, the In-Memory OLTP recovery process is highly scalable, with multiple schedulers loading data from the different checkpoint files in parallel. Usually, I/O performance becomes the limiting factor in how fast SQL Server can recover memory-optimized data.

Recovery performance becomes even more important if a database has a low recovery time objective (RTO) metric in its service level agreement (SLA). Even though databases with an In-Memory OLTP filegroup support piecemeal restore with the Enterprise Edition, SQL Server must bring all In-Memory OLTP data online together with the PRIMARY filegroup. You cannot postpone In-Memory OLTP filegroup recovery to a later stage in the restore.

One of the ways to improve recovery performance is to create multiple containers in the In-Memory OLTP filegroup, placing them in different disk arrays using different HBA adapters and, in the case of network storage, different access paths. SQL Server spreads checkpoint files across containers and will load them in parallel from multiple drives.

Listing 12-1 shows how to create a database with two containers in an In-Memory OLTP filegroup, placing them into the H:\HKData and K:\HKData folders, respectively.

Listing 12-1. Creating a Database with Two Containers in an In-Memory OLTP Filegroup

```
create database HKMultiContainers
on primary
(
    name = N'HKMultiContainers'
    ,filename = N'M:\HKMultiContainers.mdf'
),
filegroup HKData CONTAINS MEMORY_OPTIMIZED_DATA
(
    name = N'HKMultiContainers_HKData1'
    ,filename = N'H:\HKData\HKMultiContainers'
),
(

    name = N'HKMultiContainers_HKData2'
    ,filename = N'K:\HKData\HKMultiContainers'
)
log on
(
    name = N'HKMultiContainers_Log'
    ,filename = N'L:\KMultiContainers_log.ldf'
);
```

Continuous checkpoints do not usually put an extreme load on the disk subsystem. The process utilizes a streaming API and uses a limited number of threads to write data to disk. The actual requirements, obviously, will depend on the transaction log generation rate for In-Memory OLTP transactions.

The disk subsystem, however, should provide enough bandwidth to handle the merge process in parallel with a continuous checkpoint. Usually, if the checkpoint populates the data and delta files at a given IOPS, the I/O subsystem should handle three times that IOPS to account for both the checkpoint and merge processes.

As for disk space, Microsoft recommends that you have enough space to accommodate four times the size of the data from the durable memory-optimized tables. Obviously, you need to factor in the future data growth to your analysis.

Memory

You need to have enough memory in the system to accommodate the data from all the memory-optimized tables. SQL Server fails a transaction when it cannot allocate memory for the new row objects. Usually, SQL Server performs memory allocation during INSERT and UPDATE operations; however, a DELETE operation could also fail if a table has nonclustered indexes and there is not enough memory to accommodate new delta records or perform page merge operations. Moreover, if a table has a clustered columnstore index, a DELETE operation could require allocating memory for a new row in the delete bitmap internal table.

Figure 12-1 shows an error message indicating an *out-of-memory* condition.

```
Msg 701, Level 17, State 103, Line 10
There is insufficient system memory in
resource pool 'default' to run this query.
```

Figure 12-1. *Out-of-memory error*

An out-of-memory situation essentially makes the In-Memory OLTP data read-only. You can still query the data; however, you cannot perform any data modifications until the problem is resolved. When such conditions occur, it is beneficial to check the status of the garbage collection process to make sure that it has not been deferred by the old active transactions. I will discuss how to detect such transactions later in the chapter.

In many cases, the only option to address an out-of-memory situation is to increase the amount of memory available to SQL Server and the In-Memory OLTP Engine. When this is impossible, especially with the Standard Edition of SQL Server, you should detect the largest memory consumers in In-Memory OLTP and reduce their memory footprint by either refactoring or migrating them to disk-based tables. I will talk about how to detect them later in the chapter.

■ **Note**   The Standard edition of SQL Server is limited to 32GB of memory-optimized data per database.

Estimating the Amount of Memory for In-Memory OLTP

Estimating the amount of memory required for memory-optimized tables is not a trivial task. As a rule of thumb, you can double the size of the data in the table as a basis for the estimation if the table does not have off-row columns. For a more accurate estimate, however, you should factor the memory requirements for several different components.

- *Data rows* consist of a 24-byte header, an index pointer array (which is 8 bytes per index), and the payload (actual row data). For example, if your table has 100,000,000 rows and 3 indexes and each row is about 200 bytes on average, you will need $(24 + 3 * 8 + 200) * 100,000,000 =$ ~23.1GB of memory to store the row data without any versioning overhead included in this number.

- *Hash indexes* use 8 bytes per bucket. If a table has two hash indexes defined with 150,000,000 buckets each, SQL Server will create indexes with 268,435,456 buckets, rounding the number of buckets specified in the index properties to the next power of 2. Those two indexes will use $268,435,456 * 2 * 8 = $ 4GB of memory.

- *Nonclustered index* memory usage is based on the number of unique index keys and index key size. If a table has a nonclustered index with 25,000,000 unique key values and each key value on average uses 30 bytes, it would use $(30 + 8(pointer)) * 25,000,000 = $ ~906MB of memory. You can ignore the page header and nonleaf pages in your estimation as their sizes are insignificant compared to the leaf-level row size.

- *Off-row storage* overhead depends on the number of not-null values stored in off-row internal tables. Each row-overflow value adds 64 bytes overhead, which consists of a 24-byte internal table row structure, two 8-byte range index pointers (on the leaf level and in-row), and 24 bytes to store the artificial off-row ID three times (in-row, off-row, and in the leaf level of internal table range index). In addition, LOB (max) columns introduce 16 extra bytes for the pointers to the LOB PAGE ALLOCATOR varheap where data is stored, and they have additional overhead of 32 bytes per every 8KB of data there. There is also additional memory to store internal range index data pages and a mapping table, but it is insignificant compared to the actual data. As the example, if a memory-optimized table has 10,000,000 not-null values in a row-overflow varchar(8000) column, this will require 64 * 10,000,000 = ~610MB of memory to store the data in an internal off-row table.

- *Columnstore index* memory requirements are hard to estimate. The data is usually heavily compressed and, as the rule of thumb, will consume just 10 to 15 percent of the uncompressed data size in the table. Remember, however, that In-Memory OLTP does not deallocate old versions of the rows from compressed rowgroups until about 90 percent of the rows there have expired. You should factor the volatility of the data into your analysis and fine-tune the compression_delay index option, deferring compression until the data becomes static.

- *Row versioning* memory estimation depends on the duration of the longest transactions and the average number of data modifications (inserts and updates) per second. For example, if some processes in a system have 10-second transactions and, on average, the system handles 10,000 data modifications per second, you can estimate 10 * 10,000 * 248(row size) = ~24MB of memory for row versioning storage.

Obviously, these numbers outline the minimally required amount of memory. You should factor in future growth and changes in workload and reserve some additional memory just to be safe.

As mentioned, it is also important to remember that In-Memory OLTP does not work in a vacuum; SQL Server needs to have enough memory available to the other components. Make sure to include this in your analysis.

You should also remember In-Memory OLTP memory requirements when you design high availability or disaster recovery strategies in your system. It is not uncommon to see configurations where secondary or standby servers use less powerful hardware than the primary one. This approach helps to reduce hardware costs by allowing the system to operate with degraded performance in the event of a disaster.

You should be extremely careful with such an approach if your database is using the In-Memory OLTP technology. An insufficient amount of memory on secondary servers could break synchronization between nodes or prevent you from restoring the database in the event of a disaster. The latter can also happen in scenarios when you want to bring the copy of the production database to development or testing environments where SQL Server does not have enough memory to accommodate In-Memory OLTP data from production.

Administration and Monitoring Tasks

Let's look at several common In-Memory OLTP–related database administration and monitoring tasks.

Limiting the Amount of Memory Available to In-Memory OLTP

The Enterprise Edition of SQL Server allows you to manage workload and system resource consumption by utilizing a *Resource Governor*. Internally, the Resource Governor uses *resource pools*, which represent a subset of the physical resources available to SQL Server. You can think about each resource pool as a virtual instance inside SQL Server, and you can control resources available to the resource pool by specifying its parameters. Finally, you can distribute the workload between resource pools or, to be precise, between resource pool *workgroups* using a *classification* process. Classification is done based on a user-defined function, which allows you to define complex algorithms for such a purpose.

▪ **Note** You can read more about the Resource Governor at https://docs.microsoft. com/en-us/sql/relational-databases/resource-governor/resource-governor and in my *Pro SQL Server Internal* book.

Every Resource Governor configuration has two predefined resource pools created, *internal* and *default*. As you can guess by the name, the *internal* pool handles the internal SQL Server workload, and the *default* pool handles the unclassified workload, which is all of the user workload that has not been classified to the other resource pools. You can create other resource pools as needed.

As mentioned, you can control CPU, memory, and I/O allocations between resource pools by specifying parameters, such as MIN_CPU_PERCENT and MAX_CPU_PERCENT, MIN_MEMORY_PERCENT and MAX_MEMORY_PERCENT, AFFINITY, and a few others. You can bind a database to the resource pool, which, in the case of In-Memory OLTP, will allow you to limit the amount of memory for memory-optimized data in the database. Each database can be bound to a single resource pool; however, multiple databases can share the same pool. In this case, the limit would apply to all of them.

A resource pool can utilize up to 80 percent of the system memory, which sets the limit on the amount of memory available to In-Memory OLTP. That threshold guarantees that other SQL Server components have enough system memory to work and that the system remains stable under the memory pressure.

Listing 12-2 illustrates how to create and configure the resource pool, allowing it to use 40 percent of the system memory.

Listing 12-2. Creating a Resource Pool

```
create resource pool InMemoryDataPool
with
(
    min_memory_percent=40
    ,max_memory_percent=40
);

alter resource governor reconfigure;
```

When the resource pool is created, you can bind a database to it by using the sys.sp_xtp_bind_db_resource_pool stored procedure, as shown in Listing 12-3. As I already mentioned, this will allow In-Memory OLTP to use 80 percent of the resource pool memory. In our example, resource pool memory usage is restricted to 40 percent, which allows In-Memory OLTP to utilize up to 40 * 0.80 = 32 percent of the system memory.

Listing 12-3. Binding a Database to the Resource Pool

```
exec sys.sp_xtp_bind_db_resource_pool
    @database_name = 'InMemoryOLTPDemo'
    ,@pool_name = 'InMemoryDataPool';

-- You need to take DB offline and bring it
-- back online for the changes to take effect
alter database InMemoryOLTPDemo set offline;
alter database InMemoryOLTPDemo set online;
```

Unfortunately, binding the database to a resource pool does not automatically *transfer* previously allocated memory to the new pool, and you need to take the database offline and bring it back online to do so. Remember that this leads to a recovery process, which can be time-consuming in the case of large amounts of In-Memory OLTP data.

Similarly, you can remove the binding by calling the sys.sp_xtp_unbind_db_resource_pool stored procedure, as shown in Listing 12-4. The database will be bound back to the *default* resource pool after the call.

Listing 12-4. Removing the Binding Between a Database and a Resource Pool

```
exec sys.sp_xtp_unbind_db_resource_pool
    @database_name = 'InMemoryOLTPDemo';

-- You need to take DB offline and bring it
-- back online for the changes to take effect
alter database InMemoryOLTPDemo set offline;
alter database InMemoryOLTPDemo set online;
```

You should remember that resource pool memory will be shared between In-Memory OLTP data and user sessions that were classified to the resource pool workgroups. The queries may fail with an *insufficient memory* error or be blocked and have to wait for available memory if the pool does not have enough workspace memory to allocate memory grants to queries. It is safer to separate resource pools that are used to limit In-Memory OLTP memory from the pools that handle user workloads.

■ **Tip** You can monitor RESOURCE_SEMAPHORE waits, the Memory Grants Pending performance counter, and the sys.dm_exec_query_resource_semaphores and sys.dm_exec_query_memory_grants views to troubleshoot workspace memory–related issues.

Monitoring Memory Usage for Memory-Optimized Tables

You can monitor the memory usage of the various In-Memory OLTP objects by using a set of data management views along with the "Memory Usage by Memory Optimized Objects" report in SQL Server Management Studio.

The sys.dm_db_xtp_table_memory_stats view provides high-level memory usage statistics for the user and system memory-optimized tables in the current database. Listing 12-5 illustrates the query that uses this view.

Listing 12-5. Using the sys.dm_db_xtp_table_memory_stats View

```
select
    ms.object_id
    ,s.name + '.' + t.name as [table]
    ,ms.memory_allocated_for_table_kb
    ,ms.memory_used_by_table_kb
    ,ms.memory_allocated_for_indexes_kb
    ,ms.memory_used_by_indexes_kb
from
    sys.dm_db_xtp_table_memory_stats ms
        left outer join sys.tables t on
            ms.object_id = t.object_id
        left outer join sys.schemas s on
            t.schema_id = s.schema_id
order by
    ms.memory_allocated_for_table_kb desc
```

Figure 12-2 shows the output of the query when I ran it against one of the databases. A negative object_id value would indicate the system tables (not present in the output).

	object_id	table	memory_allocated_for_table_kb	memory_used_by_table_kb	memory_allocated_for_indexes_kb	memory_used_by_indexes_kb
1	2101582525	Delivery.Orders	178048	176946	110272	40543
2	1893581784	Delivery.Addresses	72768	72285	12288	12288
3	1861581670	Delivery.Customers	7936	7812	10944	5692
4	2069582411	Delivery.OrderStatuses	128	0	8	8
5	1973582069	Delivery.RatePlans	128	0	2	2
6	2005582183	Delivery.Rates	64	0	8	8
7	2037582297	Delivery.Drivers	64	6	648	12
8	1941581955	Delivery.Services	64	0	2	2

Figure 12-2. Output from sys.dm_db_xtp_table_memory_stats view

---

■ **Note**   You can read more about the `sys.dm_db_xtp_table_memory_stats` view at
`https://docs.microsoft.com/en-us/sql/relational-databases/system-dynamic-`
`management-views/sys-dm-db-xtp-table-memory-stats-transact-sql`.

The `sys.dm_db_xtp_memory_consumers` view provides detailed information about
database-level memory consumers. You already saw this view in action in Chapters 6 and 7
where you used it to obtain information about table memory consumers. You can group the
output from the view to obtain memory usage information with the required level of detail.

Listing 12-6 illustrates the query that provides memory usage information on the
per-internal-object (`xtp_object_id`) level.

Listing 12-6. Using the sys.dm_db_xtp_memory_consumers View

```
;with MemConsumers(object_id, xtp_object_id, alloc_mb, used_mb, allocs)
as
(
    select
        mc.object_id, mc.xtp_object_id
        ,convert(decimal(9,3),sum(mc.allocated_bytes) / 1024. / 1024.)
            as [allocated (MB)]
        ,convert(decimal(9,3),sum(mc.used_bytes) / 1024. / 1024.)
            as [used (MB)]
        ,sum(mc.allocation_count) as [allocs]
    from
        sys.dm_db_xtp_memory_consumers mc
    group by
        mc.object_id, mc.xtp_object_id
)
select
    mc.object_id, mc.xtp_object_id
    ,a.minor_id, a.type_desc
    ,s.name + '.' + t.name +
        iif(a.minor_id = 0,'','.' + col.Name)
            as [Table/Column]
    ,mc.allocs as [Allocations]
    ,mc.alloc_mb as [Allocated (MB)]
    ,mc.used_mb as [Used (MB)]
from
    MemConsumers mc
        join sys.memory_optimized_tables_internal_attributes a on
            a.object_id = mc.object_id and
            a.xtp_object_id = mc.xtp_object_id
        left outer join sys.columns col on
            a.object_id = col.object_id and
            a.minor_id > 0 and
            a.minor_id = col.column_id
```

```
        left outer join sys.tables t on
            a.object_id = t.object_id
        left outer join sys.schemas s on
            s.schema_id = t.schema_id
order by
    [Allocated (MB)] desc
```

Figure 12-3 shows the output of the query. As you can see, the output includes a separate row for the internal table that stores the data for the LOB Delivery.Orders. Notes column.

	object_id	xtp_object_id	minor_id	type_desc	Table/Column	Allocations	Allocated (MB)	Used (MB)
1	2101582525	-2147483609	0	USER_TABLE	Delivery.Orders	1061227	227.438	166.737
2	1893581784	-2147483615	0	USER_TABLE	Delivery.Addresses	250002	83.063	82.572
3	2101582525	-2147483608	15	INTERNAL OFF-ROW DATA TABLE	Delivery.Orders.Notes	105063	54.125	45.656
4	1861581670	-2147483616	0	USER_TABLE	Delivery.Customers	50636	18.438	13.188
5	2037582297	-2147483611	0	USER_TABLE	Delivery.Drivers	118	0.695	0.018
6	2069582411	-2147483610	0	USER_TABLE	Delivery.OrderStatuses	5	0.133	0.008
7	1973582069	-2147483613	0	USER_TABLE	Delivery.RatePlans	3	0.127	0.002
8	2005582183	-2147483612	0	USER_TABLE	Delivery.Rates	7	0.070	0.008
9	1941581955	-2147483614	0	USER_TABLE	Delivery.Services	4	0.064	0.002

Figure 12-3. *Output from sys.dm_db_memory_consumers view*

■ **Note**   You can read more about the sys.dm_db_xtp_memory_consumers view at https://docs.microsoft.com/en-us/sql/relational-databases/system-dynamic-management-views/sys-dm-db-xtp-memory-consumers-transact-sql.

The sys.dm_xtp_system_memory_consumers view provides information about memory used by internal In-Memory OLTP components. Listing 12-7 illustrates the query that uses this view.

Listing 12-7. Using the sys.dm_xtp_system_memory_consumers View

```
select
    memory_consumer_type_desc
    ,memory_consumer_desc
    ,convert(decimal(9,3),allocated_bytes / 1024. / 1024.)
        as [allocated (MB)]
    ,convert(decimal(9,3),used_bytes / 1024. / 1024.)
        as [used (MB)]
    ,allocation_count
from
    sys.dm_xtp_system_memory_consumers
order by
    [allocated (MB)] desc
```

Figure 12-4 shows the partial output of the query in my system.

	memory_consumer_type_desc	memory_consumer_desc	allocated (MB)	used (MB)	allocation_count
1	LOOKASIDE	Transaction constraint set	86.375	86.375	35050
2	LOOKASIDE	Transaction write set	35.125	35.125	35144
3	LOOKASIDE	Transaction read set	24.438	24.438	8276
4	VARHEAP	System heap	0.875	0.378	2172
5	LOOKASIDE	Transaction	0.688	0.688	500
6	LOOKASIDE	Hash cursor	0.563	0.563	1940
7	LOOKASIDE	Transaction partially-inserted rows set	0.438	0.438	855
8	LOOKASIDE	Heap cursor	0.313	0.313	718
9	LOOKASIDE	Range cursor	0.250	0.250	315
10	LOOKASIDE	Log IO proxy	0.188	0.188	792
11	LOOKASIDE	Sequence object insert row	0.063	0.063	744
12	LOOKASIDE	Sequence object map entry	0.063	0.063	2048
13	LOOKASIDE	Sequence object values map	0.063	0.063	341
14	LOOKASIDE	Redo transaction map entry	0.000	0.000	0
15	LOOKASIDE	Transaction recent rows	0.000	0.000	0
16	LOOKASIDE	Transaction dependent ring buffer	0.000	0.000	0
17	LOOKASIDE	Transaction save-point set entry	0.000	0.000	0
18	LOOKASIDE	Transaction FK validation sets.	0.000	0.000	0
19	LOOKASIDE	Log IO completion	0.000	0.000	0
20	VARHEAP	Lookaside heap	0.000	0.000	0
21	PGPOOL	256K page pool	0.000	0.000	0
22	PGPOOL	4K page pool	0.000	0.000	0
23	LOOKASIDE	Transaction list element	0.000	0.000	0

Figure 12-4. *Output from sys.dm_xtp_system_memory_consumers view*

■ **Note** You can read more about the sys.dm_xtp_system_memory_consumers view at https://docs.microsoft.com/en-us/sql/relational-databases/system-dynamic-management-views/sys-dm-xtp-system-memory-consumers-transact-sql.

You can access the "Memory Usage by Memory Optimized Objects" report in the Reports ➤ Standard Reports section in the database context menu of the SQL Server Management Studio Object Explorer. Figure 12-5 illustrates the output of the report. As you can see, this report returns similar data to the sys.dm_db_xtp_table_memory_stats view.

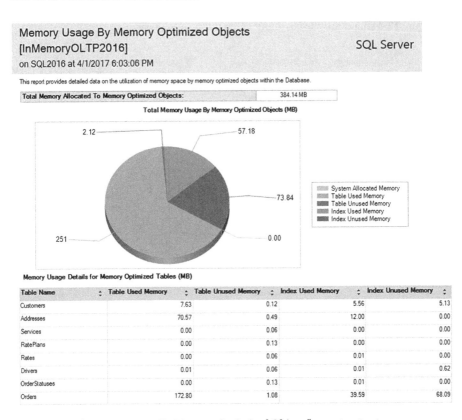

Figure 12-5. *"Memory Usage By Memory Optimized Objects" report output*

Monitoring In-Memory OLTP Transactions

The sys.dm_db_xtp_transactions view provides information about active In-Memory OLTP transactions in the system. The following are the most notable columns in the view:

- xtp_transaction_id is the internal ID of the transaction in the In-Memory OLTP Transaction Manager.

- transaction_id is the transaction ID in the system. You can use it in joins with other transaction management views, such as sys.dm_tran_active_transactions. In-Memory OLTP–only transactions, such as transactions started by natively compiled stored procedures, return a transaction_id value of 0.

- session_id indicates the session that started a transaction.

- begin_tsn and end_tsn indicate transaction timestamps.

- state and state_desc indicate the state of a transaction. The possible values are (0)-ACTIVE, (1)-COMMITTED, (2)-ABORTED, and (3)-VALIDATING.

- result and result_desc indicate the result of a transaction. The possible values are (0)-IN PROGRESS; (1)-SUCCESS; (2)-ERROR, (3)-COMMIT DEPENDENCY; (4)-VALIDATION FAILED (RR), which indicates repeatable read rules violation; (5)-VALIDATION FAILED (SR), which indicates serializable rules violation; and (6)-ROLLBACK.

- read_set_row_count, write_set_row_count, and scan_set_row_ count provide information about size of read, write, and scan sets of the transaction.

- commit_dependency_count indicates how many commits the dependency transaction has taken.

You can use the sys.dm_db_xtp_transactions view to detect long-running and orphan transactions in the system. As you probably remember, these transactions can defer the garbage collection process and lead to out-of-memory errors.

Listing 12-8 shows a query that returns information about the five oldest active In-Memory OLTP transactions in the system.

Listing 12-8. Getting Information About the Five Oldest Active In-Memory OLTP Transactions

```
select top 5
    t.session_id
    ,t.transaction_id
    ,t.begin_tsn
    ,t.end_tsn
    ,t.state_desc
    ,t.result_desc
    ,substring(
        qt.text
        ,er.statement_start_offset / 2 + 1
        ,(case er.statement_end_offset
            when -1 then datalength(qt.text)
            else er.statement_end_offset
          end - er.statement_start_offset
        ) / 2 +1
    ) as SQL
from
    sys.dm_db_xtp_transactions t
        left outer join sys.dm_exec_requests er on
            t.session_id = er.session_id
        outer apply
            sys.dm_exec_sql_text(er.sql_handle) qt
where
    t.state in (0,3) /* ACTIVE/VALIDATING */
order by
    t.begin_tsn
```

Figure 12-6 illustrates the output of the query.

	session_id	xtp_transaction_id	transaction_id	begin_tsn	end_tsn	state_desc	result_desc	SQL
1	58	775	24730	55	0	ACTIVE	IN PROGRESS	NULL
2	54	742	23026	55	0	ACTIVE	IN PROGRESS	NULL
3	56	755	23776	55	0	ACTIVE	IN PROGRESS	NULL
4	57	757	23822	55	0	ACTIVE	IN PROGRESS	NULL
5	59	801	26413	56	0	ACTIVE	IN PROGRESS	select @Cnt = count(*) from Delivery.Or

Figure 12-6. *The five oldest active In-Memory OLTP transactions in the system*

■ **Note** You can read more about the `sys.dm_db_xtp_transactions` view at `https://docs.microsoft.com/en-us/sql/relational-databases/system-dynamic-management-views/sys-dm-db-xtp-transactions-transact-sql`.

Collecting Execution Statistics for Natively Compiled Stored Procedures

In query interop mode, SQL Server collects execution statistics of the statements that access memory-optimized tables when their execution plans are cached. However, it does not collect execution statistics for natively compiled modules because of the performance impact this introduces. You can enable such a collection at the module level with `sys.sp_xtp_control_proc_exec_stats` and at the statement level with the `sys.sp_xtp_control_query_exec_stats` system stored procedures.

Both procedures accept a Boolean `@new_collection_value` parameter, which indicates whether the collection needs to be enabled or disabled. In addition, `sys.sp_xtp_control_query_exec_stats` allows you to provide `@database_id` and `@xtp_object_id` values to specify a module to monitor. It is also worth noting that SQL Server does not persist collection settings, and you will need to reenable statistics collection after each SQL Server restart.

■ **Important** Collecting execution statistics degrades the performance of the system. Do not collect execution statistics unless you are performing troubleshooting. Moreover, consider limiting collection to specific natively compiled modules to reduce the performance impact on the system.

When statistics have been collected, you can access them through the `sys.dm_exec_procedure_stats`, `sys.dm_exec_function_stats`, and `sys.dm_exec_query_stats` views.

Listing 12-9 shows the code that returns execution statistics for stored procedures using the `sys.dm_exec_procedure_stats` view. The code does not limit the output to natively compiled stored procedures; however, you can do it by joining the `sys.dm_exec_procedure_stats` and `sys.sql_modules` views and filtering by the `uses_native_compliation = 1` value.

Listing 12-9. Analyzing Stored Procedures Execution Statistics

```
select
    object_name(ps.object_id) as [Proc Name]
    ,p.query_plan
    ,ps.execution_count as [Exec Cnt]
    ,ps.total_worker_time as [Total CPU]
    ,convert(int,ps.total_worker_time / ps.execution_count)
        as [Avg CPU] -- in Microseconds
    ,ps.total_elapsed_time as [Total Elps]
    ,convert(int,ps.total_elapsed_time / ps.execution_count)
        as [Avg Elps] -- in Microseconds
    ,ps.cached_time as [Cached]
    ,ps.last_execution_time as [Last Exec]
    ,ps.sql_handle
    ,ps.plan_handle
    ,ps.total_logical_reads as [Reads]
    ,ps.total_logical_writes as [Writes]
from
    sys.dm_exec_procedure_stats ps cross apply
        sys.dm_exec_query_plan(ps.plan_handle) p
order by
    [Avg CPU] desc
```

Figure 12-7 illustrates the output of the code from Listing 12-9. As you can see, in
SQL Server 2016, both the `sql_handle` and `plan_handle` columns are populated and can
be used to obtain the stored procedure text and execution plan. It is also worth noting
that there is no I/O-related statistics provided. Natively compiled modules work with
memory-optimized tables only, and therefore there is no I/O involved.

	Proc Name	query_plan	Exec Cnt	Total CPU	Avg CPU	Total Elps	Avg Elps
1	InsertOrder	<ShowPlanXML xmlns...	2	258	129	258	129
2	DeleteCustomer	<ShowPlanXML xmlns...	5	231	46	234	46

Cached	Last Exec	sql_handle	plan_handle	Reads	Writes
2017-04-01 18:46:20.183	2017-04-01 18:46:31.583	0x0300050...	0x0A0005...	0	0
2017-04-01 18:38:43.127	2017-04-01 18:46:31.583	0x0300050...	0x0A0005...	0	0

Figure 12-7. *Data from sys.dm_exec_procedure_stats view*

Listing 12-10 shows the code that obtains execution statistics for individual
statements using the `sys.dm_exec_query_stats` view.

Listing 12-10. Analyzing Stored Procedure Statement Execution Statistics

```
select
    substring(qt.text
        ,(qs.statement_start_offset/2) + 1
        ,(case qs.statement_end_offset
```

```
            when -1 then datalength(qt.text)
            else qs.statement_end_offset
        end - qs.statement_start_offset) / 2 + 1
    ) as SQL
    ,p.query_plan
    ,qs.execution_count as [Exec Cnt]
    ,qs.total_worker_time as [Total CPU]
    ,convert(int,qs.total_worker_time / qs.execution_count)
        as [Avg CPU] -- in Microseconds
    ,total_elapsed_time as [Total Elps]
    ,convert(int,qs.total_elapsed_time / qs.execution_count)
        as [Avg Elps] -- in Microseconds
    ,qs.creation_time as [Cached]
    ,last_execution_time as [Last Exec]
    ,qs.plan_handle
    ,qs.total_logical_reads as [Reads]
    ,qs.total_logical_writes as [Writes]
from
    sys.dm_exec_query_stats qs
        cross apply sys.dm_exec_sql_text(qs.sql_handle) qt
        cross apply sys.dm_exec_query_plan(qs.plan_handle) p
where -- it is null for natively compiled SPs
    qs.plan_generation_num is null
order by
    [Avg CPU] desc
```

Figure 12-8 illustrates the output of the code from Listing 12-10.

	SQL	query_plan	Exec Cnt	Total CPU	Avg CPU
1	insert into Delivery.Orders(OrderNum,OrderDate,R...	<ShowPlanXM...	2	209	104
2	delete from Delivery.Customers where CustomerId =...	<ShowPlanXM...	3	35	11
3	delete from Delivery.Orders where CustomerId = @...	<ShowPlanXM...	3	22	7
4	delete from Delivery.Addresses where CustomerId =...	<ShowPlanXM...	3	13	4

Total Elps	Avg Elps	Cached	Last Exec	plan_handle	Reads	Writes
209	104	2017-04-01 18:46:20.183	2017-04-01 18:46:31.583	0x0A0005008...	0	0
35	11	2017-04-01 18:38:43.127	2017-04-01 18:46:31.583	0x0A000500C...	0	0
21	7	2017-04-01 18:38:43.127	2017-04-01 18:46:31.583	0x0A000500C...	0	0
13	4	2017-04-01 18:38:43.127	2017-04-01 18:46:31.583	0x0A000500C...	0	0

Figure 12-8. Data from sys.dm_exec_query_stats view

■ **Note** You can read more about the sys.sp_xtp_control_proc_exec_stats procedure at https://docs.microsoft.com/en-us/sql/relational-databases/system-stored-procedures/sys-sp-xtp-control-proc-exec-stats-transact-sql. More information about the sys.sp_xtp_control_query_exec_stats procedure is available at https://docs.microsoft.com/en-us/sql/relational-databases/system-stored-procedures/sys-sp-xtp-control-query-exec-stats-transact-sql.

Finally, it is worth noting that neither the DBCC FREEPROCCACHE nor ALTER DATABASE SCOPED CONFIGURATION CLEAR PROCEDURE_CACHE command removes natively compiled modules execution statistics from the plan cache. Statistics would be removed, however, when a module was recompiled.

In-Memory OLTP and Query Store Integration

Query Store is new SQL Server 2016 component that collects execution plans and runtime statistics for the queries in the system. Those statistics are persisted in the database, and they would survive database restart or failover, which is different from the plan cache–based execution statistics I just discussed.

Similarly to plan cache–based execution statistics, Query Store does not collect the execution statistics of natively compiled modules by default. You need to enable them with the sys.sp_xtp_control_query_exec_stats system stored procedure. Consider the performance overhead this introduces, and do not enable them unless you troubleshoot performance issues.

Figure 12-9 shows a Query Store report that works with the statements from natively compiled stored procedures. As you can see, Management Studio provides a powerful and convenient set of tools that dramatically simplify performance troubleshooting and tuning.

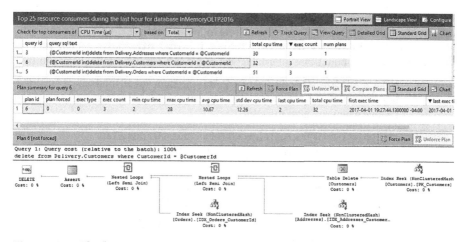

Figure 12-9. *The "Top Resource Consuming Queries" report in Query Store*

■ **Note**   The coverage of Query Store is outside the scope of this book. You can read more about it at https://docs.microsoft.com/en-us/sql/relational-databases/performance/monitoring-performance-by-using-the-query-store and in my *Pro SQL Server Internals* book.

Metadata Changes and Enhancements

In-Memory OLTP introduces a large number of changes in catalog and data management views.

Catalog Views

There are two In-Memory OLTP–related catalog views in SQL Server 2016.

sys.hash_indexes

As you can guess by the name, the sys.hash_indexes view provides information about hash indexes defined in the database. It is inherited from and has the same columns as the sys.indexes view, adding one extra column called bucket_count. You can read about this view at https://docs.microsoft.com/en-us/sql/relational-databases/system-catalog-views/sys-hash-indexes-transact-sql.

sys.memory_optimized_tables_internal_attributes

As you already know, every memory-optimized table may include additional internal tables to store off-row column data, columnstore index internal structures, and a few other objects. The sys.memory_optimized_tables_internal_attributes catalog view provides information about those internal tables, and it consists of the following columns:

- object_id is the ID of the user table. It is the same for all internal tables that belong to the user table. The object_id value does not change when you alter the table.

- xtp_object_id is internal object ID of an internal table. This value may change when you re-create the table object during table alteration.

- minor_id provides the column_id value of the table column when the internal table stores off-row column data. It is 0 in other cases.

- The type and type_description columns indicate the type of internal table. The possible values are as follows:

  - (0): DELETED_ROWS_TABLE is the delete bitmap in a columnstore index.

  - (1): USER_TABLE is the main table structure that stores in-row data.

  - (2): DICTIONARIES_TABLE is the dictionaries for a columnstore index.

  - (3): SEGMENTS_TABLE is the compressed segments for a columnstore index.

- (4): ROW_GROUPS_INFO_TABLE is the metadata about compressed rowgroups in a columnstore index.

- (5): INTERNAL_OFF_ROW_DATA_TABLE is a table that stores off-row column data. As I already mentioned, minor_id provides the column_id value of the off-row column, and it can be used in joins with the sys.columns catalog view.

- (252): INTERNAL_TEMPORAL_HISTORY_TABLE is an in-memory buffer that contains the *hot tail* of the disk-based history table. The *history* rows are inserted into this internal table first, and then they asynchronously move to the disk-based history table.

You can use sys.memory_optimized_tables_internal_attributes with the sys.dm_db_xtp_memory_consumers view when you are analyzing memory consumption of the memory-optimized tables in the system. You have already seen this in action many times in the book.

You can read more about the sys.memory_optimized_tables_internal_attributes view at https://docs.microsoft.com/en-us/sql/relational-databases/system-catalog-views/sys-memory-optimized-tables-internal-attributes-transact-sql.

Changes in Other Catalog Views

Other catalog view changes include the following:

- The sys.tables view has three new columns. The is_memory_optimized column indicates whether a table is memory-optimized. The durability and durability_desc columns indicate a durability mode for memory-optimized tables. The values are (0)-SCHEMA_AND_DATA and (1)-SCHEMA_ONLY.

- The sys.indexes view has a new possible value in the type and type_description columns, such as (7)-NONCLUSTERED HASH. Nonclustered Bw-Tree indexes use a value of (2)-NONCLUSTERED as the regular nonclustered B-Tree indexes defined on disk-based tables. Clustered columnstore indexes use a value of (5) - CLUSTERED COLUMNSTORE and an index_id value of 1.

- The sys.sql_modules and sys.all_sql_modules views have a new column called uses_native_compilation.

- The sys.table_types view has a new column called is_memory_optimized, which indicates whether a type represents a memory-optimized table variable.

- The sys.data_spaces view now has new type and type_desc values of (FX)-MEMORY_OPTIMIZED_DATA_FILEGROUP.

Data Management Views

In-Memory OLTP provides a large set of new data management views; they can be easily detected by the `xtp_` prefix in their names. The naming convention also provides information about their scope. The `sys.dm_xtp_*` views return instance-level information, and the `sys.dm_db_xtp_*` views provide database-level information. Let's look at them in more detail, grouping them by area.

Object and Index Statistics

The following data management views provide index-related and data modification-related statistics:

- `sys.dm_db_xtp_object_stats` reports the number of rows affected by data modifications along with write conflicts and unique constraint violations on a per-object basis. You can use this view to analyze the volatility of the data from memory-optimized tables, correlating it with index usage statistics. As with disk-based tables, you can improve data modification performance by removing rarely used indexes defined on volatile tables. More information about this view is available at `https://docs.microsoft.com/en-us/sql/relational-databases/system-dynamic-management-views/sys-dm-db-xtp-object-stats-transact-sql`.

- `sys.dm_db_xtp_index_stats` returns information about index usage, including the number of row-chain scans, the number of rows scanned (`rows_touched`), the number of rows returned to the client (`rows_returned`), and data about expired rows. The large discrepancy between `rows_touched` and `rows_returned` may indicate an inefficient indexing strategy with queries performing the large range scans. For hash indexes, it may also indicate the large index row chains because of an insufficient number of buckets in the hash table. You can read about this view at `https://docs.microsoft.com/en-us/sql/relational-databases/system-dynamic-management-views/sys-dm-db-xtp-index-stats-transact-sql`.

- `sys.dm_db_xtp_nonclustered_index_stats` provides information about nonclustered (range) indexes, such as the number of pages in the index, the number of delta pages, and page split and merge statistics. You can read about this view at `https://docs.microsoft.com/en-us/sql/relational-databases/system-dynamic-management-views/sys-dm-db-xtp-nonclustered-index-stats-transact-sql`.

- sys.dm_db_xtp_hash_index_stats provides information about
  hash indexes, such as the number of buckets in the index, the
  number of empty buckets, and row chain length information. This
  view is useful when you need to analyze the state of hash indexes
  and fine-tune their bucket_count allocations. You can read
  about this view at https://docs.microsoft.com/en-us/sql/
  relational-databases/system-dynamic-management-views/
  sys-dm-db-xtp-hash-index-stats-transact-sql.

Listing 12-11 shows the script that you can use to find hash indexes with a potentially
suboptimal bucket_count value.

Listing 12-11. Obtaining Information About Hash Indexes with a Potentially Suboptimal
bucket_count Value

```
select
    s.name + '.' + t.name as [Table]
    ,i.name as [Index]
    ,stat.total_bucket_count as [Total Buckets]
    ,stat.empty_bucket_count as [Empty Buckets]
    ,floor(100. * empty_bucket_count / total_bucket_count)
        as [Empty Bucket %]
    ,stat.avg_chain_length as [Avg Chain]
    ,stat.max_chain_length as [Max Chain]
from
    sys.dm_db_xtp_hash_index_stats stat
        join sys.tables t on
            stat.object_id = t.object_id
        join sys.indexes i on
            stat.object_id = i.object_id and
            stat.index_id = i.index_id
        join sys.schemas s on
            t.schema_id = s.schema_id
where
    stat.avg_chain_length > 3 or
    stat.max_chain_length > 50 or
    floor(100. * empty_bucket_count /
        total_bucket_count) > 50
```

Memory Usage Statistics

I already discussed memory usage–related views in this and other chapters. However, as a
quick overview, the views are as follows:

- sys.dm_xtp_system_memory_consumers reports information
  about system-level memory consumers in the system. More
  information about this view is available at https://docs.
  microsoft.com/en-us/sql/relational-databases/system-
  dynamic-management-views/sys-dm-xtp-system-memory-
  consumers-transact-sql.

- `sys.dm_db_xtp_table_memory_stats` provides memory usage statistics on a per-object level. You can read more at https://docs.microsoft.com/en-us/sql/relational-databases/system-dynamic-management-views/sys-dm-db-xtp-table-memory-stats-transact-sql.

- `sys.dm_db_xtp_memory_consumers` provides information about database-level memory consumers. You can use this view to analyze per-index memory allocation in the system along with the memory consumed by internal tables. The documentation is available at https://docs.microsoft.com/en-us/sql/relational-databases/system-dynamic-management-views/sys-dm-xtp-system-memory-consumers-transact-sql.

Transaction Management

The following views provide transaction-related statistics in the system:

- `sys.dm_xtp_transaction_stats` reports statistics about transactional activity in the system since the last server restart. It includes the number of transactions, information about transaction log activity, and quite a few other metrics. More information about this view is available at https://docs.microsoft.com/en-us/sql/relational-databases/system-dynamic-management-views/sys-dm-xtp-transaction-stats-transact-sql.

- `sys.dm_db_xtp_transactions` provides information about currently active transactions in the system. We discussed this view in this chapter, and you can read more about it at https://docs.microsoft.com/en-us/sql/relational-databases/system-dynamic-management-views/sys-dm-db-xtp-transactions-transact-sql.

Garbage Collection

The following views provide information about the garbage collection process in the system:

- `sys.dm_xtp_gc_stats` reports the overall statistics about the garbage collection process. More information is available at https://docs.microsoft.com/en-us/sql/relational-databases/system-dynamic-management-views/sys-dm-xtp-gc-stats-transact-sql.

- `sys.dm_xtp_gc_queue_stats` provides information about the state of garbage collection worker item queues. You can use this view to monitor whether the garbage collection deallocation process is keeping up with the system load. You can read more about this view at https://docs.microsoft.com/en-us/sql/relational-databases/system-dynamic-management-views/sys-dm-xtp-gc-queue-stats-transact-sql.

- `sys.dm_db_xtp_gc_cycle_stats` provides information about idle worker thread generation queues. I discussed this view in Chapter 11, and you can read more about it at https://docs.microsoft.com/en-us/sql/relational-databases/system-dynamic-management-views/sys-dm-db-xtp-gc-cycle-stats-transact-sql.

Checkpoint

The following views provide information about checkpoint operations in the current database:

- `sys.dm_db_xtp_checkpoint_stats` reports the overall statistics about database checkpoint operations. It includes log file I/O statistics, the amount of data processed during a continuous checkpoint, the time since the last checkpoint operation, and quite a few other metrics. More information about this view is available at https://docs.microsoft.com/en-us/sql/relational-databases/system-dynamic-management-views/sys-dm-db-xtp-checkpoint-stats-transact-sql.

- `sys.dm_db_xtp_checkpoint_files` provides information about checkpoint file pairs in the database. Appendix C shows this view in action, and you can read more about it at https://docs.microsoft.com/en-us/sql/relational-databases/system-dynamic-management-views/sys-dm-db-xtp-checkpoint-files-transact-sql.

Extended Events and Performance Counters

SQL Server has the large number of extended events and performance counters that can be used to monitor and troubleshoot In-Memory OLTP–related actions. You can use the code from Listing 12-12 to get the list of In-Memory OLTP extended events.

Listing 12-12. Analyzing In-Memory OLTP Extended Events

```
select
    xp.name as [package]
    ,xo.name as [event]
    ,xo.description as [description]
```

```
from
    sys.dm_xe_packages xp
        join sys.dm_xe_objects xo on
            xp.guid = xo.package_guid
where
    xp.name like 'XTP%' or xo.name like '%XTP%'
order by
    xp.name, xo.name
```

Figure 12-10 shows the partial output from the query. I recommend you analyze the full output from the query and get familiar with the events that may be useful for monitoring and troubleshooting purposes.

	package	event	description
1	sqlserver	temporal_xtp_ddl_period	Occurs when trying to create temporal period on memory-op
2	sqlserver	temporal_xtp_flush_task_ended	Occurs when background task for moving history data of me
3	sqlserver	temporal_xtp_flush_task_exception	Occurs when background task for moving history data of me
4	sqlserver	temporal_xtp_flush_task_started	Occurs when background task for moving history data of me
5	sqlserver	xtp_alter_table	Occurs at start of XTP table altering.
6	sqlserver	xtp_checkpoint_controller_start_scan	Fired by checkpoint controller thread whenever it is started.
7	sqlserver	xtp_close_harden_checkpoint	Fired by XTP close thread after it updates the boot page.
8	sqlserver	xtp_controller_thread_status	Indicates whether the Hekaton checkpoint controller thread
9	sqlserver	xtp_create_procedure	Occurs at start of XTP procedure creation.
10	sqlserver	xtp_create_table	Occurs at start of XTP table creation.
11	sqlserver	xtp_database_deployed	Fired after first xtp add container or create database.
32	sqlserver	xtp_storage_table_create	Occurs at just before the XTP storage table is created.
33	sqlserver	xtp_table_created	Occurs after the XTP table is created.
34	XtpCompile	cgen	Occurs at start of C code generation.
35	XtpCompile	cl_duration	Reports the duration of the C compilation.
36	XtpCompile	invoke_cl	Occurs prior to the invocation of the C compiler.
37	XtpCompile	keyword_map	Event grouping keywords
38	XtpCompile	mat_export	Occurs at start of MAT export.
39	XtpCompile	pitgen_procs	Occurs at start of PIT generation for procedures.
40	XtpCompile	pitgen_tables	Occurs at start of PIT generation for tables.
41	XtpCompile	table_update_code_path	Occurs when update statement is executed.
42	XtpEngine	after_changestatetx_event	Fires after transaction changes state.

Figure 12-10. *In-Memory OLTP extended events*

Similarly, you can see In-Memory OLTP performance counters with the query shown in Listing 12-13.

Listing 12-13. Analyzing In-Memory OLTP Performance Counters

```
select object_name, counter_name
from sys.dm_os_performance_counters
where object_name like '%XTP%'
order by object_name, counter_name
```

Figure 12-11 shows a partial output of the query. As with extended events, it is beneficial to get familiar with performance counters and use them to baseline the system workload and use them while monitoring and troubleshooting performance issues.

	object_name	counter_name
10	SQL Server 2016 XTP Cursors	Rows returned/sec
11	SQL Server 2016 XTP Cursors	Rows touched/sec
12	SQL Server 2016 XTP Cursors	Tentatively-deleted rows touched/sec
13	SQL Server 2016 XTP Garbage Collection	Dusty corner scan retries/sec (GC-issued)
14	SQL Server 2016 XTP Garbage Collection	Main GC work items/sec
15	SQL Server 2016 XTP Garbage Collection	Parallel GC work item/sec
16	SQL Server 2016 XTP Garbage Collection	Rows processed/sec
17	SQL Server 2016 XTP Garbage Collection	Rows processed/sec (first in bucket and removed)
18	SQL Server 2016 XTP Garbage Collection	Rows processed/sec (first in bucket)
19	SQL Server 2016 XTP Garbage Collection	Rows processed/sec (marked for unlink)
20	SQL Server 2016 XTP Garbage Collection	Rows processed/sec (no sweep needed)
21	SQL Server 2016 XTP Garbage Collection	Sweep expired rows removed/sec
36	SQL Server 2016 XTP Phantom Processor	Phantom rows touched/sec
37	SQL Server 2016 XTP Phantom Processor	Phantom scans started/sec
38	SQL Server 2016 XTP Storage	Checkpoints Closed
39	SQL Server 2016 XTP Storage	Checkpoints Completed
40	SQL Server 2016 XTP Storage	Core Merges Completed
41	SQL Server 2016 XTP Storage	Merge Policy Evaluations
42	SQL Server 2016 XTP Storage	Merge Requests Outstanding
43	SQL Server 2016 XTP Storage	Merges Abandoned
44	SQL Server 2016 XTP Storage	Merges Installed
45	SQL Server 2016 XTP Storage	Total Files Merged
46	SQL Server 2016 XTP Transaction Log	Log bytes written/sec
47	SQL Server 2016 XTP Transaction Log	Log records written/sec
48	SQL Server 2016 XTP Transactions	Cascading aborts/sec
49	SQL Server 2016 XTP Transactions	Commit dependencies taken/sec
50	SQL Server 2016 XTP Transactions	Read-only transactions prepared/sec

Figure 12-11. In-Memory OLTP performance counters

■ **Note** You can read about In-Memory OLTP performance counters at https://docs.microsoft.com/en-us/sql/relational-databases/performance-monitor/sql-server-xtp-in-memory-oltp-performance-counters.

Summary

Choosing the right hardware is a crucial part of achieving good In-Memory OLTP performance and transactional throughput. In-Memory OLTP uses hardware in a different manner than the Storage Engine, and you need to carefully plan the deployment and server configuration when a system uses In-Memory OLTP.

In-Memory OLTP benefits from single-threaded CPU performance. You should choose CPUs with a high base clock speed and have hyperthreading enabled in the system.

You should store In-Memory OLTP checkpoint files in the disk array, which is optimized for sequential I/O performance, preferably using SSD-based drives. You can consider using multiple containers in an In-Memory OLTP filegroup, placing them on different drives if the database recovery time is critical.

Obviously, you should have enough memory in the system to accommodate the In-Memory OLTP data, while leaving enough memory for other SQL Server components. In the Enterprise Edition of SQL Server, you can restrict In-Memory OLTP memory usage by configuring memory in the Resource Governor resource pool and binding the database there. In the Standard Edition, In-Memory OLTP is limited to 32GB of memory-optimized data per database.

In-Memory OLTP provides a large set of data management views, performance counters, and extended events that you can use for system monitoring.

CHAPTER 13

■ ■ ■

Utilizing In-Memory OLTP

This chapter discusses several design considerations for systems utilizing In-Memory OLTP and demonstrates how to benefit from the technology when migrating the existing systems is cost-ineffective. It also talks about implementing data partitioning, which can be helpful in a system with a large amount of data and mixed workload.

Design Considerations for Systems Utilizing In-Memory OLTP

Two years ago, when I worked on the first edition of the book, about half of this chapter focused on the techniques that helped to address technology limitations. Those limitations positioned In-Memory OLTP as a niche technology in SQL Server 2014 and prevented its widespread adoption because of the high implementation and refactoring cost.

Fortunately, the majority of the limitations have been removed in SQL Server 2016. Moreover, starting with SQL Server 2016 SP1, In-Memory OLTP is available in the Standard Edition of SQL Server, which allows you to benefit from the technology and maintain a single system architecture and code base across multiple editions of the product.

■ **Note** Remember that non-Enterprise editions limit the amount of memory they can utilize. For example, the Standard Edition is limited to 32GB of memory-optimized data per database.

Nevertheless, the adoption of In-Memory OLTP comes at a cost. You will need to acquire or upgrade to SQL Server 2016, spend time learning the technology, and, if you are migrating an existing system, refactor code and test the changes. It is important to perform a cost-benefits analysis to determine whether In-Memory OLTP provides you with adequate benefits to outweigh the costs.

In-Memory OLTP is hardly a magical solution that will improve server performance by simply flipping a switch and moving data into memory. It is designed to address a specific set of problems, such as latch and lock contentions on very active OLTP systems. Moreover, it helps improve the performance of the small and frequently executed OLTP queries that perform point-lookups and small-range scans.

© Dmitri Korotkevich 2017

D. Korotkevich, *Expert SQL Server In-Memory OLTP*, DOI 10.1007/978-1-4842-2772-5_13

In-Memory OLTP is less beneficial in the case of data warehouse systems with low concurrent activity, large amounts of data, and queries that require large scans and complex aggregations. In some cases, it is still possible to achieve performance improvements by moving data into memory or creating columnstore indexes on memory-optimized tables; however, you will often obtain better results by using columnstore indexes with disk-based tables, especially with dedicated data warehouse implementations.

You should remember that memory-optimized columnstore indexes are targeted toward operational analytics scenarios when you need to run infrequent reporting and analysis queries against *hot* OLTP data. Their implementation is limited compared to disk-based column-based storage. Memory-optimized columnstore indexes cannot be partitioned nor can they become the main copy of the data in the table like disk-based clustered columnstore indexes do. Also, In-Memory OLTP does not allow you to rebuild or reorganize columnstore indexes, reducing the size of the delta store and delete bitmap.

You should also remember that memory-optimized tables live completely in-memory and out-of-memory conditions would lead to system downtime. This is especially important in the case of non-Enterprise editions where you cannot scale the system with the data growth by adding extra memory to the server. In many cases, it may be beneficial to design the system utilizing data partitioning, keeping *hot* recent data in memory-optimized and *cold* historical data in disk-based tables. I will discuss such an implementation later in this chapter.

As you already know, SQL Server 2016 removes the majority of the limitations of the technology that existed in SQL Server 2014. In many cases, you can migrate disk-based tables into memory without any schema and code changes in the system. There are, however, a few important considerations and behavior differences you need to remember and factor into the decision. Let's talk about the most important ones.

Off-Row Storage

Even though In-Memory OLTP supports LOB and row-overflow columns, it works with them in a different way than the Storage Engine. With disk-based tables, the decision of which columns are stored off-row is made on a per-row basis based on the row size; all data will be stored in-row when it fits into the 8,060-byte limit. By contrast, with memory-optimized tables, the decision is made strictly based on the table schema; the off-row column data will be stored in separate internal tables for all rows, regardless of the amount of data you store there.

As you will remember from Chapter 6, an excessive number of off-row columns leads to serious performance implications because of the internal tables management that In-Memory OLTP has to perform. Moreover, off-row columns increase the memory usage; each not null off-row *value* adds 64+ bytes of overhead. You should be extremely careful with off-row columns and avoid using them in memory-optimized tables unless they are absolutely necessary.

It is common to see systems in which many text columns are defined as (n) varchar(max) *just in case*. This is a bad practice that increases query memory grants, introduces concurrency issues in the system, and complicates index management. This overhead, however, is not always noticeable, or, perhaps, it is not always correlated with the existence of off-row data.

The situation will change if you migrate those tables to In-Memory OLTP, keeping off-row columns intact. This decision could significantly increase the memory usage and slow down the queries against the table. After all, querying data from or modifying data in multiple internal tables will always be slower than working with a single table. You need to remember this behavior and analyze off-row column usage before migration. In many cases, you can change the data types to (n)varchar(N) and store those columns in-row.

You can also consider implementing vertical partitioning and storing some off-row columns in disk-based tables, as shown in Listing 13-1. The Description column is stored in a disk-based table, while all other columns are stored in a memory-optimized table. The majority of the use cases in the system would not work with the product description, and therefore, you can utilize native compilation while working with the dbo.ProductsInMem table. Moreover, moving a product description to a disk-based table will allow you to utilize the Full-Text Search feature, which is not supported for memory-optimized tables.

Listing 13-1. Vertical Partitioning

```
create table dbo.ProductsInMem
(
    ProductId int not null identity(1,1)
        constraint PK_ ProductsInMem
        primary key nonclustered hash
        with (bucket_count = 65536),
    ProductName nvarchar(64) not null,
    ShortDescription nvarchar(256) not null,

    index IDX_ProductsInMem_ProductName
    nonclustered(ProductName)
)
with (memory_optimized = on, durability = schema_and_data);

create table dbo.ProductDescriptions
(
    ProductId int not null,
    Description nvarchar(max) not null,

    constraint PK_ ProductDescriptions
    primary key clustered(ProductId)
);
```

You can hide some of the implementation details from the interop SELECT queries by defining a view, as shown in Listing 13-2. You can also define INSTEAD OF triggers on the view and use them as the target for data modifications; however, it is more efficient to update the data in the tables directly.

Listing 13-2. Creating a View That Combines Data from Both Tables

```
create view dbo.Products(ProductId, ProductName,
    ShortDescription, Description)
as
    select
        p.ProductId, p.ProductName, p.ShortDescription
        ,pd.Description
    from
        dbo.ProductsInMem p left outer join
            dbo.ProductDescriptions pd on
                p.ProductId = pd.ProductId
```

As you should notice, the view is using an outer join. This allows SQL Server to perform join elimination when the client application does not reference any columns from the dbo.ProductDescriptions table while querying the view. For example, if you ran the query from Listing 13-3, you would see the execution plan shown in Figure 13-1. As you can see, there are no joins in the plan, and the dbo.ProductDescriptions table is not accessed.

Listing 13-3. Query Against the View

```
select ProductId, ProductName
from dbo.Products
```

Query 1: Query cost (relative to the batch): 100%
select ProductId, ProductName from dbo.Products

Figure 13-1. Execution plan of the query

Unfortunately, it is impossible to define a FOREIGN KEY constraint for a disk-based table referencing a memory-optimized table; furthermore, you should support referential integrity in your code.

Listing 13-4 shows the stored procedure that inserts a row into the dbo.ProductDescriptions table. The implementation looks trivial; however, there is one very important detail. The code checks for the existence of the dbo.ProductsInMem row using the REPEATABLE READ transaction isolation level. This forces In-Memory OLTP to build the *read set* for the transaction and validate that the selected dbo.ProductsInMem row exists at the time of transaction commit. The transaction would fail with a *repeatable read validation failure* if the other session deleted the product row in between the SELECT and INSERT statements.

Listing 13-4. Enforcing Referential Integrity Between Disk-Based and Memory-Optimized Tables: Inserting the Row into the Referencing Table

```
create proc dbo.InsertProductDescription
(
    @ProductId int
    ,@Description nvarchar(max)
)
as
begin
    set nocount on

    declare
        @Exists int

    set transaction isolation level read committed
    begin tran
        -- using REPEATABLE READ isolation level
        -- to build transaction read set
        select @Exists = ProductId
        from dbo.ProductsInMem with (repeatableread)
        where ProductId = @ProductId;

        if @Exists is null
            raiserror('ProductId %d not found',16,1,@ProductId);
        else
            insert into dbo.ProductDescriptions
                (ProductId, Description)
            values(1,@Description);
    commit;
end
```

Listing 13-5 shows how to perform the deletion of the dbo.ProductsInMem row. As you can see, the SELECT statement checks for the existence of the dbo.ProductDescriptions rows using the SERIALIZABLE isolation level, which places a key range shared lock and prevents other sessions from inserting a product description with the same ProductId value.

Listing 13-5. Enforcing Referential Integrity Between Disk-Based and Memory-Optimized Tables: Deleting the Row from the Referenced Table

```
declare
    @Cnt int
    ,@ProductId int = 1

begin tran
    -- using SERIALIZABLE level to acquire the range lock
    select @Cnt = count(*)
```

```
    from dbo.ProductDescriptions with (serializable)
    where ProductId = @ProductId;

    if @Cnt > 0
        raiserror('Referential Integrity Violation',16,1);
    else
        delete from dbo.ProductsInMem with (snapshot)
        where ProductId = @ProductId;
commit;
```

You can use a similar approach when you need to enforce referential integrity in the opposite direction with memory-optimized tables referencing disk-based ones. In this case, however, the latter example (checking for the existence of the referencing rows in memory-optimized tables) would depend on *serializable validation* at the time of transaction commit rather than on locking.

With all that being said, splitting the data into memory-optimized and disk-based tables would increase the complexity of the system along as well as its development cost. It may be beneficial when a table has a large number of off-row columns that may not be moved in-row and/or when you want to utilize technologies not supported by In-Memory OLTP (Full-Text Search, for example). However, in many cases, it may be more cost-effective to keep off-row columns in memory-optimized tables, especially if you have just a handful of them.

Unsupported Data Types

Even though In-Memory OLTP in SQL Server 2016 supports the majority of data types, there are still a few unsupported types, such as xml, geometry, geography, hierarchyid, datetimeoffset, rowversion, and sql_variant. Moreover, user-defined data types are not supported either.

As the simplest workaround, you can store them either in binary or text format or, in some cases, shred them into relational data types when it is possible.

Let's look at an example. Listing 13-6 shows a disk-based table that stores event information from devices along with the locations where the events occurred.

Listing 13-6. DeviceEvents Disk-Based Table

```
create table dbo.DeviceEvents
(
    DeviceId int not null,
    EventTime datetime2(0) not null,
    Location geography not null,
    EventInfo xml not null,
);

create unique clustered index
IDX_DeviceEvents_DeviceId_EventTime
on dbo.DeviceEvents(DeviceId, EventTime);
```

Neither the geography nor xml data type is supported in In-Memory OLTP. You can address this by storing location information in a pair of decimal columns and using the varbinary column to store the xml data, as shown in Listing 13-7.

Listing 13-7. DeviceEvents Memory-Optimized Table

```
create table dbo.DeviceEvents
(
    DeviceId int not null,
    EventTime datetime2(0) not null,
    Lat decimal(9,6) not null,
    Long decimal(9,6) not null,
    EventInfo varbinary(max) not null,

    constraint PK_DeviceEvents
    primary key nonclustered(DeviceId, EventTime)
)
with (memory_optimized = on, durability = schema_and_data);
```

You can cast the data back to the geometry and xml data types and utilize the XQuery and geospatial methods when you access the table through the Interop Engine, as shown in Listing 13-8.

Listing 13-8. Working with DeviceEvents Data

```
declare
    @Loc geography =
        geography::Point(47.65600,-122.36000, 4326);

;with DeviceData(DeviceId, EventTime, Location, EventInfo)
as
(
    select
        DeviceId, EventTime
        ,geography::Point(Lat, Long, 4326) as Location
        ,convert(xml,EventInfo) as EventInfo
    from dbo.DeviceEvents
)
select
    DeviceId, EventTime
    ,Location.STDistance(@Loc) as Distance
    ,EventInfo.value('/Event[1]/@Code','int') as [Code]
    ,EventInfo.value('/Event[1]/@Sensor1','varchar(3)')
        as [Status]
from DeviceData;
```

Obviously, you can also split the data between memory-optimized and disk-based tables similarly to the dbo.ProductsInMem and dbo.ProductDescriptions tables from Listing 13-1. This may be beneficial if you need to utilize spatial or XML indexes for the data.

Unfortunately, there is no built-in support for rowversion data type behavior. Fortunately, it is easy to implement this manually. Listing 13-9 shows how you can implement optimistic concurrency in the code similarly to a disk-based implementation that relies on the rowversion column.

Listing 13-9. Implementing Optimistic Concurrency

```
create table dbo.OptimisticConcurrency
(
    ID int not null
        constraint PK_OptimisticConcurrency
        primary key nonclustered,
    Data int not null,
    RowVer uniqueidentifier not null
        constraint DEF_OptimisticConcurrency_RowVer
        default newid()
)
with (memory_optimized = on, durability = schema_only);

-- Reading data from the client
declare
    @Data int
    ,@OldRowVer uniqueidentifier

select @Data = Data, @OldRowVer = RowVer
from dbo.OptimisticConcurrency
where ID = @ID;

-- Saving data to the database
update dbo.OptimisticConcurrency
set
    Data = @NewData
    ,RowVer = newid()
where ID = @ID and RowVer = @OldRowVer;

if @@rowcount = 0
    raiserror('Row with ID: %d has been modified by other session',
        16,1,@ID);
```

Indexing Considerations

As I have already discussed in the book, an In-Memory OLTP indexing strategy and the choice between nonclustered (range) and hash indexes both greatly depend on the data and queries that utilize them. Nonclustered (range) indexes provide you with a similar experience as regular B-Tree indexes. They can be used in the same use cases, and they provide a comparable set of *SARGability* rules. The only exception is scanning an index in the opposite direction to the index sorting order. Nonclustered (range) indexes are unidirectional, and In-Memory OLTP is unable to utilize them for such scans.

Hash indexes, on the other hand, are useful only for point-lookup searches and equality joins when queries use the equality predicate on all index key columns. They may outperform range indexes in those scenarios assuming that they have a sufficient number of buckets in the hash table. However, an insufficient bucket_count value greatly affects their performance and makes the indexes inefficient.

You can use hash indexes as the primary keys in the catalog entities where the amount of data is relatively static and you can correctly estimate the number of bucket for the index. Those entities are often used in the equality joins, and a hash index can be very efficient in those scenarios. However, as the general rule, using range indexes is the safer choice, which simplifies In-Memory OLTP migration and also reduces maintenance overhead in the system.

There are a few other factors to consider. First, you should remember that indexes on memory-optimized tables point to the actual data row objects and are covering for in-row columns. They do not cover off-row columns, and In-Memory OLTP needs to perform actions conceptually similar to a Key Lookup operation to obtain off-row values. You should analyze the table structure and keep frequently selected columns in-row when you migrate a disk-based table into memory.

Second, you should try to minimize the number of indexes in the table similar to disk-based tables. Indexes add overhead during INSERT operations and slow down database recovery and the garbage collection processes. Moreover, In-Memory OLTP is using row versioning, and it creates a new version of the row every time you update it. Every extra index adds update overhead; In-Memory OLTP has to maintain the index row chains regardless of whether the index key columns were updated. This is different from disk-based B-Tree indexes, which stay intact unless you update index columns.

Let's look at the example and create memory-optimized and disk-based tables of the same structure and insert some data there. Both tables have two indexes and four columns, as shown in Listing 13-10.

Listing 13-10. Update Overhead: Tables Creation

```
create table dbo.MOTable
(
    Id int not null,
    IdxCol int not null,
    IntCol int not null,
    VarCharCol varchar(128) null,

    constraint PK_MOTable
    primary key nonclustered hash(Id)
    with (bucket_count = 2097152),

    index IDX_IdxCol nonclustered hash(IdxCol)
    with (bucket_count = 2097152),
)
with (memory_optimized=on, durability=schema_only);
```

```
create table dbo.DBTable
(
    Id int not null,
    IdxCol int not null,
    IntCol int not null,
    VarCharCol varchar(128) null,

    constraint PK_DBTable
    primary key clustered(Id)
);

create index IDX_DBTable_IdxCol on dbo.DBTable(IdxCol);

;with N1(C) as (select 0 union all select 0) -- 2 rows
,N2(C) as (select 0 from N1 as t1 cross join N1 as t2) -- 4 rows
,N3(C) as (select 0 from N2 as t1 cross join N2 as t2) -- 16 rows
,N4(C) as (select 0 from N3 as t1 cross join N3 as t2) -- 256 rows
,N5(C) as (select 0 from N4 as t1 cross join N4 as t2) -- 65,536 rows
,N6(C) as (select 0 from N5 as t1 cross join N3 as t2) -- 1,048,576 rows
,Ids(Id) as (select row_number() over (order by (select null)) from N6)
insert into dbo.MOTable(ID,IdxCol,IntCol)
    select Id, Id, Id from Ids;

insert into DBTable(Id, IdxCol, IntCol)
    select Id, IdxCol, IntCol from dbo.MOTable;
```

As the next step, let's run three UPDATE statements against each table, as shown in Listing 13-11. The first statement modifies the nonindexed fixed-length column. The second changes the value of the indexed fixed-length column. The last statement populates the empty variable-length column with a value, which increases the row size and triggers a large number of page splits in the disk-based table.

Listing 13-11. Update Overhead: Update Statements

```
update dbo.MOTable set IntCol += 1;
update dbo.MOTable set IdxCol += 1;
update dbo.MOTable set VarCharCol = replicate('a',128);

update dbo.DBTable set IntCol += 1;
update dbo.DBTable set IdxCol += 1;
update dbo.DBTable set VarCharCol = replicate('a',128);
```

Table 13-1 shows the execution time of the statements in my environment. As you can see, the execution time stays pretty much the same in the case of the memory-optimized table, and it depends on the number of indexes in the table. There is still index update overhead associated with index maintenance during the update of the index key column. In-Memory OLTP needs to calculate the hash bucket for the new index key value in hash indexes or find the new index key row chain in nonclustered indexes. This overhead, however, is relatively insignificant.

Table 13-1. *Execution Time of Update Statements*

	Memory-Optimized Table	Disk-Based Table
Update of nonindexed column	1,016 ms	1,879 ms
Update of indexed column	1,036 ms	4,586 ms
Update with row size increase	1,045 ms	3,906 ms

This is not the case with the disk-based tables where the update of the index key column leads to the update of the nonclustered index B-Tree structure. Similarly, increasing the size of the row leads to page splits. The Storage Engine has to allocate new data pages and move data there when the new versions of the rows do not fit into the original pages. This is a very expensive operation, which updates allocation map pages and leads to significant transaction log overhead.

Just to illustrate that update overhead depends on the number of indexes in a memory-optimized table, let's add another index to the table with the code from Listing 13-12.

Listing 13-12. Update Overhead: Adding Extra Index to Memory-Optimized Table

```
alter table dbo.MOTable
add index IDX_VarCharCol nonclustered(VarCharCol);
```

Table 13-2 illustrates the execution time of the update statements after creating the index. As you can see, adding an extra index adds overhead to the operation; however, all three statements take a similar amount of time.

Table 13-2. *Execution Time of Update Statements with New Index*

	Memory-Optimized Table
Update of nonindexed column	1,840 ms
Update of indexed column	1,900 ms
Update with row size increase	1,921 ms

It is beneficial to analyze the indexing strategy in a system, adjusting and redesigning it during migration. You can use the sys.dm_db_index_usage_stats and sys.dm_db_index_operational_stats data management views to obtain index usage statistics in the system. Remember that SQL Server does not persist these statistics at the time of restart. Moreover, some versions may clear them at the time of an index rebuild.

Finally, I will to discuss another SQL Server 2014 limitation, which has been removed in SQL Server 2016. As you may remember, the first release of In-Memory OLTP required you to use binary collations for the index key columns. In SQL Server 2014, this may become a breaking change in the system behavior because of the case-sensitiveness of the collation. However, in the grand scheme of things, binary collations have benefits. The comparison operations on the columns that store data in binary collations are much more efficient compared to nonbinary counterparts. You can achieve significant performance improvements when a large number of rows need to be processed.

One such example is a substring search in large tables. Consider the situation when you need to search by part of the product name in a large Products table. Unfortunately, a substring search will lead to the following predicate: WHERE ProductName LIKE '%' + @ Param + '%'. This is not *SARGable*, and SQL Server cannot use an Index Seek operation in such a scenario. The only option is to scan the data, evaluating every row in the table, which is significantly faster with binary collation.

Let's look at an example and create the table shown in Listing 13-13. The table has four text columns that store Unicode and non-Unicode data in binary and nonbinary formats. Finally, you populate it with 65,536 rows of random data.

Listing 13-13. Binary Collation Performance: Table Creation

```
create table dbo.CollationTest
(
    ID int not null,
    VarCol varchar(108) not null,
    NVarCol nvarchar(108) not null,
    VarColBin varchar(108)
        collate Latin1_General_100_BIN2 not null,
    NVarColBin nvarchar(108)
        collate Latin1_General_100_BIN2 not null,

    constraint PK_CollationTest
    primary key nonclustered hash(ID)
    with (bucket_count=131072)
)
with (memory_optimized=on, durability=schema_only);

create table #CollData
(
    ID int not null,
    Col1 uniqueidentifier not null
        default NEWID(),
    Col2 uniqueidentifier not null
        default NEWID(),
    Col3 uniqueidentifier not null
        default NEWID()
);
```

```
;with N1(C) as (select 0 union all select 0) -- 2 rows
,N2(C) as (select 0 from N1 as T1 cross join N1 as T2) -- 4 rows
,N3(C) as (select 0 from N2 as T1 cross join N2 as T2) -- 16 rows
,N4(C) as (select 0 from N3 as T1 cross join N3 as T2) -- 256 rows
,N5(C) as (select 0 from N4 as T1 cross join N4 as T2) -- 65,536 rows
,IDs(ID) as (select row_number() over (order by (select NULL)) from N5)
insert into #CollData(ID)
    select ID from IDs;

insert into dbo.CollationTest(ID,VarCol,NVarCol,VarColBin,NVarColBin)
    select
        ID
        /* VarCol */
        ,convert(varchar(36),Col1) + convert(varchar(36),Col2) +
        convert(varchar(36),Col3)
        /* NVarCol */
        ,convert(nvarchar(36),Col1) + convert(nvarchar(36),Col2) +
        convert(nvarchar(36),Col3)
        /* VarColBin */
        ,convert(varchar(36),Col1) + convert(varchar(36),Col2) +
        convert(varchar(36),Col3)
        /* NVarColBin */
        ,convert(nvarchar(36),Col1) + convert(nvarchar(36),Col2) +
        convert(nvarchar(36),Col3)
    from
        #CollData
```

As the next step, run the queries from Listing 13-14, comparing the performance of a search in different scenarios. All the queries scan the table varheap, evaluating the predicate for every row in the table.

Listing 13-14. Binary Collation Performance: Test Queries

```
declare
    @Param varchar(16)
    ,@NParam varchar(16)

-- Getting substring for the search
select
    @Param = substring(VarCol,43,6)
    ,@NParam = substring(NVarCol,43,6)
from
    dbo.CollationTest
where
    ID = 1000;
```

```
select count(*)
from dbo.CollationTest
where VarCol like '%' + @Param + '%';

select count(*)
from dbo.CollationTest
where NVarCol like '%' + @NParam + N'%';

select count(*)
from dbo.CollationTest
where VarColBin like '%' + upper(@Param) + '%'
          collate Latin1_General_100_Bin2;

select count(*)
from dbo.CollationTest
where NVarColBin like '%' + upper(@NParam) + N'%'
          collate Latin1_General_100_Bin2;
```

Table 13-3 shows the execution time of all queries in my system. As you can see, the queries against the binary collation columns are significantly faster, especially in the case of Unicode data.

Table 13-3. *Binary Collation Performace: Test Results*

Varchar Column with Nonbinary Collation	Varchar Column with Binary Collation	Nvarchar Column with Nonbinary Collation	Nvarchar Column with Binary Collation
135 ms	75 ms	624 ms	34 ms

Remember that binary collations are case-sensitive. You may want to create another binary collation column and store the copy of the data there, converting it to uppercase or lowercase when needed.

Finally, it is worth noting that this behavior is not limited to memory-optimized tables. You will get a similar level of performance improvement with disk-based tables when binary collations are used.

Maintainability and Management Overhead

In SQL Server 2014 and SQL Server 2016 RTM, In-Memory OLTP was included only in the Enterprise Edition of the product. Starting with SQL Server 2016 SP1, you can use In-Memory OLTP in every edition of SQL Server. It is also available in the premium tiers of Microsoft Azure SQL Databases. While this allows you to maintain a single architecture and code across multiple SQL Server editions, there is the hidden danger in this approach.

In-Memory OLTP is hardly a "set it and forget it" type of technology. Database professionals should actively participate in system monitoring and maintenance after deployment. They need to monitor system memory usage, analyze data, re-create hash indexes if the bucket counts need to be adjusted, recompile natively compiled modules to address data distribution and statistic changes, and perform other tasks as well.

The memory usage monitoring is, perhaps, the most important task. In-Memory OLTP consumes system memory, which may affect the performance of the other SQL Server components. For example, a large amount of data in memory-optimized tables may reduce the size of the buffer pool, which will increase physical I/O and reduce query performance against disk-based tables. Similarly, it may reduce the size of the plan cache, which will lead to recompilations and increase CPU load in the system. Ironically, in the Standard Edition, 32GB of memory-optimized data would not affect buffer pool memory when the server has enough RAM to accommodate both of them.

You should also remember that data in memory-optimized tables will become read-only if In-Memory OLTP does not have enough memory to proceed. This may lead to prolonged system outages, especially in non-Enterprise instances of SQL Server. You cannot address the issue by adding more memory and exceeding the edition limit. The only option is to reduce the amount of data in memory-optimized tables.

■ **Important**   Abandoned uncommitted transactions may defer the garbage collection process and lead to out-of-memory conditions in the system.

You should also consider In-Memory OLTP memory usage when you design a high availability strategy in your system. It is not uncommon to have the implementations with secondary nodes be less powerful than the primary ones. This decreases the implementation cost of the solution and may provide a required high availability even though the system would operate with a reduced performance after failover.

The situation changes if secondary nodes do not have enough memory to accommodate In-Memory OLTP data. This will break the synchronization between the nodes and may affect the availability of the system.

The cross-edition support of the technology in SQL Server 2016 SP1 and above allows you to architect the system once and upgrade editions as the amount of data and the load increase. It is not targeted for independent software vendors who develop products that need be deployed to a large number of customers who may or may not have DBA teams to support the system. In-Memory OLTP is not the best choice in that scenario.

Using In-Memory OLTP in Systems with Mixed Workloads

In-Memory OLTP can provide significant performance improvements in OLTP systems. However, with data warehouse workloads, the results may vary. The memory-optimized columnstore indexes may help to improve the performance of some data warehouse and operational analytics queries; however, memory-optimized columnstore indexes still have plenty of limitations compared to disk-based column-based storage.

When you run a query against a memory-optimized columnstore index, In-Memory OLTP has to perform a scan of all the index row groups. Even though SQL Server may skip some of the row groups based on segment metadata, you should not rely on that behavior.

By contrast, disk-based columnstore indexes may be partitioned, and entire partitions can be eliminated from the scan. This may significantly reduce the amount of data to process when a system has a long data retention policy and queries work with just subset of the data.

Keeping the *old* data in memory-optimized tables also negatively affects the performance of OLTP queries. It increases the length and slows down the scans of the index row chains. More importantly, it will consume SQL Server memory. Even though memory is relatively cheap nowadays, NUMA servers partition the memory on a per-socket basis, and in some cases, you will have to add more CPUs to utilize the memory. This may require you to license them, which is expensive.

Finally, there is another, less obvious aspect of the problem. Different data in the system may have different availability requirements. For example, current *hot* data may have a 99.99 percent or higher SLA in the mission-critical systems, while the availability requirements for the old *cold* data may be significantly lower.

The Enterprise Edition of SQL Server allows you to utilize *piecemeal restore*, bringing the database online on a per-filegroup basis. This can significantly reduce the downtime in the case of a disaster. However, a piecemeal restore requires the In-Memory OLTP filegroup to be online for the database to become partially available. Keeping a large amount of old *cold* data in-memory would slow down the recovery process.

It is often beneficial to build separate data warehouse environments to handle analysis and reporting for the system. However, there are still many cases when systems need to retain data for a long time and support mixed OLTP and data warehouse workloads against the same data. Moving the data completely into memory is usually not the best option, especially when you expect the amount of data grow over time.

One of the solutions in this scenario is to partition the data between memory-optimized and disk-based tables. You can put recent *hot* data into memory-optimized tables, keeping old *cold* data disk-based. This allows you to create a different set of indexes and utilize different technologies based on workload, obtaining the biggest performance gain and reducing the size of the data on disk.

Figure 13-2 shows an example of the architecture that partitions data in the system. Obviously, the criteria for partitioning should depend on the system workload and other requirements.

Figure 13-2. *Example of data partitioning*

The *hot operational* data is stored in memory-optimized tables. This data is customer-facing, and it handles the majority of OLTP activity in the system. The *warm* data for several previous operational periods could be stored in disk-based B-Tree tables. There is usually some degree of OLTP and data warehouse workload against such data.

The *cold historical* data mainly handles data warehouse workloads. It may be stored in the tables with clustered columnstore indexes, potentially with COLUMNSTORE_ARCHIVE compression. It is also possible to create nonclustered B-Tree indexes on such tables if you need to support OLTP use cases. Finally, if the data is static, it is beneficial to put it in a read-only filegroup and exclude it from the regular FULL database backups.

Let's look at an example of such an implementation and assume that you have an imaginary order entry system where the majority of OLTP transactions occur for the current month's data. Figure 13-3 shows the data partitioning that may exist in the system as of June 2017.

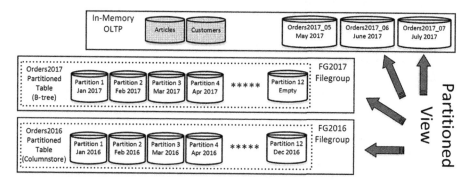

Figure 13-3. *Order entry system: data partitioning*

The *hot* data for the current (June 2017), previous (May 2017), and next (July 2017) operation periods are stored in the memory-optimized tables. The *warm* data from January to April 2017 is stored in a B-Tree table on the FG2017 filegroup. Lastly, the *cold* data for 2016 is stored in the table with the clustered columnstore index on the FG2016 filegroup. The catalog entities, such as Articles and Customers, are implemented as memory-optimized tables, which will allow you to utilize native compilation when you are working with the *hot* orders.

It is also beneficial to partition disk-based tables according to operational periods. This will help to manage data movement between the tables when the period changes. You will see this shortly.

Listing 13-15 illustrates this implementation. I am omitting the dbo.Orders2017_07 table to save the space in the book. However, you should always have the table for the next (future) operational period to avoid downtime in the system.

Listing 13-15. Data Partitioning: Object Creation

```
create table dbo.Customers
(
    CustomerId int not null
        constraint PK_Customers
        primary key nonclustered hash
        with (bucket_count=65536),
    Name nvarchar(256) not null,

    index IDX_Customers_Name nonclustered(Name)
)
with (memory_optimized=on, durability=schema_and_data);

-- Storing data for 2017_06
create table dbo.Orders2017_06
(
    OrderId bigint identity(1,1) not null,
    OrderDate datetime2(0) not null,
    CustomerId int not null,
    Amount money not null,
    Status tinyint not null,

    /* Other columns */
    constraint PK_Orders2017_06
    primary key nonclustered (OrderId),

    index IDX_Orders2017_06_CustomerId
    nonclustered hash(CustomerId)
    with (bucket_count=65536),

    constraint CHK_Orders2017_06
    check (OrderDate >= '2017-06-01' and OrderDate < '2017-07-01'),

    constraint FK_Orders2017_06_Customers
    foreign key(CustomerId)
    references dbo.Customers(CustomerId)
)
with (memory_optimized=on, durability=schema_and_data);

-- Storing data for 2017_05
create table dbo.Orders2017_05
(
    OrderId bigint identity(1,1) not null,
    OrderDate datetime2(0) not null,
    CustomerId int not null,
    Amount money not null,
    Status tinyint not null,
```

```
    /* Other columns */
    constraint PK_Orders2017_05
    primary key nonclustered (OrderId),

    index IDX_Orders2017_05_CustomerId
    nonclustered hash(CustomerId)
    with (bucket_count=65536),

    constraint CHK_Orders2017_05
    check (OrderDate >= '2017-05-01' and OrderDate < '2017-06-01'),

    constraint FK_Orders2017_05_Customers
    foreign key(CustomerId)
    references dbo.Customers(CustomerId)
)
with (memory_optimized=on, durability=schema_and_data);
go

create partition function pf2017(datetime2(0))
as range right for values
('2017-02-01','2017-03-01','2017-04-01','2017-05-01','2017-06-01','2017-07-01'
,'2017-08-01','2017-09-01','2017-10-01','2017-11-01','2017-12-01','2018-01-01');
go

create partition scheme ps2017
as partition pf2017
all to ([FG2017]);
go

-- Storing data for 2017
create table dbo.Orders2017
(
    OrderId bigint not null,
    OrderDate datetime2(0) not null,
    CustomerId int not null,
    Amount money not null,
    Status tinyint not null,

    constraint CHK_Order2017_01_05 check (OrderDate >= '2017-01-01' and
OrderDate < '2017-05-01'),
    constraint CHK_Order2017_01_06 check (OrderDate >= '2017-01-01' and
OrderDate < '2017-06-01'),
    constraint CHK_Order2017_01_07 check (OrderDate >= '2017-01-01' and
OrderDate < '2017-07-01'),
    constraint CHK_Order2017_01_08 check (OrderDate >= '2017-01-01' and
OrderDate < '2017-08-01'),
```

```
    constraint CHK_Order2017_01_09 check (OrderDate >= '2017-01-01' and
OrderDate < '2017-09-01'),
    constraint CHK_Order2017_01_10 check (OrderDate >= '2017-01-01' and
OrderDate < '2017-10-01'),
    constraint CHK_Order2017_01_11 check (OrderDate >= '2017-01-01' and
OrderDate < '2017-11-01'),
    constraint CHK_Order2017_01_12 check (OrderDate >= '2017-01-01' and
OrderDate < '2017-12-01'),
    constraint CHK_Order2017 check (OrderDate >= '2017-01-01' and OrderDate
< '2018-01-01')
);

create unique clustered index IDX_Orders2017_OrderDate_OrderId
on dbo.Orders2017(OrderDate, OrderId)
with (data_compression=row)
on ps2017(OrderDate);

create nonclustered index IDX_Orders2017_CustomerId
on  dbo.Orders2017(CustomerId)
with (data_compression=row)
on ps2017(OrderDate);

create nonclustered index IDX_Orders2017_OrderId
on  dbo.Orders2017(OrderId)
with (data_compression=row)
on ps2017(OrderDate);
go

create partition function pf2016(datetime2(0))
as range right for values
('2016-02-01','2016-03-01','2016-04-01','2016-05-01','2016-06-01','2016-07-01'
,'2016-08-01','2016-09-01','2016-10-01','2016-11-01','2016-12-01','2017-01-01');
go

create partition scheme ps2016
as partition pf2016
all to ([FG2016]);
go

create table dbo.Orders2016
(
    OrderDate datetime2(0) not null,
    OrderId bigint not null,
    CustomerId int not null,
    Amount money not null,
    Status tinyint not null,
```

```
    constraint CHK_Order2016 check (OrderDate >= '2016-01-01' and OrderDate
< '2017-01-01'),
)
on ps2016(OrderDate);

create clustered columnstore index CCI_Orders2016
on dbo.Orders2016
with (data_compression=columnstore_archive)
on ps2016(OrderDate);

create nonclustered index IDX_Orders2016_CustomerId
on  dbo.Orders2016(CustomerId)
include(Amount)
with (data_compression=row)
on ps2016(OrderDate);
go

create view dbo.Orders(OrderDate, OrderId, CustomerId, Amount, Status)
as
    select OrderDate, OrderId, CustomerId, Amount, Status
    from dbo.Orders2017_06

    union all

    select OrderDate, OrderId, CustomerId, Amount, Status
    from dbo.Orders2017_05

    union all

    select OrderDate, OrderId, CustomerId, Amount, Status
    from dbo.Orders2017

    union all

    select OrderDate, OrderId, CustomerId, Amount, Status
    from dbo.Orders2016;
```

You can hide implementation details from read-only reporting queries by implementing a partitioned view that combines data from all the tables there. *Each table should have the* CHECK *constraint that indicates what data is stored in the table.* This will allow SQL Server to skip processing unnecessary tables when you reference a view in the queries. Do not focus on multiple CHECK constraints in the dbo.Orders2017 table now; I will explain the need for them later.

Listing 13-16 illustrates several queries against a partition view.

Listing 13-16. Data Partitioning: Querying Partitioned View

```
select count(*)
from dbo.Orders
where OrderDate between '2017-06-02' and '2017-06-03';

select count(*)
from dbo.Orders
where OrderDate >= '2017-01-01';

select count(*) from dbo.Orders;
```

Figure 13-4 shows the execution plans for the queries. As you can see, SQL Server is able to eliminate the scan of unnecessary tables during query execution.

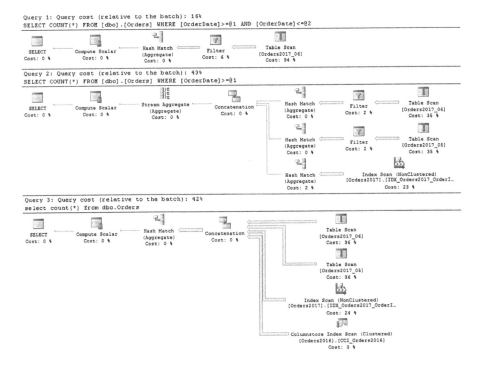

Figure 13-4. *Execution plan of the query*

As you have probably noticed, the memory-optimized tables define an `OrderId` column as `identity(1,1)`. In-Memory OLTP requires you to use a `SEED` value of 1 when you define the identity column. Fortunately, you can re-seed it and enforce key uniqueness by implementing `identity_insert` of the dummy row immediately after table creation.

Listing 13-17 shows this approach. It assumes that the system handles fewer than 100,000,000 new orders per month.

Listing 13-17. Data Partitioning: Changing Identity SEED Property

```
set identity_insert dbo.Orders2017_06 on

insert into dbo.Orders2017_06(OrderDate, OrderId, CustomerId, Amount, Status)
values('2017-06-01',201706000000000,1,1,1);

delete from dbo.Orders2017_06;

set identity_insert dbo.Orders2017_06 off;
```

As with any multitable data partitioning implementation, you should support the data migration across the tables. As time goes on, the orders need to be moved from memory-optimized to disk-based tables.

It is possible to use an INSERT..SELECT approach; however, the statement would move the *snapshot* of the data taken when the transaction started. You will subsequently need to move the data changes that occur during and after the statement execution. You can capture those changes by defining triggers on the memory-optimized tables.

Let's look at an example of data movement assuming that you want to move the last-month (May 2017) data to a disk-based table. Listing 13-18 shows the first step in the process, which inserts data into the separate disk-based staging table to avoid data duplication in the system. This also creates two tables to keep the OrderId values of updated and deleted rows using the triggers to populate them (I am assuming that there are no inserts into the last-month table).

Listing 13-18. Data Movement: Step 1

```
create table dbo.Orders2017_05_Tmp
(
    OrderId bigint not null,
    OrderDate datetime2(0) not null,
    CustomerId int not null,
    Amount money not null,
    Status tinyint not null,

    check (OrderDate >= '2017-05-01' and OrderDate < '2017-06-01')
)
on [FG2017];

create unique clustered index IDX_Orders2017_05_Tmp_OrderDate_OrderId
on dbo.Orders2017_05_Tmp(OrderDate, OrderId)
with (data_compression=row)
on [FG2017];
```

```
create nonclustered index IDX_Orders2017_05_Tmp_CustomerId
on  dbo.Orders2017_05_Tmp(CustomerId)
with (data_compression=row)
on [FG2017];

create nonclustered index IDX_Orders2017_05_Tmp_OrderId
on  dbo.Orders2017_05_Tmp(OrderId)
with (data_compression=row)
on [FG2017]
go

create table dbo.OrdersUpdateQueue
(
    ID int not null identity(1,1)
        constraint PK_OrdersUpdateQueue
        primary key nonclustered hash
        with (bucket_count=262144),
    OrderId bigint not null,
)
with (memory_optimized=on, durability=schema_and_data)
go

create table dbo.OrdersDeleteQueue
(
    ID int not null identity(1,1)
        constraint PK_OrdersDeleteQueue
        primary key nonclustered hash
        with (bucket_count=262144),
    OrderId bigint not null
)
with (memory_optimized=on, durability=schema_and_data)
go

create trigger trgAfterUpdate on dbo.Orders2017_05
with native_compilation, schemabinding
after update
as
begin atomic with
(
    transaction isolation level = snapshot
    ,language = N'English'
)
    insert into dbo.OrdersUpdateQueue(OrderId)
        select OrderId from inserted;
end
go
```

```
create trigger trgAfterDelete on dbo.Orders2017_05
with native_compilation, schemabinding
after delete
as
begin atomic with
(
    transaction isolation level = snapshot
    ,language = N'English'
)
    insert into dbo.OrdersDeleteQueue(OrderId)
        select OrderId from deleted;
end
go

-- Step 1: Copy data to the staging table
insert into dbo.Orders2017_05_Tmp(OrderDate, OrderId, CustomerId, Amount,
Status)
    select OrderDate, OrderId, CustomerId, Amount, Status
    from dbo.Orders2017_05 with (snapshot);
```

The OrderId of the rows that were updated and deleted during the INSERT..SELECT execution are stored in the dbo.OrdersUpdateQueue and dbo.OrdersDeleteQueue tables. You can apply those data modifications to the staging table by using the code from Listing 13-19. Depending on the volatility of the data in your system, you may need to run it several times until the tables are almost empty.

Listing 13-19. Data Movement: Step 2

```
declare
    @MaxUpdateId int
    ,@MaxDeleteId int

select @MaxUpdateId = max(ID)
from dbo.OrdersUpdateQueue with (snapshot);

select @MaxDeleteId = max(ID)
from dbo.OrdersDeleteQueue with (snapshot);

begin tran
    if @MaxUpdateId is not null
    begin
        update t
        set t.Amount = s.Amount, t.Status = s.Status
        from
            dbo.OrdersUpdateQueue q with (snapshot) join
                dbo.Orders2017_05 s with (snapshot) on
                    q.OrderId = s.OrderId
```

```
        join dbo.Orders2017_05_Tmp t on
                t.OrderId = s.OrderId
    where
        q.ID <= @MaxUpdateId;

    delete from dbo.OrdersUpdateQueue with (snapshot)
        where ID <= @MaxUpdateId;
end;

if @MaxDeleteId is not null
begin
    delete from t
    from
        dbo.OrdersDeleteQueue q with (snapshot) join
            dbo.Orders2017_05_Tmp t on
                t.OrderId = q.OrderId
    where
        q.ID <= @MaxDeleteId;

    delete from dbo.OrdersDeleteQueue with (snapshot)
        where ID <= @MaxDeleteId;
end
commit;
```

Finally, you need to drop the dbo.Orders2017_05 table, switch the staging table as the partition to the dbo.Orders2017 table, and change the partition view. You should prevent client access to the May 2017 data during those operations. Fortunately, the duration of the downtime will be very short; both update and delete queue tables are almost empty, and other operations will be done on the metadata level, as shown in Listing 13-20.

■ **Note** If you access the data in the dbo.Orders2017_05 table through the T-SQL (interop) stored procedures, you can alter them at the beginning of the transaction and obtain a schema modification (Sch-M) lock on them. This will block clients from calling stored procedures until a transaction is committed.

Listing 13-20. Data Movement: Final Step

```
-- Disconnect clients before running those steps.
-- Alternatively, if the Data Access Tier uses Interop
-- stored procedures, you can start the transaction and
-- alter SPs before the updates. This will block clients
-- from calling those SPs.
```

```
update t
set t.Amount = s.Amount, t.Status = s.Status
from
    dbo.OrdersUpdateQueue q with (snapshot)
        join dbo.Orders2017_05 s with (snapshot) on
            q.OrderId = s.OrderId
    join dbo.Orders2017_05_Tmp t on
            t.OrderId = s.OrderId;

delete from t
from
    dbo.OrdersDeleteQueue q with (snapshot) join
        dbo.Orders2017_05_Tmp t on
            t.OrderId = q.OrderId;

alter table dbo.Orders2017
    drop constraint CHK_Order2017_01_05
go

alter table dbo.Orders2017_05_Tmp
switch to dbo.Orders2017 partition 5
go

alter view dbo.Orders(OrderDate, OrderId, CustomerId, Amount, Status)
as
    select OrderDate, OrderId, CustomerId, Amount, Status
    from dbo.Orders2017_06

    union all

    select OrderDate, OrderId, CustomerId, Amount, Status
    from dbo.Orders2017

    union all

    select OrderDate, OrderId, CustomerId, Amount, Status
    from dbo.Orders2016
go

drop table dbo.Orders2017_05;
```

One of the things you need to do during this process is change the CHECK constraints on the dbo.Orders2017 table indicating that the table stores May 2017 data now. Unfortunately, SQL Server always scans one of the indexes in the table to validate new CHECK constraints, holding the schema modification (SCH-M) lock and preventing access to the table during the scan.

One of the ways to address such a problem is by creating multiple CHECK constraints—one constraint per month—as part of the CREATE TABLE statement. Every time you move another month data into the table, you are dropping a constraint, which is a metadata operation, rather than creating a new one. SQL Server evaluates all constraints during optimization and picks the most restrictive one. This is the reason why you created nine CHECK constraints in the dbo.Orders2017 table in Listing 13-15.

■ **Note**   You can look at a more comprehensive and detailed version of the code in the companion materials of the book.

While implementing data partitioning requires additional effort, it pays off in the long run. It allows you to utilize the best technologies for each workload, simplifies database administration and maintenance, improves system availability, and helps to reduce the hardware and storage costs. Consider implementing it when you expect to store a large amount of data in the system.

■ **Note**   My *Pro SQL Server Internals* book includes a detailed chapter about data partitioning. It shows how to implement tiered storage and move data between different tables and filegroups while keeping it transparent to the users.

Thinking Outside the In-Memory Box

You can benefit from In-Memory OLTP even without fully utilizing the technology and migrating the data into memory. Let's look at several examples.

Importing Batches of Rows from Client Applications

In Chapter 13 of my book *Pro SQL Server Internals*, I compare the performance of several methods that inserted a batch of rows from the client application into the database. I looked at the performance of calling individual INSERT statements, encoding the data into XML and JSON and passing it to a stored procedure, using the .NET SqlBulkCopy class, and passing the data to a stored procedure utilizing table-valued parameters. Table-valued parameters became the clear winner of the tests, providing performance on par with the SqlBulkCopy implementation plus the flexibility of using stored procedures during the import.

Listing 13-21 illustrates the database schema and stored procedure I used in the tests.

Listing 13-21. Importing a Batch of Rows: Table, TVP, and Stored Procedure

```
create table dbo.Data
(
    ID int not null,
    Col1 varchar(20) not null,
    Col2 varchar(20) not null,
    /* Seventeen more columns Col3 - Col19*/
    Col20 varchar(20) not null,

    constraint PK_DataRecords
    primary key clustered(ID)
)
go

create type dbo.tvpData as table
(
    ID int not null,
    Col1 varchar(20) not null,
    Col2 varchar(20) not null,
    /* Seventeen more columns: Col3 - Col19 */
    Col20 varchar(20) not null,

    primary key(ID)
)
go

create proc dbo.InsertDataTVP
(
    @Data dbo.tvpData readonly
)
as
    insert into dbo.Data
    (
        ID,Col1,Col2,Col3,Col4,Col5,Col6,Col7
        ,Col8,Col9,Col10,Col11,Col12,Col13,Col14
        ,Col15,Col16,Col17,Col18,Col19,Col20
    )
        select ID,Col1,Col2,Col3,Col4,Col5,Col6
            ,Col7,Col8,Col9,Col10,Col11,Col12
            ,Col13,Col14,Col15,Col16,Col17,Col18
            ,Col19,Col20
        from @Data;
```

Listing 13-22 shows the ADO.NET code that performed the import in the case of a table-valued parameter.

Listing 13-22. Importing a Batch of Rows: Client Code

```
using (SqlConnection conn = GetConnection())
{
    /* Creating and populating DataTable object with dummy data */
    DataTable table = new DataTable();
    table.Columns.Add("ID", typeof(Int32));
    for (int i = 1; i <= 20; i++)
        table.Columns.Add("Col" + i.ToString(), typeof(string));
    for (int i = 0; i < packetSize; i++)
        table.Rows.Add(i, "Parameter: 1"
            ,"Parameter: 2"
            /* Other columns */
            ,"Parameter: 20");

    /* Calling SP with TVP parameter */
    SqlCommand insertCmd =
        new SqlCommand("dbo.InsertDataTVP", conn);
    insertCmd.Parameters.Add("@Data", SqlDbType.Structured);
    insertCmd.Parameters[0].TypeName = "dbo.tvpData";
    insertCmd.Parameters[0].Value = table;
    insertCmd.ExecuteNonQuery();
}
```

You can improve performance even further by making the dbo.tvpData table type memory-optimized, which is transparent to the stored procedure and client code. Listing 13-23 shows the new type definition.

Listing 13-23. Importing a Batch of Rows: Defining a Memory-Optimized Table Type

```
create type dbo.tvpData as table
(
    ID int not null,
    Col1 varchar(20) not null,
    Col2 varchar(20) not null,
    /* Seventeen more columns: Col3 - Col19 */
    Col20 varchar(20) not null,

    primary key nonclustered hash(ID)
    with (bucket_count=65536)
)
with (memory_optimized=on);
```

The degree of performance improvement depends on the table schema, and it grows with the size of the batch. In my test environment, I got about 5 to 10 percent improvement on the small 5,000-row batches, 20 to 25 percent improvement on the 50,000-row batches, and 45 to 50 percent improvement on the 500,000-row batches.

Moreover, memory-optimized tables do not utilize tempdb, which may reduce tempdb page allocation contention (PAGELATCH waits) on very busy systems and improve performance even further. They, however, cannot spill to tempdb, which can be dangerous in the case of very large batches and with servers with an insufficient amount of memory. You should also define the bucket_count value for the indexes based on a typical batch size, as discussed in Chapter 4 of this book.

■ **Note** You can download the test application from this book's companion materials and compare the performance of the various import methods.

Using Memory-Optimized Objects as Replacements for Temporary and Staging Tables

Memory-optimized tables and table variables can be used as replacements for disk-based temporary and staging tables. However, the level of performance improvement may vary, and it greatly depends on the table schema, workload patterns, and amount of data in the table.

Let's look at a few examples and first compare the performance of a memory-optimized table variable with disk-based temporary objects in a simple scenario that you will often encounter in OLTP systems. Listing 13-24 shows stored procedures that insert up to 256 rows into an object, scanning it afterward.

Listing 13-24. Comparing Performance of a Memory-Optimized Table Variable with Disk-Based Temporary Objects

```
create table dbo.TestRows
(
    Id int not null
        primary key nonclustered hash
        with (bucket_count=512),
)
with (memory_optimized=on, durability=schema_only)
go

;with N1(C) as (select 0 union all select 0) -- 2 rows
,N2(C) as (select 0 from N1 as t1 cross join N1 as t2) -- 4 rows
,N3(C) as (select 0 from N2 as t1 cross join N2 as t2) -- 16 rows
,N4(C) as (select 0 from N3 as t1 cross join N3 as t2) -- 256 rows
,Ids(Id) as (select row_number() over (order by (select null)) from N4)
insert into dbo.TestRows(Id)
    select Id from Ids;
go
```

```
create type dbo.InMemTV as table
(
    Id int not null
        primary key nonclustered hash
        with (bucket_count=512),
    Placeholder char(255)
)
with (memory_optimized=on)
go

create proc dbo.TestInMemTempTables(@Rows int)
as
    declare
        @ttTemp dbo.InMemTV
        ,@Cnt int

    insert into @ttTemp(Id)
        select Id
        from dbo.TestRows with (snapshot)
        where Id <= @Rows;

    select @Cnt = count(*) from @ttTemp;
go

create proc dbo.TestTempTables(@Rows int)
as
    declare
        @Cnt int

    create table #TTTemp
    (
        Id int not null primary key,
        Placeholder char(255)
    )

    insert into #TTTemp    (Id)
        select Id
        from dbo.TestRows with (snapshot)
        where Id <= @Rows;

    select @Cnt = count(*) from #TTTemp;
go

create proc dbo.TestTempVars(@Rows int)
as
    declare
        @Cnt int
```

```
declare
    @ttTemp table
    (
        Id int not null primary key,
        Placeholder char(255)
    )

insert into @ttTemp(Id)
    select Id
    from dbo.TestRows with (snapshot)
    where Id <= @Rows;

select @Cnt = count(*) from @ttTemp;
```

Table 13-4 illustrates the execution time of the stored procedures called 10,000 times in the loop. I ran the tests in two environments, using Intel i7-4770HQ and AMD Opteron 6328 CPUs. As you can see, the memory-optimized table variable outperformed disk-based objects even in the system with a very fast PCI-e SSD drive. The level of performance improvements grew with the amount of data when the disk-based tables needed to allocate more data pages to store the data. This is also a good example that demonstrates that In-Memory OLTP is usually CPU-bound and benefits from the faster single-threaded performance provided by an Intel CPU.

Table 13-4. *Execution Time of Stored Procedures (10,000 Executions)*

	16 Rows	64 Rows	256 Rows
Memory-Optimized Table Variable (i7-4770HQ)	843 ms	1,016 ms	1,850 ms
Memory-Optimized Table Variable (AMD Opteron 6328)	980 ms	1,360 ms	2,617 ms
Table Variable	1,450 ms	3,054 ms	8,390 ms
Temporary Table	6,267 ms	8,020 ms	12,546 ms

It is also worth mentioning that performance improvements can be even more significant in systems with heavy concurrent tempdb loads because of the possible allocation maps contention.

You should remember that memory-optimized table variables do not keep index statistics, similar to disk-based table variables. The Query Optimizer generates execution plans with the assumption that they store just a single row. This cardinality estimation error can lead to highly inefficient plans, especially when with a large amount of data and joins.

Similar to disk-based table variables, the statement-level recompile with OPTION (RECOMPILE) allows the Query Optimizer to obtain a number of rows in memory-optimized table variables. It does not provide the information about data distribution, however, because of the missing statistics histogram. This behavior may lead to inefficient execution plans even with a statement-level recompile involved.

Let's look at an example of cardinality estimations with and without a statement-level recompile by using the code from Listing 13-25.

Listing 13-25. Memory-Optimized Table Variables and Statement-Level Recompile

```
declare
        @InMemTV dbo.InMemTV;

insert into @InMemTV(Id)
        select Id from dbo.TestRows with (snapshot);

select count(*) from @InMemTV;
select count(*) from @InMemTV option (recompile);
select count(*) from @InMemTV where ID > 0 option (recompile);
```

You can see the cardinality estimations for the Index Scan and Filter operators in Figure 13-5. Without a statement-level recompile, SQL Server assumed that the memory-optimized table variable has just a single row. The statement-level recompile allowed SQL Server to obtain the information about the number of rows in the table. However, there is no information about data distribution in the table, and adding the where clause led to the cardinality estimation error. This behavior matches the behavior of disk-based table variables.

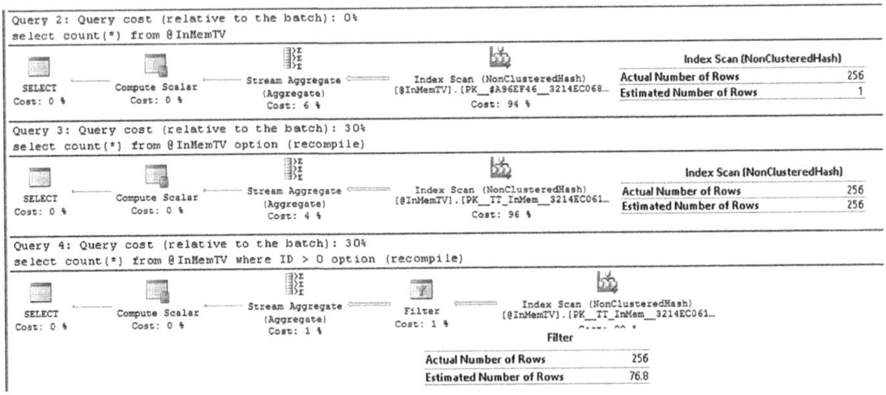

Figure 13-5. *Memory-optimized table variables and cardinality estimations*

Memory-optimized tables can be used as the staging area for ETL processes. As a general rule, they outperform disk-based tables in INSERT performance, especially if the process imports the data from the multiple sources in parallel. The lock- and latch-free nature of memory-optimized tables will eliminate latch contention and will provide a significant increase of insert throughput. You already saw a similar example in Chapter 2 of the book.

In-Memory OLTP will also reduce I/O and transaction log overhead. Moreover, in the case of nondurable memory-optimized tables, it will eliminate all disk and transaction log activity generated by the staging tables.

The data modification overhead is different between technologies. As you already know, with memory-optimized tables, the UPDATE overhead depends on the number of indexes in the table. With disk-based tables, it depends on what columns were updated and the number of page splits it generated.

Scan performance, on the other hand, greatly depends on the use case. In SQL Server 2014, In-Memory OLTP did not support parallelism and varheap scans, which greatly affected scan performance. Traversing memory pointers is a fast operation, and it is significantly faster compared to getting a page from the buffer pool. However, on-page row access could be faster than traversing long memory pointer chains. In SQL Server 2014, it was possible that with the small data rows and large number of rows per page, disk-based tables outperformed memory-optimized tables during the scans, especially with the parallel execution plans for the queries.

Fortunately, both limitations have been removed in SQL Server 2016, and in the majority of the cases, memory-optimized table scans would outperform B-Tree disk-based tables. Nevertheless, the results may vary based on the data, hardware, and ETL logic.

You should also remember that parallelism and varheaps scans are supported only in query interop mode. You should compare the performance of natively compiled code responsible for ETL logic with the interop T-SQL implementation. Those limitations may offset the performance benefits provided by native compilation and make the interop approach more efficient in the case of large scans and complex ETL transformations.

With all that being said, you can achieve the best results by adjusting ETL processes to In-Memory OLTP. Consider the situation when you need to import data to a data warehouse using many flat files as the source. In-Memory OLTP will allow you to perform the import from multiple files in parallel without any latch contention overhead. Moreover, you can achieve better results by performing the processing and transformation of the data using large batches rather than doing it on per-file basis.

■ **Tip** Consider using a separate staging database when you utilize In-Memory OLTP for ETL processes. This will allow you to avoid creating an In-Memory OLTP filegroup with checkpoint files in the main database.

Using In-Memory OLTP as Session or Object State Store

Modern software systems have become extremely complex. They consist of a large number of components and services responsible for various tasks, such as interaction with users, data processing, integration with other systems, reporting, and quite a few others. They must be scalable and redundant, they need to be able to handle load growth, and they need to be able to survive hardware failures and crashes.

A common approach to solving scalability and redundancy issues is to design the systems in a way that permits you to deploy and run multiple instances of individual services. This allows you to add more servers and instances as the load grows and helps you survive hardware failures by distributing the load across other active servers. The services are usually implemented in a stateless way, and they don't store or rely on any local data.

Most systems, however, have data that needs to be shared across instances. For example, front-end web servers usually need to maintain web session states. Back-end processing services often need to have a shared cache with some data.

Historically, there were two approaches to address this issue. The first one was to use a dedicated storage/cache and host it somewhere in the system. Remember the old ASP.NET model that used either a SQL Server database or a separate web server to store session data? The problem with this approach was limited scalability and redundancy. Storing session data in web server memory is fast, but it is not redundant. A SQL Server database, on the other hand, can be protected, but it does not scale well under the load because of page latch contention and other issues.

Another approach was to replicate the content of the cache across multiple servers. Each instance worked with a local copy of the cache, while another background process distributed the changes to the other servers. Several solutions on the market provide such a capability; some are open source, and others are commercial products.

If your system is using SQL Server as the database back end, you have an option of utilizing In-Memory OLTP as the session or object store in your system. This may not necessarily be the best option because of the extra load it adds to SQL Server; however, it may be one of the simplest approaches, especially if SQL Server has enough extra bandwidth to handle the load.

In the nutshell, it looks similar to the ASP.NET SQL Server session-store model; however, In-Memory OLTP throughput and performance improvements address the scalability issues of the old disk-based solution. You can improve the performance even further by using nondurable memory-optimized tables. Even though the data will be lost when there is failover, this is acceptable in many cases.

Listing 13-26 shows the table and natively compiled stored procedures that you can use to store and manipulate the data in the database. The client application calls the LoadObjectFromStore and SaveObjectToStore stored procedures to load and save the data. The PurgeExpiredObjects stored procedure removes expired rows from the table, and it can be called from a SQL Agent or other process based on the schedule.

The serialized object data is stored in a varbinary(max) column. You can achieve slightly better performance by using an in-row varbinary(8000) data type if your objects will not exceed 8,000 bytes. Alternatively, you can use separate tables for large and small objects if needed. Consider, however, the development and maintenance overhead and the possibility of future object growth; it is entirely possible that the small performance improvements gained by eliminating the off-row internal table is not worth the effort.

Listing 13-26. Implementing Session Store: Database Schema

```
create table dbo.ObjStore
(
    ObjectKey uniqueidentifier not null,
    ExpirationTime datetime2(2) not null,
    Data varbinary(max) not null,
```

```
    constraint PK_ObjStore
    primary key nonclustered hash(ObjectKey)
    with (bucket_count = 131072),
)
with (memory_optimized = on, durability = schema_only);

create proc dbo.SaveObjectToStore
(
    @ObjectKey uniqueidentifier
    ,@ExpirationTime datetime2(2)
    ,@Data varbinary(max)
)
with native_compilation, schemabinding, exec as owner
as
begin atomic with
(
    transaction isolation level = snapshot
    ,language = N'English'
)
    -- @ObjectKeys are randomly generated and unique across
    -- multiple sessions
    update dbo.ObjStore
    set Data = @Data, ExpirationTime = @ExpirationTime
    where ObjectKey = @ObjectKey;

    if (@@rowcount = 0)
        insert into dbo.ObjStore(ObjectKey, ExpirationTime, Data)
        values(@ObjectKey, @ExpirationTime, @Data)
end;

create proc dbo.LoadObjectFromStore
(
    @ObjectKey uniqueidentifier not null
    ,@Data varbinary(max) output
)
with native_compilation, schemabinding, exec as owner
as
begin atomic
with
(
    transaction isolation level = snapshot
    ,language = N'English'
)
    select @Data = t.Data
    from dbo.ObjStore t
    where t.ObjectKey = @ObjectKey and
        ExpirationTime >= sysutcdatetime();
end;
```

```
create proc dbo.PurgeExpiredObjects
with native_compilation, schemabinding, exec as owner
as
begin atomic
with
(
    transaction isolation level = snapshot
    ,language = N'English'
)
    declare @CurrentTime
        datetime2(2) = sysutcdatetime();

    delete dbo.ObjStore
    where ExpirationTime < @CurrentTime
end
```

The client implementation includes several static classes. The ObjStoreUtils class provides two methods to serialize and deserialize objects into the byte arrays. You can see the implementation in Listing 13-27.

Listing 13-27. Implementing Session Store: ObjStoreUtils Class

```
public static class ObjStoreUtils
{
    /// <summary>
    /// Serialize object of type T to the byte array
    /// </summary>
    public static byte[] Serialize<T>(T obj)
    {
        if (obj == null)
            return null;
        using (var ms = new MemoryStream())
        {
            var formatter = new BinaryFormatter();
            formatter.Serialize(ms, obj);

            return ms.ToArray();
        }
    }

    /// <summary>
    /// Deserialize byte array to the object
    /// </summary>
    public static T Deserialize<T>(byte[] data)
    {
        if (data == null || data.Length == 0)
            return default(T);
```

```
        using (var output = new MemoryStream(data))
        {
            var binForm = new BinaryFormatter();
            return (T) binForm.Deserialize(output);
        }
    }
}
```

The ObjStoreDataAccess class shown in Listing 13-28 loads and saves binary data to and from the database. It utilizes another static class called DBConnManager, which returns the SqlConnection object to the target database. This class is not shown in the listing.

Listing 13-28. Implementing Session Store: ObjStoreDataAccess Class

```
public static class ObjStoreDataAccess
{
    /// <summary>
    /// Saves serialized object to the database
    /// </summary>
    public static void SaveObjectData(Guid key,
                DateTime expirationTime, byte[] obj)
    {
        using (var cnn = DBConnManager.GetConnection())
        {
            using (var cmd = cnn.CreateCommand())
            {
                cmd.CommandText = "dbo.SaveObjectToStore";
                cmd.CommandType = CommandType.StoredProcedure;
                cmd.Parameters.Add("@ObjectKey",
                    SqlDbType.UniqueIdentifier).Value = key;
                cmd.Parameters.Add("@ExpirationTime",
                    SqlDbType.DateTime2).Value = expirationTime;
                cmd.Parameters.Add("@Data",
                    SqlDbType.VarBinary,-1).Value = obj;

                cmd.ExecuteNonQuery();
            }
        }
    }

    /// <summary>
    /// Load serialized object from the database
    /// </summary>
    public byte[] LoadObjectData(Guid key)
    {
        using (var cnn = DBConnManager.GetConnection())
        {
            using (var cmd = cnn.CreateCommand())
```

```
                {
                    cmd.CommandText = "dbo.LoadObjectFromStore";
                    cmd.CommandType = CommandType.StoredProcedure;
                    cmd.Parameters.Add("ObjectKey",
                        SqlDbType.UniqueIdentifier).Value = key;
                    cmd.Parameters.Add("@Data",
                        SqlDbType.VarBinary,-1).Direction =
                            ParameterDirection.Output;
                    cmd.ExecuteNonQuery();
                    return (byte[])cmd.Parameters[1].Value;
                }
            }
        }
}
```

Finally, the ObjStoreService class shown in Listing 13-29 puts everything together and manages the entire process. It implements two simple methods, Load and Save, calling the helper classes defined earlier.

Listing 13-29. Implementing Session Store: ObjStoreService Class

```
public static class ObjStoreService
{
    /// <summary>
    /// Saves object in the object store
    /// </summary>
    public static void Save(Guid key,
                DateTime expirationTime, object obj)
    {
        var objectBytes = ObjStoreUtils.Serialize(obj);
        ObjStoreDataAccess.SaveObjectData(key, expirationTime, objectBytes);
    }

    /// <summary>
    /// Loads object from the object store
    /// </summary>
    public static T Load<T>(Guid key) where T: class
    {
        var obj = ObjStoreDataAccess.LoadObjectData(key);
        if (obj == null)
            return default(T); // Object not found
        return ObjStoreUtils.Deserialize<T>(objectBytes);
    }
}
```

Obviously, this is an oversimplified example, and the production implementation could be significantly more complex, especially if there is the possibility that multiple sessions can update the same object simultaneously. You can implement retry logic or create some sort of object locking management in the system if this is the case.

It is also worth mentioning that you can compress binary data before saving it into the database. The compression will introduce unnecessary overhead in the case of small objects; however, it could provide significant space savings and performance improvements if the objects are large.

I did not include the compression code in the example, although you can easily implement it with the GZipStream or DeflateStream class.

■ **Note**   The code and test application are included in the companion materials of this book.

Summary

SQL Server 2016 removes the majority of In-Memory OLTP limitations that existed in the first release of the technology. However, migrating to In-Memory OLTP still incurs an implementation cost. You should perform a cost-benefit analysis, making sure that the cost is acceptable.

In-Memory OLTP can dramatically improve the performance of OLTP systems. It is not necessarily the best choice for data warehouse workloads and in-memory data warehouse implementations. You may consider implementing data partitioning and combining the data from memory-optimized and disk-based tables to get the most from all the SQL Server technologies.

You can benefit from the technology even if you do not perform a full In-Memory OLTP migration. To name just a few use cases, memory-optimized table variables can be used as a replacement of disk-based temporary objects. Memory-optimized table-valued parameters are the fastest way to pass the batch of the rows between the client and T-SQL routines. Memory-optimized tables can be used as the staging area for ETL processes.

Remember, however, that In-Memory OLTP is not a "set it and forget it" technology and may require administration and monitoring after it is deployed to production.

APPENDIX A

■ ■ ■

Memory Pointer Management

This chapter explains how SQL Server works with memory pointers that link In-Memory OLTP objects together.

Memory Pointer Management

The In-Memory OLTP Engine relies on memory pointers, using them to link objects together. For example, pointers embedded into data rows link them into the data row chains, which, in turn, are referenced by the hash and nonclustered index objects.

The lock- and latch-free nature of In-Memory OLTP adds the challenge of managing memory pointers in highly volatile environments where multiple sessions can try to simultaneously change them, overwriting each other's changes.

Consider the situation when multiple sessions are trying to insert rows into the same data row chain. Each session traverses that chain to locate the last row and update its pointer with the address of the newly created row. SQL Server must guarantee that every row will be added to the chain even when multiple sessions from the different parallel threads are trying to perform that pointer update simultaneously.

SQL Server uses `InterlockedCompareExchangePointer` API functions to guarantee that multiple sessions cannot update the same pointer and thus overwrite each other's changes, thereby losing references to each other's objects. `InterlockedCompareExchangePointer` functions change the value of the pointer, checking that the existing (*pre-update*) value matches the expected (*old)* value provided as another parameter. Only when the check succeeds is the pointer value updated. All of those operations are completed as a single CPU instruction.

To illustrate this, assume you have two sessions that want to simultaneously insert new delta records for the same nonclustered index leaf page. As a first step, shown in Figure A-1, the sessions create delta records and set their pointers to a page based on the address from the mapping table.

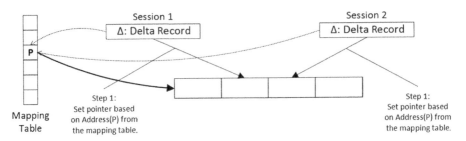

Figure A-1. *Data modifications and concurrency: step 1*

In the next step, both sessions call the `InterlockedCompareExchangePointer` function to try to update the mapping table by changing the reference from a page to the delta records the sessions just created. `InterlockedCompareExchangePointer` serializes the update of the mapping table element and changes it only if its current pre-update value matches the old pointer (address of the page) provided as the parameter. The first `InterlockedCompareExchangePointer` call succeeds. The second call, however, fails because the mapping table element references the delta record from another session rather than the page.

Figure A-2 illustrates such a scenario.

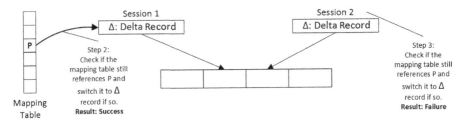

Figure A-2. *Data modifications and concurrency: steps 2 and 3*

At this time, the second session will need to repeat the action. It will read the address of the session 1 delta page from the mapping table and repoint its own delta page to reference this delta page. Finally, it will call `InterlockedCompareExchangePointer` again using the address of the session 1 delta page as the *old pointer* value during the call. Figure A-3 illustrates that.

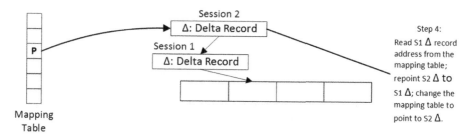

Figure A-3. *Data modifications and concurrency: final steps*

As you can see, with the exception of a short serialization during the InterlockedCompareExchangePointer call, there is no locking or latching of the data during the modifications.

SQL Server uses the same approach with InterlockedCompareExchangePointer every time the pointer chain needs to be preserved, such as when it creates another version of a row during an update, when it needs to change a pointer in the index mapping or hash tables, and in quite a few other cases.

Summary

SQL Server uses an InterlockedCompareExchangePointer mechanism to guarantee that multiple sessions cannot update the same memory pointers simultaneously, losing references to each other's objects.

InterlockedCompareExchangePointer functions change the value of the pointer, checking that the existing (*pre-update*) value matches the expected (*old*) value provided as another parameter. Only when the check succeeds is the pointer value updated. All of those operations are completed as a single CPU instruction.

■ ■ ■

Page Splitting and Page Merging in Nonclustered Indexes

This appendix provides an overview of the internal operations of nonclustered index, such as page splitting and page merging.

Internal Maintenance of Nonclustered Indexes

The In-Memory OLTP engine has several internal operations that maintain the structure of nonclustered indexes. As you already know from Chapter 5, *page consolidation* rebuilds the nonclustered index page, consolidating all changes defined by the page delta records. It helps avoid the performance hit introduced by long delta record chains. The newly created page has the same PID in the mapping table and replaces the old page, which is marked for garbage collection.

Two other processes can create new index pages, page splitting and page merging. Both are complex actions and deserve detailed explanations of their internal implementation.

Page Splitting

Page splitting occurs when a page does not have enough free space to accommodate a new data row. Even though the process is similar to a B-Tree disk-based index page split, there is one conceptual difference. In B-Tree indexes, the page split moves the part of the data to the new data page, freeing up space on the original page. In Bw-Tree indexes, however, the pages are nonmodifiable, and SQL Server replaces the old page with two new ones, splitting the data between them.

Let's look at this situation in more detail. Figure B-1 shows the internal and leaf pages of a nonclustered index. Let's assume that one of the sessions wants to insert a row with a key of value Bob.

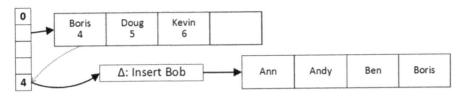

Figure B-1. *Page splitting: initial state*

When the delta record is created, SQL Server adjusts the delta record statistics on the index page and detects that there is no space on the page to accommodate the new index value once the delta records are consolidated. It triggers a page split process, which is done in two atomic steps.

In the first step, SQL Server creates two new leaf-level pages and splits the old page values between them. After that, it repoints the mapping table to the first newly created page and marks the old page and the delta records for garbage collection.

Figure B-2 illustrates this state. At this state, there are no references to the second newly created leaf-level page from the internal pages. The first leaf-level page, however, maintains the link between pages (through the mapping table), and SQL Server is able to access and scan the second page if needed.

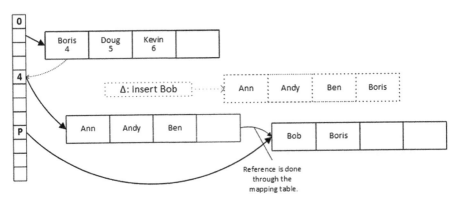

Figure B-2. *Page splitting: first step*

During the second step, SQL Server creates another internal page with key values that represent the new leaf-level page layout. When the new page is created, SQL Server switches the pointer in the mapping table and marks the old internal page for garbage collection. Figure B-3 illustrates this action.

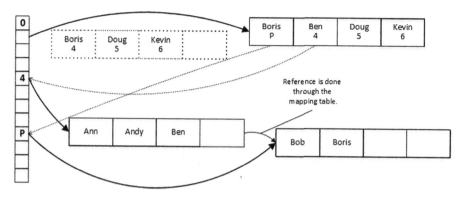

Figure B-3. *Page splitting: second step*

Eventually, the old data pages and delta records are deallocated by the garbage collection process.

Page Merging

Page merging occurs when a delete operation leaves an index page less than 10 percent from the maximum page size, which is 8KB now, or when an index page contains just a single row. During this operation, SQL Server merges the data from two adjacent index pages, replacing them with the new, combined data page.

Assume you have the page layout shown in Figure B-3 and you want to delete the index key value Bob, which means that all data rows with the name Bob have been already deleted. This leaves an index page with the single value Boris, which triggers page merging.

In the first step, SQL Server creates a delete delta record for Bob and another special kind of delta record called a *merge delta*. Figure B-4 illustrates the layout after the first step.

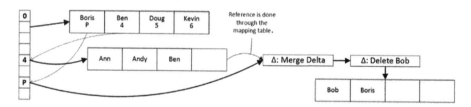

Figure B-4. *Page merging: first step*

During the second step of page merging, SQL Server creates a new internal page that does not reference the leaf-level page that it is about to be merged. After that, SQL Server switches the mapping table to point to the newly created internal page and marks the old page for garbage collection. Figure B-5 illustrates this action.

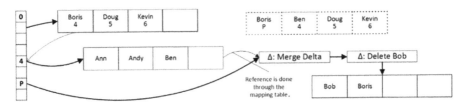

Figure B-5. *Page merging: second step*

Finally, SQL Server builds a new leaf-level page, copying the Boris value there. After the new page is created, it updates the mapping table and marks the old pages and delta records for garbage collection.

Figure B-6 shows the final data layout after page merging is completed.

Figure B-6. *Page merging: third (final) step*

You can get page consolidation, merging, and splitting statistics from the sys.dm_db_ xtp_nonclustered_index_stats view.

■ **Note**   You can read documentation about the sys.dm_db_xtp_nonclustered_index_ stats view at https://docs.microsoft.com/en-us/sql/relational-databases/ system-dynamic-management-views/sys-dm-db-xtp-nonclustered-index-stats- transact-sql.

Summary

The In-Memory OLTP Engine uses several internal operations to maintain the structure of nonclustered indexes. Page consolidation rebuilds the index page, combining page data with the delta records. It helps avoid the performance impact introduced by long delta records chains.

Page splitting occurs when the index page does not have enough space to accommodate the new rows. In contrast to page splitting in disk-based B-Tree indexes, which moves part of the data to the new page, Bw-Tree page splitting replaces the old data page with new pages that contain the data.

Page merging occurs when an index page is less than 10 percent of the maximum page size or when it has just a single row. SQL Server merges the data from adjacent data pages and replaces them with the new page with the merged data.

APPENDIX C

∎ ∎ ∎

Analyzing the States of Checkpoint Files

SQL Server persists data from durable memory-optimized tables in checkpoint files. This appendix demonstrates how to analyze the states of checkpoint files using the sys.dm_db_xtp_checkpoint_files view and shows how the state transitions throughout a file's lifetime.

sys.dm_db_xtp_checkpoint_files View

The sys.dm_db_xtp_checkpoint_files view provides information about database checkpoint files, including their state, size, and physical location. You will use this view extensively in this appendix. Let's look at the most important columns:

- The container_id and container_guid columns provide information about the FILESTREAM container to which a checkpoint file belongs. The container_id column corresponds to the file_id column in the sys.database_files view.

- checkpoint_file_id is a GUID that represents the ID of the file.

- checkpoint_pair_file_id is the ID of the second, data or delta, file in the pair.

- relative_file_path shows the relative file path in the container.

- state and state_desc describe the state of the file. As you already know from Chapter 10, the checkpoint files can be in one of the following states (the number represents the state column value): 0 for PRECREATED, 1 for UNDER CONSTRUCTION, 2 for ACTIVE, 3 for MERGE TARGET, and 8 for WAITING FOR LOG TRUNCATION.

- file_type and file_type_desc describe the type of file: -1 for FREE, 0 for DATA, 1 for DELTA, 2 for ROOT, and 3 for LARGE_DATA.

© Dmitri Korotkevitch 2017
D. Korotkevitch, *Expert SQL Server In-Memory OLTP*, DOI 10.1007/978-1-4842-2772-5

- `lower_bound_tsn` and `upper_bound_tsn` indicate the timestamp of the earliest and latest transactions covered by the file. These columns are populated only for the `ACTIVE` and `MERGE TARGET` states.

- `file_size_in_bytes` and `file_size_used_in_bytes` provide information about the file size and space used in the file. The `file_size_used_in_bytes` value is updated at the time of the checkpoint event.

- `logical_row_count` provides the number of rows in the data and delta files.

It is worth noting that in some cases, especially with early SQL Server 2016 builds, the view may provide slightly outdated data. For example, the SQL Server 2016 RTM build may omit information about some of `PRECREATED` files in the database.

Let's use this view to analyze the state transitions of the checkpoint files.

The Lifetime of Checkpoint Files

As the first step in this test, let's enable the undocumented trace flag T9851 using the `DBCC TRACEON(9851,-1)` command. This trace flag disables the automatic merge process, which will allow you to have more control over your test environment.

■ **Important**   Do not set T9851 in production.

Let's create a database with an In-Memory OLTP filegroup and perform a full backup, starting the backup chain, as shown in Listing C-1. I am doing this in a test environment and not following best practices (such as placing In-Memory OLTP and disk-based data on different drives, creating secondary filegroups for disk-based data, and a few others). Obviously, you should remember to follow best practices when you design your real databases.

Listing C-1. Creating a Database and Performing a Backup

```
create database [InMemoryOLTP2016_AppendixC]
on primary
(
    name = N'AppendixC'
    ,filename = N'C:\Data\AppendixC.mdf'
),
filegroup HKData CONTAINS MEMORY_OPTIMIZED_DATA
(
    name = N'AppendixC_HKData'
    ,filename = N'C:\Data\HKData\AppendixC'
)
```

```
log on
(
    name = N'AppendixC_Log'
    ,filename = N'C:\Data\AppendixC_log.ldf'
)
go

create table InMemoryOLTP2016_AppendixC.dbo.T(ID int);
go

backup database [InMemoryOLTP2016_AppendixC]
to disk = N'C:\Data\Backups\AppendixC.bak'
with noformat, init, name = 'AppendixC - Full', compression;
```

The database is currently empty; therefore, it does not have any checkpoint files created. You can confirm this by querying the sys.dm_db_xtp_checkpoint_files view, as shown in Listing C-2.

Listing C-2. Checking Checkpoint Files

```
use [InMemoryOLTP2016_AppendixC]
go

select
    checkpoint_file_id
    ,checkpoint_pair_file_id
    ,file_type_desc
    ,state_desc
    ,file_size_in_bytes / 1024 / 1024 as [size MB]
    ,relative_file_path
from
    sys.dm_db_xtp_checkpoint_files;
```

Figure C-1 shows that the resultset is empty and that the sys.dm_db_xtp_checkpoint_files view does not return any data.

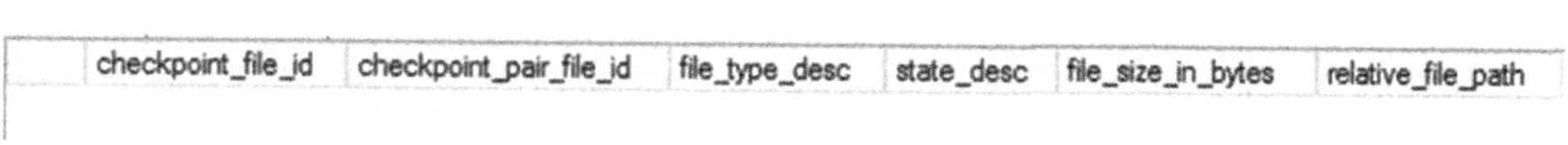

checkpoint_file_id	checkpoint_pair_file_id	file_type_desc	state_desc	file_size_in_bytes	relative_file_path

Figure C-1. *State of checkpoint files after database creation*

As the next step, let's create a durable memory-optimized table, as shown in Listing C-3.

Listing C-3. Creating a Durable Memory-Optimized Table

```
create table dbo.HKData
(
    ID int not null,
    Placeholder char(8000) not null,

    constraint PK_HKData
    primary key nonclustered hash(ID)
    with (bucket_count=8192),
)
with (memory_optimized=on, durability=schema_and_data);
```

If you check the state of the checkpoint files now and run the code from Listing C-2 again, you will see the output shown in Figure C-2. The size of the files may be different in your environment and will depend on the hardware. My test machine has 16 CPUs and 256GB of RAM, so SQL Server preallocated 128MB for data, 64MB for large data, 8MB for delta files, and 16MB for root files. The root file was created in ACTIVE state; all other file types were empty and in a PRECREATED state.

	checkpoint_file_id	checkpoint_pair_file_id	file_type_desc	state_desc	size MB	relative_file_path
1	C189EDEC-224F-4C15-BD01-2E3BC89BD738	NULL	FREE	PRECREATED	128	$HKv2\{C189EDEC-224F-4C15-BD01-2E3BC89BD738}.hkckp
2	A89BC18D-2ACC-446E-A076-E7AB873EF694	NULL	FREE	PRECREATED	64	$HKv2\{A89BC18D-2ACC-446E-A076-E7AB873EF694}.hkckp
3	9F707AE3-1067-4C48-A984-2C9021D1B928	NULL	FREE	PRECREATED	64	$HKv2\{9F707AE3-1067-4C48-A984-2C9021D1B928}.hkckp
4	72E9B85B-F903-47AC-8B16-87D63AB0BB32	NULL	ROOT	ACTIVE	16	$HKv2\{72E9B85B-F903-47AC-8B16-87D63AB0BB32}.hkckp
5	5FD977AE-A63C-49B1-B898-BB56644DE1D4	NULL	DELTA	PRECREATED	8	$HKv2\{5FD977AE-A63C-49B1-B898-BB56644DE1D4}.hkckp
6	FE3A9407-2545-4F95-A5F5-321EEAAA5809	NULL	FREE	PRECREATED	16	$HKv2\{FE3A9407-2545-4F95-A5F5-321EEAAA5809}.hkckp
7	8CF5904A-32F8-4758-AFBF-30DB82CC4DC5	NULL	FREE	PRECREATED	8	$HKv2\{8CF5904A-32F8-4758-AFBF-30DB82CC4DC5}.hkckp
8	3A1F8AD8-DED3-42E3-ADED-D7E72A166168	NULL	DATA	PRECREATED	128	$HKv2\{3A1F8AD8-DED3-42E3-ADED-D7E72A166168}.hkckp
9	36E48A3E-8F2A-4104-BA79-C7DF140932E9	NULL	FREE	PRECREATED	64	$HKv2\{36E48A3E-8F2A-4104-BA79-C7DF140932E9}.hkckp
10	1AED22C4-D09B-4F62-BEB9-37F13B4F52B2	NULL	FREE	PRECREATED	8	$HKv2\{1AED22C4-D09B-4F62-BEB9-37F13B4F52B2}.hkckp
11	8C01FEE3-2A96-43DF-8C5A-D8AF567C2A7C	NULL	FREE	PRECREATED	8	$HKv2\{8C01FEE3-2A96-43DF-8C5A-D8AF567C2A7C}.hkckp
12	AE2ACA64-31F5-422C-87A7-18485FF175CB	NULL	FREE	PRECREATED	128	$HKv2\{AE2ACA64-31F5-422C-87A7-18485FF175CB}.hkckp
13	912C0D7D-19F1-497C-B25B-07E49FF092C0	NULL	FREE	PRECREATED	16	$HKv2\{912C0D7D-19F1-497C-B25B-07E49FF092C0}.hkckp
14	033D53FB-0231-42EE-BB09-AB5D77BD23DE	NULL	DELTA	PRECREATED	8	$HKv2\{033D53FB-0231-42EE-BB09-AB5D77BD23DE}.hkckp
15	F7CD2061-420A-45B5-BD6D-2FF3C192ABA6	NULL	DATA	PRECREATED	128	$HKv2\{F7CD2061-420A-45B5-BD6D-2FF3C192ABA6}.hkckp
16	E206E3D7-52C7-42A2-B3C3-ECDC80F9D662	NULL	FREE	PRECREATED	128	$HKv2\{E206E3D7-52C7-42A2-B3C3-ECDC80F9D662}.hkckp
17	E8DDC239-A11C-4C3B-81A5-3426FF20004F	NULL	FREE	PRECREATED	16	$HKv2\{E8DDC239-A11C-4C3B-81A5-3426FF20004F}.hkckp

Figure C-2. *State of checkpoint files after creating the durable memory-optimized table*

Let's enlarge the output for some of the files, as shown in Figure C-3.

	checkpoint_file_id	checkpoint_pair_file_id	file_type_desc
1	C189EDEC-224F-4C15-BD01-2E3BC89BD738	NULL	FREE
2	A89BC18D-2ACC-446E-A076-E7AB873EF694	NULL	FREE
3	9F707AE3-1067-4C48-A984-2C9021D1B928	NULL	FREE

state_desc	size MB	relative_file_path
PRECREATED	128	$HKv2\{C189EDEC-224F-4C15-BD01-2E3BC89BD738}.hkckp
PRECREATED	64	$HKv2\{A89BC18D-2ACC-446E-A076-E7AB873EF694}.hkckp
PRECREATED	64	$HKv2\{9F707AE3-1067-4C48-A984-2C9021D1B928}.hkckp

Figure C-3. *Checkpoint files (enlarged)*

The relative_file_path column provides the path to the file relative to the FILESTREAM container in the In-Memory OLTP filegroup. Figure C-4 shows the checkpoint files in the folder on the disk.

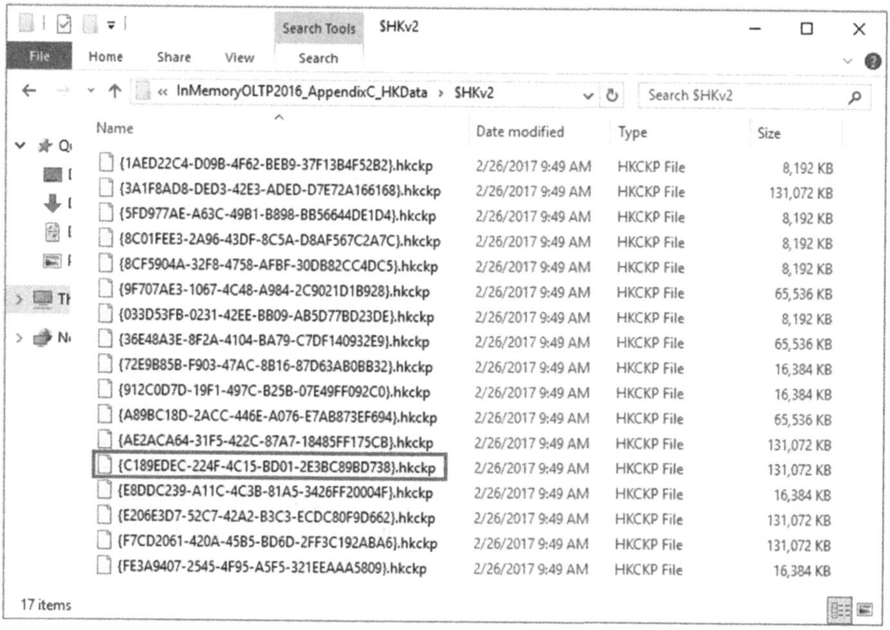

Figure C-4. *Checkpoint files on disk*

Now, let's populate the dbo.HKData table with 1,000 rows and check the status of the checkpoint files, as shown in Listing C-4. The query filters out the checkpoint files in PRECREATED state from the output. The listing also inserts the data into the disk-based table to generate the log record and force the checkpoint controller thread to scan the log and start the In-Memory OLTP checkpoint process.

Listing C-4. Populating the dbo.HKData Table and Checking the States of the Checkpoint Files

```
;with N1(C) as (select 0 union all select 0) -- 2 rows
,N2(C) as (select 0 from N1 as t1 cross join N1 as t2) -- 4 rows
,N3(C) as (select 0 from N2 as t1 cross join N2 as t2) -- 16 rows
,N4(C) as (select 0 from N3 as t1 cross join N3 as t2) -- 256 rows
,N5(C) as (select 0 from N4 as t1 cross join N4 as t2) -- 65,536 rows
,Ids(Id) as (select row_number() over (order by (select null)) from N5)
insert into dbo.HKData(Id, Placeholder)
    select Id, Replicate('0',8000)
    from ids
    where Id <= 1000;
```

```
insert into dbo.T values(0);

select
    checkpoint_file_id
    ,checkpoint_pair_file_id
    ,file_type_desc
    ,state_desc
    ,lower_bound_tsn
    ,upper_bound_tsn
    ,file_size_in_bytes / 1024 / 1024 as [size MB]
    ,file_size_used_in_bytes / 1024 / 1024 as [size used MB]
    ,logical_row_count
from
    sys.dm_db_xtp_checkpoint_files
where
    state_desc <> 'PRECREATED'
order by
    file_type, lower_bound_tsn;
```

As you can see in Figure C-5, SQL Server converted two PRECREATED files to an UNDER CONSTRUCTION state and inserted 1,000 rows into the data file there. The lower_bound_tsn and upper_bound_tsn columns indicate the range of transactions that the files cover. You can also see that the checkpoint_file_pair_id column indicates the corresponding data or delta file in the pair.

	checkpoint_file_id	checkpoint_pair_file_id	file_type_desc	state_desc
1	5FD977AE-A63C-49B1-B898-BB56644DE1D4	F7CD2061-420A-45B5-BD6D-2FF3C192ABA6	DELTA	UNDER CONSTRUCTION
2	F7CD2061-420A-45B5-BD6D-2FF3C192ABA6	5FD977AE-A63C-49B1-B898-BB56644DE1D4	DATA	UNDER CONSTRUCTION
3	72E9B85B-F903-47AC-8B16-87D63AB0BB32	NULL	ROOT	ACTIVE

lower_bound_tsn	upper_bound_tsn	size MB	size used MB	logical_row_count
0	3	8	0	0
0	3	128	0	1000
0	0	16	0	0

Figure C-5. *UNDER CONSTRUCTION files*

Let's run a manual CHECKPOINT and check the status of checkpoint files, as shown in Listing C-5.

Listing C-5. Forcing CHECKPOINT and Checking the Status of Checkpoint Files

```
checkpoint
go
select
    checkpoint_file_id
    ,checkpoint_pair_file_id
    ,file_type_desc
    ,state_desc
```

```
    ,lower_bound_tsn
    ,upper_bound_tsn
    ,file_size_in_bytes / 1024 / 1024 as [size MB]
    ,file_size_used_in_bytes / 1024 / 1024 as [size used MB]
    ,logical_row_count
from
    sys.dm_db_xtp_checkpoint_files
where
    state_desc <> 'PRECREATED'
order by
    file_type, lower_bound_tsn;
```

As you can see in Figure C-6, the CHECKPOINT operation transitioned the UNDER CONSTRUCTION files to an ACTIVE state. It also created the new root file and switched the old file to a WAITING FOR LOG TRUNCATION state.

	checkpoint_file_id	checkpoint_pair_file_id	file_type_desc	state_desc
1	F7CD2061-420A-45B5-BD6D-2FF3C192ABA6	5FD977AE-A63C-49B1-B898-BB56644DE1D4	DATA	ACTIVE
2	5FD977AE-A63C-49B1-B898-BB56644DE1D4	F7CD2061-420A-45B5-BD6D-2FF3C192ABA6	DELTA	ACTIVE
3	912C0D7D-19F1-497C-B25B-07E49FF092C0	NULL	ROOT	ACTIVE
4	72E9B85B-F903-47AC-8B16-87D63AB0BB32	NULL	ROOT	WAITING FOR LOG TRUNCATION

lower_bound_tsn	upper_bound_tsn	size MB	size used MB	logical_row_count
0	4	128	7	1000
0	4	8	0	0
0	4	16	0	0
0	0	16	0	0

Figure C-6. *The file state after CHECKPOINT*

Let's insert another 1,000 rows into the dbo.HKData table and check the status of the files. Listing C-6 shows the code to perform this.

Listing C-6. Populating the dbo.HKData Table with Another Batch of Rows and Checking the States of the Files Afterward

```
;with N1(C) as (select 0 union all select 0) -- 2 rows
,N2(C) as (select 0 from N1 as t1 cross join N1 as t2) -- 4 rows
,N3(C) as (select 0 from N2 as t1 cross join N2 as t2) -- 16 rows
,N4(C) as (select 0 from N3 as t1 cross join N3 as t2) -- 256 rows
,N5(C) as (select 0 from N4 as t1 cross join N4 as t2) -- 65,536 rows
,Ids(Id) as (select row_number() over (order by (select null)) from N5)
insert into dbo.HKData(Id, Placeholder)
    select 1000 + Id, Replicate('0',8000)
    from ids
    where Id <= 1000;

insert into dbo.T values(1);
```

281

```
select
    checkpoint_file_id
    ,checkpoint_pair_file_id
    ,file_type_desc
    ,state_desc
    ,lower_bound_tsn
    ,upper_bound_tsn
    ,file_size_in_bytes / 1024 / 1024 as [size MB]
    ,file_size_used_in_bytes / 1024 / 1024 as [size used MB]
    ,logical_row_count
from
    sys.dm_db_xtp_checkpoint_files
where
    state_desc <> 'PRECREATED'
order by
    file_type, lower_bound_tsn;
```

Figure C-7 shows the states of the checkpoint files after the second insert. As you can see, SQL Server transitioned another set of data and delta files to the UNDER CONSTRUCTION state with lower_bound_tsn = 4.

	checkpoint_file_id	checkpoint_pair_file_id	file_type_desc	state_desc
1	F7CD2061-420A-45B5-BD6D-2FF3C192ABA6	5FD977AE-A63C-49B1-B898-BB56644DE1D4	DATA	ACTIVE
2	5FD977AE-A63C-49B1-B898-BB56644DE1D4	F7CD2061-420A-45B5-BD6D-2FF3C192ABA6	DELTA	ACTIVE
3	912C0D7D-19F1-497C-B25B-07E49FF092C0	NULL	ROOT	ACTIVE
4	72E9B85B-F903-47AC-8B16-87D63AB0BB32	NULL	ROOT	WAITING FOR LOG TRUNCATION
5	3A1F8AD8-DED3-42E3-ADED-D7E72A166168	033D53FB-0231-42EE-BB09-AB5D77BD23DE	DATA	UNDER CONSTRUCTION
6	033D53FB-0231-42EE-BB09-AB5D77BD23DE	3A1F8AD8-DED3-42E3-ADED-D7E72A166168	DELTA	UNDER CONSTRUCTION

lower_bound_tsn	upper_bound_tsn	size MB	file_size_used_in_bytes	logical_row_count
0	4	128	8196096	1000
0	4	8	4096	0
0	4	16	8192	0
0	0	16	8192	0
4	5	128	0	1000
4	5	8	0	0

Figure C-7. *States of the files after the second INSERT*

Another CHECKPOINT would transition the UNDER CONSTRUCTION files to the ACTIVE state, as shown in Figure C-8. You can force it by running the code from Listing C-5 again. At this point, you have two ACTIVE checkpoint file pairs covering different ranges of transaction timestamps.

	checkpoint_file_id	checkpoint_pair_file_id	file_type_desc	state_desc
1	F7CD2061-420A-45B5-BD6D-2FF3C192ABA6	5FD977AE-A63C-49B1-B898-BB56644DE1D4	DATA	ACTIVE
2	5FD977AE-A63C-49B1-B898-BB56644DE1D4	F7CD2061-420A-45B5-BD6D-2FF3C192ABA6	DELTA	ACTIVE
3	912C0D7D-19F1-497C-B25B-07E49FF092C0	NULL	ROOT	WAITING FOR LOG TRUNCATION
4	E8DDC239-A11C-4C3B-81A5-3426FF20004F	NULL	ROOT	ACTIVE
5	72E9B85B-F903-47AC-8B16-87D63AB0BB32	NULL	ROOT	WAITING FOR LOG TRUNCATION
6	3A1F8AD8-DED3-42E3-ADED-D7E72A166168	033D53FB-0231-42EE-BB09-AB5D77BD23DE	DATA	ACTIVE
7	033D53FB-0231-42EE-BB09-AB5D77BD23DE	3A1F8AD8-DED3-42E3-ADED-D7E72A166168	DELTA	ACTIVE

lower_bound_tsn	upper_bound_tsn	size MB	file_size_used_in_bytes	logical_row_count
0	4	128	8196096	1000
0	4	8	4096	0
0	4	16	8192	0
0	6	16	8192	0
0	0	16	8192	0
4	6	128	8196096	1000
4	6	8	4096	0

Figure C-8. *States of the files after second CHECKPOINT*

As the next step, let's delete 99 percent of the rows from the table, as shown in Listing C-7. In this listing, you are also running the query that combines the information about the data and delta files and demonstrates that both checkpoint file pairs are mostly empty. You also need to perform CHECKPOINT to update the logical_row_count column in the delta files, which would generate another empty checkpoint file pair in the ACTIVE state.

Listing C-7. Deleting 99 Percent of the Rows from the Table

```
delete from dbo.HKData
where ID % 100 <> 0;

checkpoint
go

select
    data.checkpoint_file_id
    ,data.state_desc
    ,data.lower_bound_tsn
    ,data.upper_bound_tsn
    ,data.file_size_in_bytes
    ,data.file_size_used_in_bytes
    ,data.logical_row_count
    ,delta.logical_row_count
    ,convert(decimal(5,2),
        iif(data.logical_row_count = 0,0,
            100. - 100. * delta.logical_row_count /
                data.logical_row_count))
        as [% Full]
from
    sys.dm_db_xtp_checkpoint_files data join
        sys.dm_db_xtp_checkpoint_files delta on
            data.checkpoint_pair_file_id = delta.checkpoint_file_id
```

```
where
    data.file_type_desc = 'DATA' and
    data.state_desc <> 'PRECREATED'
order by
    data.lower_bound_tsn
```

As you can see in Figure C-9, the data files are almost empty, and they are perfect candidates for the merge.

	checkpoint_file_id	state_desc	lower_bound_tsn	upper_bound_tsn
1	F7CD2061-420A-45B5-BD6D-2FF3C192ABA6	ACTIVE	0	4
2	3A1F8AD8-DED3-42E3-ADED-D7E72A166168	ACTIVE	4	6
3	C189EDEC-224F-4C15-BD01-2E3BC89BD738	ACTIVE	6	8

file_size_in_bytes	file_size_used_in_bytes	logical_row_count	logical_row_count	% Full
134217728	8196096	1000	990	1.00
134217728	8196096	1000	990	1.00
134217728	4096	0	0	0.00

Figure C-9. *File states after deletion*

As the next step, let's turn on the automatic merge process by switching off trace flag T9851 with the DBCC TRACEOFF(9851,-1) command. After that, you will issue another CHECKPOINT command to trigger the merge process.

Figure C-10 illustrates the state of the checkpoint file pairs after the merge was initiated. As you can see, SQL Server created the new checkpoint file pair in the MERGE TARGET state and merged data from four ACTIVE file pairs that cover a transaction range from 0 to 9.

	checkpoint_file_id	checkpoint_pair_file_id	file_type_desc	state_desc	lower_bound_tsn	upper_bound_tsn	size MB	file_size_used_in_bytes	logical_row_count
1	50128D48-32E9-4C	NULL	ROOT	ACTIVE	0	9	16	12288	0
2	5FD977AE-A63C-4!	F7CD2061-420A-45B5-BC	DELTA	ACTIVE	0	4	8	24576	990
3	F7CD2061-420A-45	5FD977AE-A63C-49B1-B{	DATA	ACTIVE	0	4	128	8196096	1000
4	033D53FB-0231-42	3A1F8AD8-DED3-42E3-A	DELTA	ACTIVE	4	6	8	24576	990
5	3A1F8AD8-DED3-4	033D53FB-0231-42EE-BE	DATA	ACTIVE	4	6	128	8196096	1000
6	1AED22C4-D09B-4	C189EDEC-224F-4C15-B{	DELTA	ACTIVE	6	8	8	4096	0
7	C189EDEC-224F-4	1AED22C4-D09B-4F62-B{	DATA	ACTIVE	6	8	128	4096	0
8	8C01FEE3-2A96-4:	E206E3D7-52C7-42A2-B:	DELTA	ACTIVE	8	9	8	4096	0
9	E206E3D7-52C7-4:	8C01FEE3-2A96-43DF-8C	DATA	ACTIVE	8	9	128	4096	0
10	8CF5904A-32F8-47	AE2ACA64-31F5-422C-87	DELTA	MERGE TARGET	NULL	NULL	8	NULL	NULL
11	AE2ACA64-31F5-4;	8CF5904A-32F8-4758-AFI	DATA	MERGE TARGET	NULL	NULL	128	NULL	NULL
12	912C0D7D-19F1-4{	NULL	ROOT	WAITING FOR LO	0	4	16	8192	0
13	72E9B85B-F903-47	NULL	ROOT	WAITING FOR LO	0	0	16	8192	0
14	FE3A9407-2545-4F	NULL	ROOT	WAITING FOR LO	0	8	16	8192	0
15	E8DDC239-A11C-4	NULL	ROOT	WAITING FOR LO	0	6	16	8192	0

Figure C-10. *The state of checkpoint files after the merge is initiated*

The next CHECKPOINT will transition the checkpoint files that participated in the merge from ACTIVE to WAITING FOR LOG TRUNCATION and from MERGE TARGET to ACTIVE. Figure C-11 demonstrates this. As you can see, the new ACTIVE (formerly MERGE TARGET) data file covers a range from 0 to 9 and now has only 20 data rows. The delta file in the pair is empty.

	checkpoint_file_id	checkpoint_p...	file_type_desc	state_desc	lower_bound_tsn	upper_bound_tsn	file_size_in_bytes	file_size_used_in_bytes	logical_row_count
1	8CF5904A-32F8-4758-...	AE2ACA64-3...	DELTA	ACTIVE	0	9	8388608	4096	0
2	AE2ACA64-31F5-422...	8CF5904A-3...	DATA	ACTIVE	0	9	134217728	167936	20
3	3579B972-0DA7-4A2...	NULL	ROOT	ACTIVE	0	18	16777216	12288	0
4	7E31A312-527F-44C2...	C7DF2548-D...	DELTA	ACTIVE	9	18	8388608	4096	0
5	C7DF2548-D7B6-426...	7E31A312-5...	DATA	ACTIVE	9	18	134217728	4096	0
6	14FF0150-87DB-4279...	48DDF69B-F...	DATA	MERGE TARGET	NULL	NULL	134217728	NULL	NULL
7	48DDF69B-F7DC-440...	14FF0150-8...	DELTA	MERGE TARGET	NULL	NULL	8388608	NULL	NULL
8	F7CD2061-420A-45B5...	5FD977AE-A...	DATA	WAITING FOR LO(	0	4	134217728	8196096	0
9	912C0D7D-19F1-497...	NULL	ROOT	WAITING FOR LO(	0	4	16777216	8192	0
10	50128D48-32E9-4D7F...	NULL	ROOT	WAITING FOR LO(	0	9	16777216	12288	0
11	72E9B85B-F903-47AC...	NULL	ROOT	WAITING FOR LO(	0	0	16777216	8192	0
12	5FD977AE-A63C-49B...	F7CD2061-4...	DELTA	WAITING FOR LO(	0	4	8388608	24576	0
13	FE3A9407-2545-4F95-...	NULL	ROOT	WAITING FOR LO(	0	8	16777216	8192	0
14	E8DDC239-A11C-4C3...	NULL	ROOT	WAITING FOR LO(	0	6	16777216	8192	0
15	3A1F8AD8-DED3-42E...	033D53FB-0...	DATA	WAITING FOR LO(	4	6	134217728	8196096	0
16	033D53FB-0231-42EE...	3A1F8AD8-...	DELTA	WAITING FOR LO(	4	6	8388608	24576	0
17	C189EDEC-224F-4C1...	1AED22C4-...	DATA	WAITING FOR LO(	6	8	134217728	4096	0
18	1AED22C4-D09B-4F6...	C189EDEC-...	DELTA	WAITING FOR LO(	6	8	8388608	4096	0
19	8C01FEE3-2A96-43D...	E206E3D7-5...	DELTA	WAITING FOR LO(	8	9	8388608	4096	0
20	E206E3D7-52C7-42A...	8C01FEE3-2...	DATA	WAITING FOR LO(	8	9	134217728	4096	0

Figure C-11. *The state of the checkpoint files after the merge is completed*

After the transaction log backup is taken, the log records are transmitted to secondary nodes, and the checkpoint event occurs, then the files in a WAITING FOR LOG TRUNCATION state will be deleted or recycled back to a FREE state. Listing C-8 performs a transaction log backup along with CHECKPOINT.

Listing C-8. Performing Log Backup and Forcing Garbage Collection

```
backup log [InMemoryOLTP2016_AppendixC]
to disk = N'C:\Data\Backups\AppendixC.bak'
with noformat, noinit, name = 'AppendixC - Log', compression
go

checkpoint;
```

■ **Note** In reality, it could take more than one log backup and checkpoint event to deallocate files in the WAITING FOR LOG TRUNCATION state. You can execute the code from Listing C-8 multiple times if this happens on your system.

Figure C-12 illustrates that some of the files were deleted.

	checkpoint_file_id	checkpoint_pair_file_id	file_type_desc	state_desc	lower_bound_tsn	upper_bound_tsn	file_size_in_bytes	file_size_used_in_bytes	logical_row_count
1	96CFF776-124E-4109-8C76-C8C1997EFA39	FDF6CA04-562D-49C0-8347-9A66CF40501E	DATA	ACTIVE	0	19	134217728	167936	20
2	FDF6CA04-562D-49C0-8347-9A66CF40501E	96CFF776-124E-4109-8C76-C8C1997EFA39	DELTA	ACTIVE	0	19	8388608	4096	0
3	FDC60C78-0579-463B-BC94-608F6B6EEC87	NULL	ROOT	ACTIVE	0	20	16777216	12288	0
4	7DE5E828-398B-4CB9-805D-7B7BF6EDECF9	95BDA51B-3576-4329-ABB6-D8DA5BE7D25E	DELTA	ACTIVE	19	20	8388608	4096	0
5	95BDA51B-3576-4329-ABB6-D8DA5BE7D25E	7DE5E828-398B-4CB9-805D-7B7BF6EDECF9	DATA	ACTIVE	19	20	134217728	4096	0
6	09325213-8193-4C74-8437-5812C0E8DABB	DDFD4717-22E2-49C8-A0E7-08AE4771404D	DELTA	MERGE TARGET	NULL	NULL	8388608	NULL	NULL
7	DDFD4717-22E2-49C8-A0E7-08AE4771404D	09325213-8193-4C74-8437-5812C0E8DABB	DATA	MERGE TARGET	NULL	NULL	134217728	NULL	NULL
8	48DDF69B-F7DC-4404-B331-3E274DF3EA3C	14FF0150-87DB-4279-9E0A-1C736442D7D8	DELTA	WAITING FOR LOG TRUNCATION	0	18	8388608	4096	0
9	8CF5904A-32F8-4758-AFBF-30DB82CC4DC5	AE2ACA64-31F5-422C-87A7-18485FF175CB	DELTA	WAITING FOR LOG TRUNCATION	0	9	8388608	4096	0
10	AE2ACA64-31F5-422C-87A7-18485FF175CB	8CF5904A-32F8-4758-AFBF-30DB82CC4DC5	DATA	WAITING FOR LOG TRUNCATION	0	9	134217728	167936	0
11	07865E4C-686B-49A5-B794-100BD814BDA8	NULL	ROOT	WAITING FOR LOG TRUNCATION	0	15	16777216	12288	0
12	14FF0150-87DB-4279-8E0A-1C736442D7D8	48DDF69B-F7DC-4404-B331-3E274DF3EA3C	DATA	WAITING FOR LOG TRUNCATION	0	18	134217728	167936	0
13	35798B72-0DA7-4A2E-9694-099296A72C13	NULL	ROOT	WAITING FOR LOG TRUNCATION	0	18	16777216	12288	0
14	C70F2548-D7B6-426E-8945-681D28686B39	7E31A312-527F-44C2-8AEB-E3DA55E47B2F	DATA	WAITING FOR LOG TRUNCATION	9	18	134217728	4096	0
15	7E31A312-527F-44C2-8AEB-E3DA55E47B2F	C70F2548-D7B6-426E-8945-681D28686B39	DELTA	WAITING FOR LOG TRUNCATION	9	18	8388608	4096	0
16	9A4BD489-7DC6-4ACE-B353-B67DE3A6B237	7CFCE32A-48B2-46E5-B632-017858EFD375	DELTA	WAITING FOR LOG TRUNCATION	18	19	8388608	4096	0
17	7CFCE32A-48B2-46E5-B632-017858EFD375	9A4BD489-7DC6-4ACE-B353-B67DE3A6B237	DATA	WAITING FOR LOG TRUNCATION	18	19	134217728	4096	0

Figure C-12. *Checkpoint files after backup/log truncation*

Summary

Every checkpoint file transitions through various states during its lifetime. You can analyze these states using the sys.dm_db_xtp_checkpoint_files data management view. This view returns information about individual checkpoint files, including their type, size, state, transaction interval they cover, number of rows there, and quite a few other properties.

The merge process merges information from the ACTIVE checkpoint files that have a large percent of deleted rows, creating a new checkpoint file pair. This helps to reduce the size of the data on disk and speed up the database recovery process.

Merged checkpoint files should be included in the log backup before they are deallocated. Regular transaction log backups will reduce the size of the In-Memory OLTP data on disk. Make sure to design a database backup strategy in a way that accounts for such behavior.

■ ■ ■

In-Memory OLTP Migration Tools

This appendix discusses several SQL Server 2016 tools that help with In-Memory OLTP migration.

"Transaction Performance Analysis Overview" Report

One of the challenges during In-Memory OLTP migration is determining the list of objects that will benefit the most from it. The *Pareto principle* can be easily applied here: if the migration targets are identified correctly, you can achieve 80 percent of possible gains by spending 20 percent of your time.

SQL Server 2016 provides you with a "Transaction Performance Analysis Overview" report, which can help you to identify migration targets in the system. It shows the tables that suffer from lock and latch contention along with frequently executed stored procedures that consume the most CPU resources on the server. This report is similar to the SQL Server 2014 version; however, it does not require you to set up a management data warehouse. All the work is done by SQL Server automatically.

Let's look at the information provided by the "Transaction Performance Analysis Overview" report. In this appendix, I am using the demo application and the WebRequests*_Disk tables from Chapter 2 of this book. I also added several unsupported constructs to the tables and stored procedure to illustrate how tools provide information about them.

You can access the report from the Standard Reports pop-up menu item in the database you are analyzing, as shown in Figure D-1. As you can guess, this report works on a per-database basis.

© Dmitri Korotkevitch 2017

D. Korotkevitch, *Expert SQL Server In-Memory OLTP*, DOI 10.1007/978-1-4842-2772-5

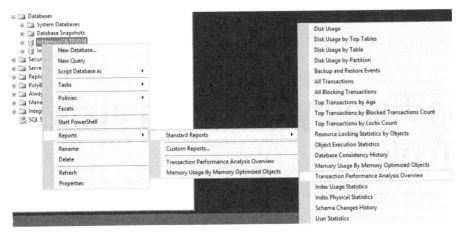

Figure D-1. *Accessing the "Transaction Performance Analysis Overview" report*

Figure D-2 shows the report.

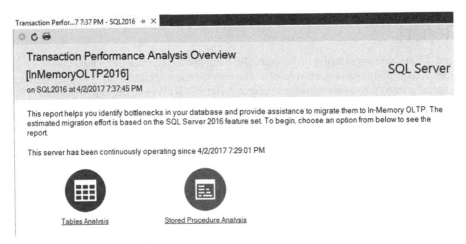

Figure D-2. *The "Transaction Performance Analysis Overview" report*

From this page, you have access to two drill-down reports. "Tables Analysis" provides table-related statistics based on how often tables are accessed and how much they suffer from lock and latch contention.

Figure D-3 illustrates the output of the "Table Analysis" report. As you can see, it displays the output in four quadrants based on the amount of work required for the migration and the estimated performance gain it will provide. Migrating the objects in the upper-right quadrant will provide the most performance gain with the lowest amount of work involved.

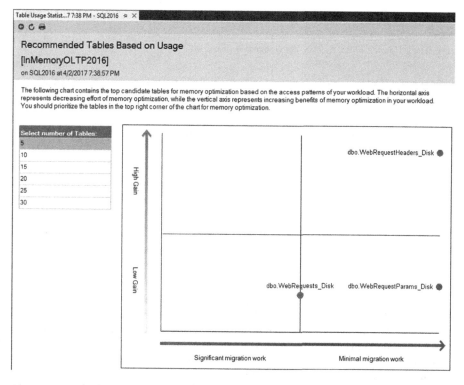

Figure D-3. *The "Table Analysis" report*

You can see the statistics on the table level by clicking the object in the graph. Figure D-4 shows the details for the WebRequestHeaders_Disk table in the system. The first output shows lock- and latch-related statistics for the table. The table suffers from a large number of page latches, as you saw in Chapter 2.

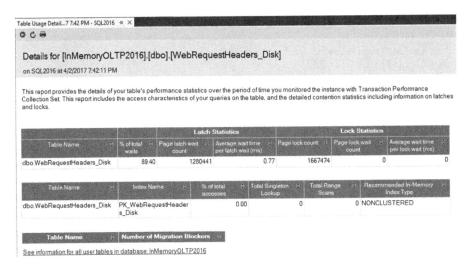

Figure D-4. Table-level statistics

The second output illustrates access method–related statistics. The demo application does not read the data from the table, which affects the numbers you see in the output.

Finally, the third output illustrates the number of migration blockers and issues that need to be addressed before migration. The table does not have any incompatibilities and can be migrated into memory without any schema changes.

Similarly, the "Stored Procedure Analysis" report shows stored procedure usage based on the amount of CPU time they consumed. Figure D-5 illustrates the output of the report. The demo application called just a single procedure, which is displayed here.

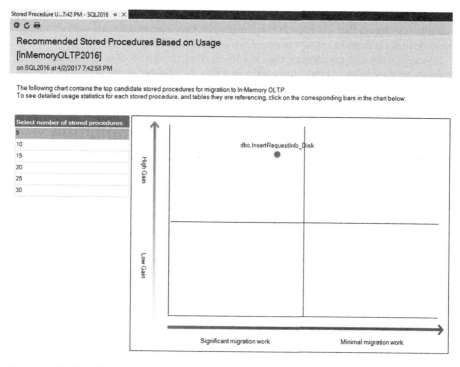

Figure D-5. *The "Procedure Usage Analysis" report*

You can drill down to the procedure-level statistics, which displays the execution count, execution time metrics, and tables that are referenced by the stored procedure. Figure D-6 illustrates this page.

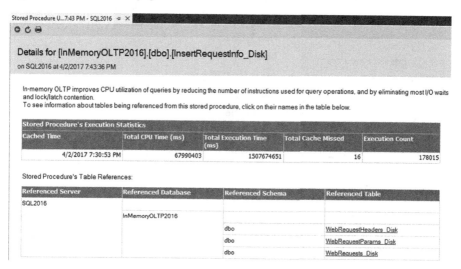

Figure D-6. *Procedure-level statistics*

The "Transaction Performance Analysis Overview" report is a great tool that can help you identify objects that will benefit from migration. However, you should not rely solely on its results. Look and analyze the entire system before making any decisions.

Finally, it is worth mentioning that, as with any tool, the quality of output greatly depends on the quality of input. You need to run this report either on the production server or in a test environment with a workload similar to production to get accurate results.

Memory Optimization and Native Compilation Advisors

In addition to the "Transaction Performance Analysis Overview" report, SQL Server 2016 includes two other tools that can help with In-Memory OLTP migration. The Memory Optimization and Native Compilation Advisors analyze database tables, stored procedures, and user-defined functions to identify unsupported constructs. Moreover, the Memory Optimization Advisor can perform the actual migration, creating an In-Memory OLTP filegroup and memory-optimized table, and move data from the disk-based table there.

You can access both advisors from the object context menu in SSMS. Figure D-7 shows the table context menu with the Memory Optimization Advisor menu item highlighted.

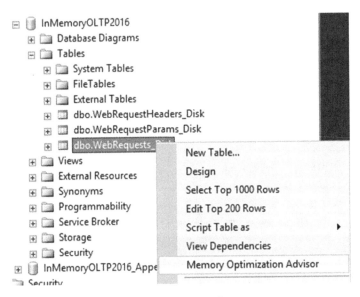

Figure D-7. *The Memory Optimization Advisor menu*

As the first step, the wizard analyzes the table and displays constructs that are unsupported by In-Memory OLTP. Figure D-8 shows the output of the validation on the WebRequests_Disk table. As mentioned, I added xml and geography columns to the table, which were reported by the advisor.

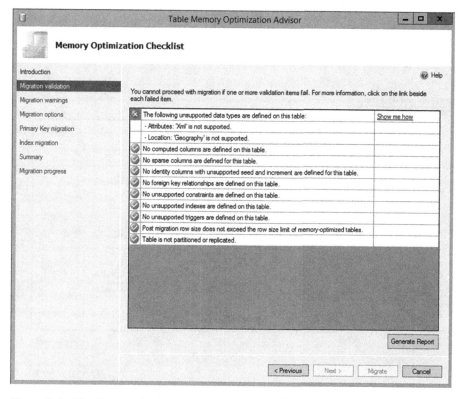

Figure D-8. *The Memory Optimization Advisor validation results*

If the table does not use any unsupported constructs, the advisor proceeds with the option of creating an In-Memory OLTP filegroup and performing the actual table migration.

The simplicity of the wizard, however, is a two-edged sword. It can simplify the migration process and, in some cases, allow the enabling of In-Memory OLTP and moving data into memory with a few mouse clicks. However, as you already know, In-Memory OLTP deployments require careful hardware and infrastructure planning, redesigning of indexing strategies, changes in database maintenance and monitoring, and quite a few other steps to be successful. An improperly done migration can lead to suboptimal results, and the simplicity of the advisor increases that chance.

The advisor is a useful tool for identifying migration roadblocks. You should be careful, however, when relying on it to perform the actual migration process.

As the opposite of the Memory Optimization Advisor, the Native Compilation Advisor does not create a natively compiled version of the modules. It just analyzes whether the modules have unsupported constructs that prevent native compilation.

Figure D-9 illustrates the output of the Native Compilation Advisor for the InsertRequestInfo_Disk stored procedure defined in Chapter 2 with an additional MERGE statement added.

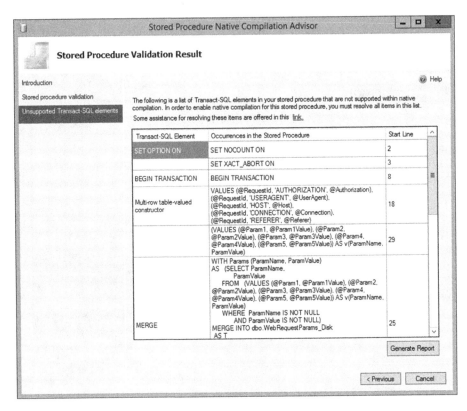

Figure D-9. *Native Compilation Advisor output*

The Generate Report button will create an HTML file with the results of the analysis, similar to what is shown in the advisor window.

Finally, Management Studio allows you to run the Memory Optimization and Native Compilation Advisors for multiple database objects using the In-Memory OLTP Migration Checklists Wizard. You can access this wizard through the Tasks menu item in the database pop-up menu, as shown in Figure D-10.

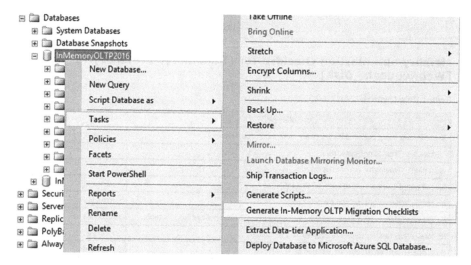

Figure D-10. *Generate In-Memory OLTP Migration Checklists menu item*

The Generate In-Memory OLTP Migration Checklists Wizard allows you to choose the list of database objects to validate, as shown in Figure D-11.

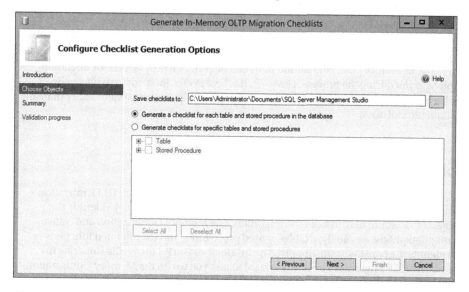

Figure D-11. *Generate In-Memory OLTP Migration Checklists Wizard's parameters*

After the process is complete, SQL Server generates the set of HTML files—one per object—and saves them in a defined location. Each file will contain a report similar to what is produced by the Memory Optimization and Native Compilation Advisors, as shown in Figure D-12.

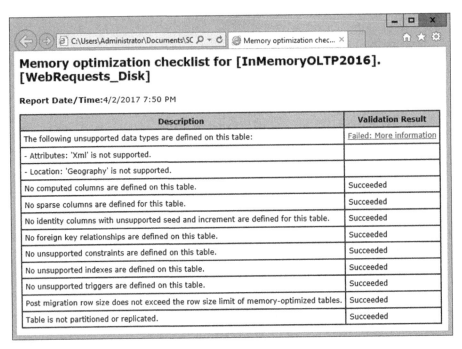

Figure D-12. *Generate In-Memory OLTP Migration Checklists Wizard's report file*

The In-Memory OLTP migration tools can help you identify targets for migration and help you during the process. However, it is best to take their advice with a grain of salt and not explicitly rely on their output. After all, you know your system better than any automatic tool does.

Summary

SQL Server 2016 provides several tools that can help with In-Memory OLTP migration. The "Transaction Performance Analysis Overview" report allows you to identify the objects that would benefit from the migration. The Memory Optimization and Native Compilation Advisors analyze tables, stored procedures, and user-defined functions to identify the constructs unsupported by In-Memory OLTP. Finally, the Generate In-Memory OLTP Migration Checklists Wizard allows you to run the Memory Optimization and Native Compilation Advisors for multiple database objects.

Those tools are beneficial and can save you a good amount of time during the migration process. However, you should not rely strictly on their output when you perform the analysis. You need to analyze the entire system, including the infrastructure and hardware, indexing strategies, database maintenance routines, and other factors to achieve the best results with In-Memory OLTP.

Again, thank you very much for your interest in the technology! It was a pleasure to write for you!

Index

■ V, W

■ X, Y, Z

Get the eBook for only $5!

Why limit yourself?

With most of our titles available in both PDF and ePUB format, you can access your content wherever and however you wish—on your PC, phone, tablet, or reader.

Since you've purchased this print book, we are happy to offer you the eBook for just $5.

To learn more, go to http://www.apress.com/companion or contact support@apress.com.

Printed in the United States
By Bookmasters